ALSO BY KYLE D. PRUETT

The Nurturing Father: Journey Toward the Complete Man

Me, Myself, and I: How Children Build Their Sense of Self: 18 to 36 Months

FATHERNEED

*Why Father Care
Is as Essential
as Mother Care
for Your Child*

KYLE D. PRUETT, M.D.

The Free Press

NEW YORK   LONDON   SYDNEY   SINGAPORE

*f*P

THE FREE PRESS
A Division of Simon & Schuster Inc.
1230 Avenue of the Americas
New York, NY 10020

10 9 8 7 6 5 4 3 2 1

Library of Congress Cataloging-in-Publication Data

Pruett, Kyle D.
  Fatherneed : why father care is as essential as
mother care for your child / Kyle D. Pruett.
       p.   cm.
  Includes bibliographical references and index.
  1. Fatherhood—United States.   2. Father and child
—United States.   I. Title.
HQ756.P77 2000
306.874′2—dc21
                                                99-050214
                                                    CIP

ISBN 0-684-85775-8

To assure the privacy of the families depicted in this
book, and to protect their anonymity while staying
faithful to their stories, their names and other identifying characteristics have been changed.

To my wife
the gifted, beloved, passionate,
and magical Marsha

for inspiring and helping me write this book,
and your loving, protective vigilance to our
family during the irony of my writing about,
instead of, fathering

AMOR VINCIT OMNIA

Contents

Acknowledgments

WALLACE STEVENS explored the varieties of life given to children by mother and father in his superb poem, *Auroras of Autumn* (1950). A favorite excerpt:

> *The mother invites humanity to her house*
> *And table. The father fetches tellers of tales*
> *And musicians who mute much, muse much,*
> *on those tales.**

I want to thank those tellers and musicians who have breathed life into this father's tale:

None of us would be on this page without the families who endure our questions, intrusions, and expectant vigils. Their selflessness in giving of their trust, privacy, and time in the service of understanding has been deeply appreciated, and never assumed. Thank you and your children.

To my father, Ozie Douthitt Pruett, and my father-in-law, Steve Kline, for their devotion and sacrifice to their lucky and blessed children, whose fatherneed rarely languished. Choosing the right parents is half the battle. To my granddad, Horace, for not smacking me senseless

*From Wallace Stevens, *The Collected Poems*, Vintage, New York, 1990, p. 415.

when my first turn at the John Deere's steering wheel destroyed Grandmother's strawberry crop in Shawnee. You all taught me how to father first and think about it second.

To my colleagues and friends whose support, respectful criticism, skills, and enthusiasm in the fathering field, made this book better than it could have been without you: Henry Biller, Ken Canfield, Marti Erickson, Betty Friedan, Vivian Gadsby, Carol Gilligan, Alan Gurwitt, Irving Harris, Jan Johnston, Michael Lamb, James Levine, Frank Pedersen, Norma Radin, Fred Rogers, Dwaine Simms, Ralph Smith, and Barbara Tinney.

Father to Father and Zero to Three's boards and staff, especially T. Berry Brazelton and Emily Fenichel, who supported my work before fatherhood was sufficiently retro.

My Yale Child Study Center associations have been yeasty and challenging, beginning with Al Solnit, and ably sustained by Donald Cohen. Kirsten Dahl, Julian Ferholt, Michael Kaplan, Jim Leckman, Steve Marans, Barbara Nordhaus, Sally Provence, Sam Ritvo, John Schowalter, Sara Sparrow, and Ed Zigler, have made it a fertile environment in which to explore the ideas and science that led to this book.

To the Whiffenpoofs of 1965, who doggedly erased any hint of self-satisfaction or self-importance from the final draft, and whose companionship still sustains.

Finally to Peggy Allen, Mary Fiore, Mel Berger, and Philip Rappaport, whose skills and talents helped me find the way from *Lifetime* to The Free Press.

Introduction

THE MOST STUNNING CHANGE in the American family over the past generation is neither marital nor economic; it is how men and women have changed their expectations and behavior toward fathering. Co-parenting, a radical concept for most of our parents, is now a major expectation among newly marrying couples. And the children say it's about time. Over the course of sixteen years, Joseph Pleck at the University of Illinois compared changing survey responses by newly marrying couples who were asked to rank-order certain values they planned to instill in their marriages. He finds that co-parenting—parents' sharing in the physical and emotional care of their infants and children as well as in the responsibilities and decision making—has moved from the eleventh priority out of fifteen topics in 1981 to the second priority in 1997, a startling shift in values in less than one generation.

And this is not just talk. "Father care" is now as common in American families as all forms of day care combined. Acceptance of paternity by unmarried men is up threefold from 1995. Men from Wall Street to homeless shelters speak with conviction about wanting to father their children more actively than they themselves were fathered. As a senior manager at the investment house Goldman Sachs puts it, "I don't want my son to feel the same void in his heart where his father belongs that I do in mine."

Research from the child's side of the aisle shows that kids yearn deeply for dads. Infants in the first months of life can tell the difference between a mother's and a father's style of care. Furthermore, children thrive when they experience those different styles throughout all the developmental stages of life. Developmental research clearly shows that children are born with a drive to find and connect to their fathers, and fathers have the internal capacity, the *instinct,* to respond. Children and fathers hunger for each other early, often, and for a very long time.

Yet even as newly married Americans embrace co-parenting aspirations, the shape of the American family continues to shift. Census data often awaken us to half-felt trends, and this one is an eye-opener: just 34 percent of all children born in America in the last three years of the twentieth century will reach the age of eighteen living with both biological parents. The bottom line: nearly two-thirds of our kids will reach majority in a nonnuclear family configuration. If co-parenting is indeed the dominant expectation during this era when nuclear families are becoming so uncommon, then we have an urgent need to understand how kids and their dads and moms are going to stay connected to each other during the time when it matters most to the healthy development of our country's children.

A prime example of why we need to understand soon: census data show that households headed by single fathers are the fastest-growing family type. U.S. Census Bureau data released in early 1999 indicate that the number of single fathers raising children increased by 25 percent in just three years while the number of single mothers remained the same (showing a slight slip in the 5 to 1 ratio). As single mothers tell us, parenting without a partner is not an easy way to raise children.

But more importantly, whether they are in a traditional family arrangement or not, parents are groaning under the strain of childrearing these days. Recent polls by Zero to Three, the national young child and family advocacy think tank, and by *Newsweek* magazine confirm precisely what I see and hear in my national speaking experiences: stress- and worry-eroded parental self-esteem is reaching epidemic proportions just about everywhere. Mothers feel uncertain and alone, and fathers feel excluded, relegated to the margins of their kids' lives, and incompetent even when they are far from it. It is precisely this strained and worry-filled climate surrounding the family that has strengthened interest in the father as a rich and enduring emotional resource in the nurturing domain, both inside and outside marriage.

Although families hunger for information about how men and children ought and need to be connected to each other for the benefit of the family, the parenting books on the bookstore shelves have let them down. While many of these otherwise helpful guides, some written by friends and teachers of mine, include *father* in the index and mention fathers in the introduction and maybe in a chapter here and there, they have not consistently included fathers, page by page, topic by topic, problem by problem, in their discussions on parenting. There is no definitive guide to the well-being of children that speaks as compellingly to men as it does to women. Consequently, many a parenting book, even those with much helpful advice on how to raise wonderful kids, gathers dust on dad's nightstand (usually after mom bought and read it first before handing it to him). In spite of the well-intentioned efforts of the authors of such parenting books, fathers usually stop reading them, because they cannot find themselves or their relationship with their children anywhere between the covers. When Dad seems to disappear from a parenting book after a few pages, fathers feel that "something's missing here" and are likely to close the book for good.

Fathers *and* mothers have asked me to write this book to explain exactly what it is that children need from their fathers, why a father has so powerful an influence on the kind of person a child eventually becomes, and why women need to encourage the profound father–child connection. So here it is, the first definitive guide to fatherneed from the point of view of kids and parents. This book began as a nagging question that first drew me into the homes of eighteen families in the early eighties: What *is* the effect of men, especially fathers, on the development of children? Today in America there is a new father speaking, and his children are listening carefully, sometimes to his and his partner's amazement.

From Madison Avenue to government bureaucracies and courthouses, we see signs that the importance of the paternal presence to our well-being as a culture is increasingly recognized. Tylenol, OshKosh B'Gosh, GantU.S.A., and Estee Lauder, to name just a few companies, have poured significant resources into creating new advertising campaigns featuring images of competent fathers and their children. Highly competitive, young MBA hopefuls being recruited at my university are increasingly bold in asking about paternity leave, flextime, and job sharing policies—all questions that would have been perceived as evidence of a lack of "real commitment" and would therefore have sunk their father's (and mother's) hiring chances or career ambitions only a generation ago. Rappers have begun to record CDs that provide evidence that the streets, too, are beginning to embrace real, and not simply reproductive, fatherhood.

Former governor Roy Romer made public service announcements on fatherhood and earmarked budget resources to promote responsible fatherhood in Colorado. Maryland, Massachusetts, and Minnesota are among a growing number of states implementing programs to discourage the widespread phenomenon of father exclusion from such preschool programs as Head Start, Early Head Start, and Healthy Start.

Michigan, California, Florida, and Connecticut are a few of the states that regularly include the topic of the father's influence on child development in annual judicial education courses. A senior jurist took me aside after a recent judicial education lecture I gave in Hartford to say, "You have vastly raised my awareness of the potential benefits to children of making it possible for their dads to stay in their lives. Likewise, you've made me feel plenty guilty about all those cases where I did the opposite!"

Increasing numbers of states have measures similar to Minnesota's and Colorado's "responsible fatherhood initiative," which supports legislative and judicial practices based on the presumption of a positive, ongoing role of the father in the life of his children (and vice versa) before, during, and after marriage. The Clinton White House asked Lisa Mallory, deputy director of its Partnership to Re-Invent Government, to implement the president's memorandum and Executive Order to Strengthen Fatherhood. She established an office that monitors all government regulations, policies, executive orders, and directives that potentially affect father–family and father–child access and mutual benefit. Its purpose is to prevent government from making it harder for mothers and fathers to co-parent their kids in ways that make sense to them, not to the government. This has been especially important in monitoring the cynical Catch-22 inherent in establishing paternity and encouraging fathering connections for the sole purpose of collecting child support to ease the government's economic burdens.

Worthy though these initiatives may be, they are far from universal and are frequently opposed by conservative politicians and community leaders wary of intruding on the privacy of the family. Most of us understand the wisdom of promoting responsible fatherhood, yet we remain uncertain about how to extend or reliably apply what we know to the lives of all our children. Judges remain confused about how to decide child custody or foster parent disputes in ways that protect and sustain the well-being of the child and the father–child relationship. Corporations anxious to protect their human resource investments debate their obligations to unhappy young mothers *and* fathers over parental leave and on-site day-care benefits.

Despite our earnest desire to understand these changes, we are unsettled about what we do *not* know about what is evolving as a result of sociocultural and political forces. Twenty years ago I began to wonder about the impact on children of a father who is the primary caregiver. I had begun to see the number of families in my clinic who were choosing this intriguing alternative slowly increase, thanks to the fresh infusion of creativity pumped into families by the women's movement. About five years into this pattern, one of my medical students raised her hand after I had delivered my standard lecture on the importance of attachment to consistent caregivers in the first months of life, and asked, "If I return to my practice after our child is three months old and my husband stays home to raise him or her, what would be the effect on the child's development?" Great question. Halfway into my answer I stopped, because I realized I was making the whole thing up. I hadn't a clue. I suggested we take her wonderful question to our local reference librarian. As the librarian predicted, we found absolutely nothing in the world-renowned Yale University Library system (containing more than twelve million volumes) about the impact of fathers on child development. We found over nine hundred citations dealing with fruit fly genes but zip on the developmental impact on children of the primary caregiving by the male contributor of half of their genes.

My student's question came as a shot across my smug academic bow, riveting my attention to a huge, almost immoral oversight about the role that men play in the lives of their children. Consequently, two years later, I began the only ongoing study of men in intact families who stayed home in the early months and years of their children's lives. I did so in an effort to understand what it is that men and children actually do or do not have going for them from the first moments of life and whether they are or are not good for each other. Throughout this book you will hear the stories of these families and the fascinating lessons they taught me about fatherneed. The study continues as those children now enter adolescence, and I sit by, anxious to learn more and more.

What little literature did connect fathers with their children back then, before I began my study, almost always had to do with father absence, not presence. It was as though fathers mattered more when they were not fathering than when they were. Indeed, father absence remains exquisitely painful for the nineteen million children who are currently growing up without their father. Earlier sexual and drug activity, higher rates of school failure, school dropout, teen suicide, and juvenile delinquency stalk these children's histories. If science has shown us that father absence adds such a burden of risk factors, what on earth does father presence add?

Despite the pioneering work of child development experts and colleagues—Michael Lamb, Frank Pedersen, Joseph Pleck, Henry Biller, Ross Parke, Norma Radin, James Levine, Tiffany Field, William Marsiglio, and a handful of others—the field of father–infant relationships is just now leaving its own infancy as we quarry this domain for its intellectual cornerstones. In a scathing critique of the entire academic child development field, University of Connecticut's Vicky Phares reported in the nation's leading psychology journal that in scientific reports on the relationship between family and child development, fathers are not even mentioned half of the time! Furthermore, when fathers are included in research designs of important problems like attention deficit disorder, autism, childhood depression, or teen suicide, the author usually fails to discuss how the father might be considered part of the solution to the problem addressed. Interestingly, in the 25 percent of all the literature Phares reviewed that did analyze the father's influence on the problem being studied, the writers always found something relevant and important to understand. In other words, when we bother to look for the father's impact, we find it—always. Not looking at the impact of fathers and children on each other has given the entire field (and the best-selling parenting books it produces) a myopic and worrisomely distorted view of child development, a view with staggering blind spots.

Fathers were practically nonexistent in the early writings of Spock, Brazelton, Leach, and White. To varying degrees, they each began to nod more often in the father's direction, particularly Brazelton, but in their souls they couldn't get past the old seduction of the sacred mother–infant bond. They all missed the fatherneed boat as the children kept boarding, departure after departure. We need to ask ourselves, How on earth could this have happened? These are not shallow thinkers, and it appears to have taken considerable effort to avoid studying this question. As a psychiatrist trained in understanding both adult and child mental health, behavior, and illness, I've learned to look at blind spots and wonder why we are not supposed to look there and, if we do, what we are forbidden to see. My own hunch: in order to look *at* the father, one must look *away* from the mother, behavior that can raise normal anxiety early in life. Will Mom be there when I look back? Will it hurt her feelings if I look or turn away from her, even for a moment? Maybe I'd best not risk it. Is this early pattern, this ambivalence, sufficient to preserve the black hole of ignorance surrounding father care, its effects, and its impact on a child's growth? Perhaps. Maybe the grown-ups among us who are studying children have some lingering maternal separation experiences and feelings that need further attention and resolution if we are to get the science right this time.

Things have improved, as pioneering fatherhood researcher Michael Lamb points out in his 1997 third edition of *The Role of the Father in Child Development*. The first edition was the field's first classic, and by the third the available references in the field could themselves fill a book. So, thankfully, we now know some things worth knowing.

In this book we shall see how fatherneed works in the lives of real mothers and fathers raising their children in a wide variety of circumstances and trying to do the best they can. I will show you what you can do on a daily basis to provide your children with father care that touches them deeply, changing their lives—and yours—for the better. By its end, you will understand what fatherneed is in yourself, your children, and your partner or spouse and what makes it such a remarkably compelling force in our emotions and behaviors, longing and growth, sorrow and joy. It is certainly not magic: the force of biology would never entrust something so crucial to something as ephemeral as magic. It is a thoroughly understandable physical and emotional force that pulls men to children just as it pulls children to men, related or not, to shape, enrich, and perpetuate each other's lives. Hence, the double meaning of the term *fatherneed* mirrors reality, as the warp of the need in fathers for children is woven together with the weft of the need of children for their father.

In Chapter 1, Fathers Do Not Mother, I explain how different father care is from mother care and how and why it matters so much to kids. We now understand that children from the first moments of life are equipped to find their father and distinguish him from their mother, even before their vision is twenty-twenty. At six weeks of age, infants can tell the difference between their mother's and father's voice. At 8 weeks of age, they can anticipate the complex differences in their mother's and father's caretaking and handling styles.

An infant's capacity to recognize father care in its own right so early in life alerts us to how critical connecting to the father is to the healthy development of the child. And this is only the beginning. Children often utter their word (or sound) for "father" before their "mother" word, and no one really knows why. Is it because the mother and child are so close that the mother does not need a name whereas the slightly more separate father entity does? By the time kids can walk and talk, they search out their father on their own.

Toddlers are particularly insistent in expressing fatherneed; they look for their father, say his name when he's not there, puzzle over his voice on the phone, and explore every inch of his face and body if given half a chance. School-age kids long to be with their father at work, to know his friends, to challenge his skills and strengths. Teenagers express fatherneed in yet more complex ways, competing with their father and confronting his values, beliefs, and, of course, limits. For so many sons and daughters, it is only at the death of the father that they discover the intensity and longevity of their fatherneed, especially when it has gone begging.

In addition to the child's contribution to the father–child relationship, the father's response to that contribution shapes the relationship even further. To begin with, father care differs from mother care in ways that are tremendously interesting to children. In Chapter 1, I describe the fascinating science that I and others have discovered about father care. I show you how fathers, compared to mothers, spend more of their time with their children in play that involves few toys and that encourages exploration and less of their time in play that is simply for the purpose of entertainment or distraction alone. Mothers, even when not home full-time, play less with their children, spend more of their time in giving physical care, and emphasize instruction and self-control. Fathers are more likely to encourage their kids to tolerate frustration and master tasks on their own before they offer help, whereas mothers tend to assist a fussing child earlier.

Dads discipline less with shame and disappointment and more with real-life consequences. Seven-year-old Morgan told me, "Dad makes me stop messing around without making me feel bad. I just stop without feeling ashamed." A retort more typical of a father than a mother is "Stop whining about the homework not being fair. Your teacher will not be impressed." Moms, however, tend to emphasize the emotional costs of misbehavior: "I can't believe you would throw your milk. How do you think I feel having to clean this mess up?" Fathers also tend to activate their kids emotionally and physically more than moms do, but with mixed results; the father who turns his toddler on just before bedtime and then complains when the child won't settle down and go to sleep is a classic source of maternal frustration.

We know now that fathers are in fact pulling more of their own weight, even though they are not mothering. The 1998 survey on shared parenting by the Work and Families Institute of New York shows a remarkable increase, compared to data collected thirty years ago, in the percentage of child care provided by fathers: whereas fathers used to provide less than 25 percent of the child care provided by mothers, they now provide 75 percent of the care that mothers provide.

Because children who have been raised with an involved father are different from those who have not, we are seeing more and more evidence of the impact that involved men have on their child's development. In Chapter 2, The Dad Difference in Child Development, I examine how father involvement actually works to promote a child's emotional, physical, and intellectual development.

Children whose dad has regularly changed their diapers, burped them and rocked them to sleep, and read to them enjoy a reserve of strength in dealing with stress and the frustrations of everyday life. They are less rigid in their gender stereotyping of their peers and in their response to other children and to society in general. They enjoy measurable intellectual benefits, especially in school readiness. Eight-year-old Ben says, "I feel bad for kids without Dads. Mine taught me how to read, but not like a teacher—more like a reader." He's referring to an instructional style more common among fathers than mothers. I find in my own research a tendency among fathers to be as interested in the process of finding an answer as in the correctness of the answer itself. Perhaps that is why math competence in girls often seems to be associated with early connections to the father.

Interestingly, all of these positive effects are even stronger and endure longer when they are complemented by a mother's support of her partner's active contribution to her child's emotional, social, and intellectual life. Even more intriguing is a finding by Jay Belsky of the University of Pennsylvania that the parental competence of fathers is more sensitive to marital satisfaction than is that of mothers; that is, a mutually satisfying marriage seems to amplify the father's, but not the mother's, positive effects. At the other end of the spectrum, we see a mirror image: studies show that the caretaking ability of women in highly dysfunctional families and marriages suffers, placing the child's development at particular risk; if the father in such a family is able to function reasonably well and continues to provide for his children emotionally and physically, he can buffer the children from some of the more toxic effects of the dysfunction.

There is an expectation among children whose father was involved in their daily life that diligence of effort pays off and that frustrations need not defeat. Interest in the novel and the challenging seems slightly keener in children whose fatherneed is gratified; they tend to assume that there is usually more than one way to skin any cat. John Snarey's four-decade-long study of fathers who supported their daughters and sons in less conventional ways—for example, by encouraging athletic competence and achievement in girls and being emotionally close to their young sons—had daughters who were more successful in school, work, and career and sons who eventually achieved more academically and in their careers down the line than did the children of fathers who supported them in more conventional ways.

If father involvement changes kids this much, how does it change kids when fathers are so involved with them that they are in fact their mainstay? Chapter 3, Dad as the Primary Caregiver, shares wonderful stories from my long-term study of intact families in which men served as the primary caregiver when their children were infants. The results of this unique study are published here for the first time; they offer a clear picture of the powerful impact of the paternal presence on children and families. The children in that study, now preteens, are described in vivid journalistic detail as we hear them talk about their experience of having been raised primarily by their father in their early years. The benefits and burdens of this arrangement on the children, mothers, and fathers give a crystalline clarity to the power of satisfied fatherneed.

Although the proportion of children who are raised by their father as the primary caretaker is relatively small and probably will always be so, the actual number, now over two million, is growing steadily. The experience of this parental arrangement is a profound one for the entire family, and the stories of individual experiences are so riveting and intriguing in what they teach us that they shine like beacons.

The kids in my study often felt a bit strange knowing their dads so well and feeling so close to them when they realized that the fathers of most of their friends were relegated to the margins of their lives. Many of the lessons I learned are not what I expected. For example, even when a father is changing diapers, cleaning, and cooking, he still plays with and disciplines the child in ways that differ from a mother's approach, but his gender stereotyping tendencies disappear! It is the mother who begins to reinforce some of the old stereotypes; it is as though she is getting her kids ready for the "outside world."

What especially characterizes most of these children now as preteens is the closeness of their friendships with opposite-sex peers. As they begin to become reproductive males and females, they are surprised to discover that their fathers are actually parents who are *males* and not just parents. Sound familiar, Mom?

Chapter 4, Fatherneed Throughout Life, is rooted in the notion, always a surprise when first discovered, that parents are changed by their children nearly as much as children are changed by their parents. The requirements of parenting are so demanding that none of us is good at all of it at all developmental stages all of the time. The dance between adult and child development requires that the lead change frequently without losing the rhythm or forward motion of personal growth. This chapter takes aim at how fatherneed in children and childneed in men are expressed across the changing landscape of the life span.

The greatest challenge to a father's parenting competence, however, is not aging but, rather, the separation of his life from his child's. In America that usually means divorce, which affects nearly half of all families. Divorce is such a critical topic that Chapter 5, Divorce: Challenge to Fatherneed, plays a central role in this book. The topic of divorce connects what we know about how important fathering is to the well-being of children and what we now know of the huge cost to children and fathers when the fatherneed goes unmet or is damaged.

Conventional wisdom to date has been far too cavalier about the cost of divorce to children. Research and clinical observations made by my wife, Dr. Marsha Kline Pruett, my own original research on divorce involving children aged six and under, and my experience as expert witness on child custody matters across the country have given me a searingly clear view of what happens when divorce threatens, or far too often destroys, fathering. Men who must work to support two families lose time with their children—and not only because they must now spend more time at work in order to meet the expenses of two households. Often the court won't give them more time with their children *because* they are too busy working to support two families to have enough time to be with their children. In this context, the concept of quality time is a cruel joke.

But divorce need not destroy fathering, ever. What terrifies children is what terrifies fathers: losing each other. What the kids want most is for their mom and dad to be "friends enough," as six-year-old Sambra said, speaking for herself and her three-year-old brother, "so they let each other love us the way we need loving." The adversarial process and litigation itself are seen by even preschool children as bad forces that destroy their parents' ability to stay "friends enough." Judicial caprice and the tattered reputation of family law practice itself combine to create the frighteningly out-of-control sensation that haunts so many divorcing couples and deprives them of the reassurance they so desperately seek, namely, the reassurance that they will not lose their life with their children.

Accounts of the experiences of divorcing men and the voices of their children fill Chapter 5, which also includes action plans that help families preserve competent postdivorce fathering (which are not too dissimilar to parenting plans that preserve competent mothering). The chapter closes with mention of new legal and judicial reforms that are more successful in sustaining contact between children and fathers, such reforms as shared custody, shared legal custody, divorce mediation, judicial education, and the use of special masters, (experienced, retired judges or attorneys who act as mediators).

Chapter 6, Expressions of Fatherneed, shows that fathering, like mothering, comes in an infinite variety of hues and shapes. Cultural and ethnic variety sculpt fatherhood in intriguing ways. African-American fathers, for example, are often more present in their child's community and neighborhood than in the home; looking closely, we see that nonresidential does not mean absent. Hundreds of thousands of fathers over age fifty are fathering and grandfathering kids in ways they could not imagine in their twenties; a certain relaxed freedom, even grace, characterizes their fathering now that they have either made it or not in their careers (or care less about making it than they did in their youth). Abandoning and teenage fathers are both being better understood.

Over 90 percent of teenage fathers in most studies want to stay involved in the life of their child and the child's mother. Those who do are more likely to finish school, stay employed, and avoid contact with the law. We are getting better at recovering these fathers, and in Chapter 9, I describe how. Incarceration poses special threats but, in some cases, provides opportunities to face one's role as a father. Cultural and ethnic variations in fathering are fascinating, as are those from the new age of assisted reproductive technology. Gay fathering, though politically controversial, is becoming less so clinically, and I explain why in Chapter 6.

Of course, what makes a man a father is a mother, and what women think and feel about the men with whom they create children strongly shapes fathering opportunities. Chapter 7, Mothers and Fatherneed, takes us into the lives of mothers, sharing what they feel, think, and remember about their relationship with their own father, a relationship that powerfully shapes a woman's expectations, hopes, and fears about her mate's role in the life of their shared child. Mothers also wield great power as gatekeepers to their child's world, beginning in the very first days of their baby's existence, and they have been culturally supported in this for eons. For biological and social reasons, mothers play a larger role in promoting competent fathering than fathers do in promoting competent mothering. Of course, the competence of each parent is intimately connected with and interacts with that of the other, but women do need to loosen their grip on the gate latch if they want their men and babies to fall in love with each other and stay in love.

Of course, not all children have a father in their life on a regular (or even irregular) basis. In this situation, how does a mother address her child's fatherneed? In fact, it is practically impossible for a mother to fill this need by herself, just as it is for a father to fill the motherneed in his motherless child. With the support of the caring, competent men in her life and in her community, however, a mother can provide her child with opportunities for ongoing and predictable physical, intellectual, spiritual, and emotional interaction with men, experiences from which her child will benefit measurably. Part of fatherneed in boys is the hunger to understand and practice maleness; in girls there is a wish to experience and explore its difference from femaleness.

Oppressions from her past can complicate a mother's desire or ability to embrace the idea of a healthy paternal presence in the life of her child. Such struggles and pain need to be respected and acknowledged, as must the right of her children to a potentially better experience of a paternal presence in their own growing up. Encouraging and supporting male involvement in child care settings, schools, camps, after-school activities, and events sponsored by one's faith community are wonderful ways to address male deficits in the life of a child. Mothers can encourage programs such as Read Boston, where men support literacy in the schools by reading regularly to classrooms of kids. A single mother can ask her married friends to include her child in their family outings and gatherings; most folks are happy to be asked.

Fatherneed does not doom fatherless or under-fathered kids. It does mean that we must support single mothers in their struggle to provide caring male relationships for their kids. And it means we can alert these mothers to the hunger in their kids for such relationships if their own hunger has been somehow damaged or wounded, tempting them to close the gate after their kids. Chapter 7 closes with how to keep this vital gate open, both within and outside marriage.

If father care can do so much for kids, the next question that arises is, What can it do for men? What are the effects on men of being so involved with kids? Chapter 8, How Fathering Changes Men for Good, provides some answers. Women are often the first to notice that a baby has changed a man. "More responsible" is the most common report, but "more patient," "more gentle," "more emotional," "nicer," "mellow," and "settled" are not far behind. Men enjoy better overall health after becoming fathers—despite the reduction in sleep. Reduced contact with the law and increased work productivity are also reported for all social groups. There don't seem to be many downsides to fatherhood for men.

There is compelling evidence that men who feel involved in their child's life are much less likely to default on child support—or, for that matter, mother support after divorce. When a divorced man feels that he has significant input into his child's everyday life and relationships, the financial and emotional commitment and sacrifice make more sense to him and feel less punitive.

Father care also appears to exert strong influence on the father's health. In a four-year National Institute of Mental Health (NIMH) study of dual-earner couples, Wellesley College's Rosalind Barnett found that men who worried about their children were more likely to experience job fatigue, anxiety, headache, low back pain, and sleeplessness. But involved fathers also have fewer accidental deaths, fewer premature deaths overall, less substance abuse, and fewer hospital admissions. Being positively involved seems to affect men's well-being so strongly that their diminished worry improves their health-related behavior.

Buddy Fite, one of America's greatest living guitar players, had decided to let his throat cancer kill him. Then his son Michael was born. Buddy wrote a lullaby, fell in love with the baby, changed his mind, and had a life-saving laryngectomy to remove the cancer. His incredible story serves as star witness to the thesis of Chapter 8.

We all play a part in satisfying our children's inborn need for their father. But beyond gatekeeping there are countless barriers in our culture itself that discourage competent fathering within and outside families: the glass ceiling for the fathers of young children who seek flextime and paternity leave; the child care and educational settings that hold parent conferences only during work hours; bureaucracies involved in the healthcare of children whose forms do not even have a place for the father's name; the media treatment of fathers as fools or jerks, even for our youngest audiences. Chapter 9, Fulfilling Fatherneed, explores proven strategies to create father-friendly environments, from day care to boardroom, for fathers married and not.

Public policy has far-reaching implications for individual lives. Child support enforcement laws are a cookie-cutter approach to an enormously complex problem, resulting in shallow and devaluing stereotypes such as the deadbeat dad. Legal advocacy must be reworked so that men who want to establish paternity for their children are not garnisheed back into poverty in a draconian Catch-22 that punishes them for trying to do the right thing for their kids. Judicial reform is sorely needed for fathers like the sixteen-year-old who wants to establish paternity so that he can support his child and girlfriend but dares not lest he face statutory rape charges because the consenting girlfriend was fourteen years old.

In the last chapter, The Kids Get the Last Word, we see that no one can tell us about who fathers are, or what having a father means, and say it with more passion or conviction than kids. Four-year-old Stacey, one of twins born to a mother by donor insemination, eloquently sums up the meaning of fatherhood in a remark made after returning home from a birthday party hosted by a friend's parents: "Mommy, what did you do with my Daddy? I need a daddy or I can't be a kid!" The differences between fathers and mothers are understood best by the children themselves; eight-year-old Julie puts it this way: "Mom just yells, but Dad means it." The difference between the divorces that work for kids and the ones that don't are most clearly expressed by the kids; David, nine years old, says, "Mom makes it impossible for Dad to be her friend because all she wants to do is hurt him, get back at him. He's not perfect, but I need him, and she uses me to get even with him. I end up with the busted heart." I close Chapter 10 with the ideas and advice kids have for other kids on how to stay close to a dad without hurting a mom, within and outside marriage.

This is the first book to address what fathering actually does to children and to men. It combines science and common sense with the realities of daily life. I am a practicing clinician who has also researched and solved some of the problems you face, and I have worked hard with remarkable men and women to change the public policies that impede competent fathering. In the following chapters we will look at fathering's rich diversity, see how it works, and, finally, understand what it means to, and how it profoundly affects, us all. From deep within their biological and psychological being, children need to connect to fathers and fathers to their children to live life whole.

1

Fathers Do Not Mother

ABE HAD BEEN home half-time now for a month with his six-week-old daughter, Sally. In the other half of his life, he was sharing a full-time software engineering job with his wife, Deb. In their late twenties, Abe and Deb were thrilled to have this great little gal enter their world. They were also shocked by how much work she was; they felt lovingly invaded by the ceaseless demands of caring for her well. Both firstborns, Abe and Deb fondly remembered doing some nurturing of their younger siblings and cousins; consequently, they tried to help each other master the surprisingly complex task of raising an infant.

Deb was a little worried, however, that Abe was not as happy fathering as she was mothering. When they discussed it, Abe said he had just come to an important realization: "I've been trying to copy the way you are with her, do what you do, and it just doesn't work for me." He went on to explain that he was reading Sally's signals a little differently than Deb was. He wasn't always sure Sally was hungry or tired or that a particular cry meant she needed a change of diaper. He liked to play with her, he said, and felt Sally liked it, too, just when Deb felt it was time to settle down. He knew that Deb felt he was too rough with Sally when he changed her or put her in the infant car seat. Abe admitted to Deb that the weekends, when they both cared for Sally, seemed harder because of these differences and that he'd begun to experiment with his

own parenting style on the weekdays when he and Sally were alone together. He was feeling better about his skills, he told Deb, but he'd been
feeling a little guilty about going his own way—although Sally, meanwhile, seemed to be just fine. Abe then described the internal comfort he
was feeling about his deepening connection with the baby. To Deb's
credit, she listened to him quietly, then simply said, "Go for it. My way
seems to work for me, and she obviously loves being with you. Neither
one of us has to be perfect in this."

Thus begins my tale about how fathers do not mother. It needn't be
that big a surprise. Clearly, mothers do not father. But since our cultural
expectation is that mothers will be competent from the moment the
umbilical cord is cut, it takes work to fully comprehend how it is that
men can become nurturing beings and how fathering differentiates itself from mothering. Herein lies a central question for this book: If fathering differs from mothering in fundamental ways, are there things
that only fathers can give their children?

In my twenty-five years of clinical work with families and children,
I have observed, with increasing amazement, an infinite variety of caretaking styles, arrangements, and structures used by families to raise
their young in the best way they can. I also now realize that most of the
enduring parental skills are probably, in the end, not dependent on gender. Once we look closely, we see nurturing skills in both mothers and
fathers. In fact, the very essence of nurturing—the ability to be selfless
and patient, loving yet consistent, tolerant but expectant, and, above all,
the capacity to share and make sacrifices of one's own emotional, spiritual, material, intellectual assets—ultimately transcends gender. Our
own personal history, cultural preparation, religion, and family values
may predispose us toward, or away from, the expression of such abilities, and consequently are not gender's exclusive domain. As Erik Erikson explained in *Dimensions of a New Identity*:

> In youth you find out what you care to do and who you care to
> be—even in changing roles. In young adulthood you learn whom
> you care to be with—at work and in private life, not only exchang-
> ing intimacies, but sharing intimacy. In adulthood, however, you
> learn to know *what* and *whom* you can take care of. [emphasis
> added].

Beyond gender itself, the forces that shape fathering, though easy
to catalogue, get harder to track across the life span of a father–child re-

lationship. What I mean by fathering is *involved* fathering. This is male behavior beyond insemination that promotes the well-being and healthy development of one's child and family in active ways. Although a list of behaviors can't possibly encompass all important aspects of fathering, it should include the following everyday characteristics:

1. Feeling and behaving responsibly toward one's child
2. Being emotionally engaged
3. Being physically accessible
4. Providing material support to sustain the child's needs
5. Exerting influence in child rearing decisions

Practically speaking, fathering means helping with, or paying, the bills; participating in infant care by changing diapers, bathing, and feeding; disciplining, bandaging cuts, helping with homework, driving to and from after-school and weekend activities, making trips to the pediatrician; and knowing your child's friends, passions, fears, and loves. As Abe put it, fathering is "almost anything that I wish my dad had done with me but didn't."

Historian Robert Griswold has described how the characteristics of fathering fit together in very different proportions across cultures and political eras. Breadwinning gained salience during the Industrial Revolution, when fathers disappeared from homes in a mass migration to factories, absenting themselves from their children for the first time in American history. Today, fathering behaviors, as convincingly documented by Wellesley College's Joseph Pleck, combine with rising coparenting expectations among both men and women as we witness greater opportunity and responsibility for care of young children by men.

Particular fathering traits and behaviors are shaped in the individual man by a rich diversity of emotional and historical forces, none of them occurring in isolation from the others. Some of the more influential forces derive from the past. I know from my own research, as well as from other original investigations (e.g., by Harvard's John Snarey and Pennsylvania State's Jay Belsky), that happy memories of being fathered by an involved and nurturing dad encourage sons toward identifying with and modeling such behavior as they father their own children. Paradoxically, an uninvolved or ineffective father may encourage a compensatory process in a son to father his own children in exactly the opposite way, thus causing the son to become the father he wishes he had had.

Research also reveals that a more subtle support may come from the past in less obvious ways. It is possible to predict a new father's parenting skills by measuring how much he perceived his own father's support of his autonomy and independence while he was growing up and how sensitive he felt his mother was to his needs as a child. In a study by Michael Cox, the quality of a father-to-be's relationship with his own father was found to be the most important predictor of the younger man's subsequent sensitivity to the baby and the appropriateness of his responses to him or her (not surprisingly, a young woman's relationship with her mother was an important predictor of her own maternal behavior).

Those of us in the fathering research field find children themselves to be a very powerful force in shaping fathering behavior in men. The temperamental fit between father and child can go a long way toward helping each of them feel competent in relating to the other: two quiet, reflective types can tolerate each other's predilection for calm and passivity rather well, and two boisterous and loud characters may find each other irresistible when it comes to exploring and roughhousing.

But more important than fit may be the amount of time alone that father and child have together. While at the NIMH, psychologist Frank Pedersen studied firstborns of working- and middle-class families and found that a father and his infant develop an enhanced relationship through interactions that occur between the two of them in the absence of the mother. In fact, the studies found that a father's broad repertoire of skills in actively engaging the infant is a consequence of such time alone. Infants who have time alone with dad show richer social and exploratory behavior than children not exposed to such experiences. They smile more frequently in general, and they more frequently present toys to their dad. They also spend more time looking at and manipulating objects as part of heightened exploratory behavior. Overall, writes Pedersen, "more extensive experience between father and infant in the absence of the mother promoted more positive interactional patterns for both partners." (The next chapter will explore the effect of involved fathering on child development.)

Biogenetics, the role that biological compounds play in expressing genetic material, also has a hand in influencing fathering behavior, albeit in ways yet to be fully explained in humans. At least two hormones are involved in stimulating nurturing behavior in males in certain species. Male tamarin monkeys of South America, known to be particularly nurturing fathers to their young, have been found by Charles Snowdon, a primatologist at the University of Wisconsin, to produce high levels of the hormone *prolactin*. This is a protein synthesized in the pituitary gland, which is deep within the brain and best known for its role in stimulating lactation and breast growth during pregnancy in female primates. But the hormone is also present in the human male brain as well. Snowdon noticed that as the tamarin male's prolactin levels rose, he acquired more caregiving experience, suggesting that the hormone may be as much an effect as a cause of paternal nurturing.

Lower down the evolutionary ladder is the example of the uxorious vole and his hormonal transformation from naïve male to affectionate and protective father by another brain protein. NIMH neuroscientist Thomas Insel found that the hormone *vasopressin*, also found in the pituitary gland of the human brain, improved the male vole's tendency to huddle over pups, groom them, and carry them to safety. Notably, vasopressin is closely related biochemically to the human hormone *oxytocin*, the hormone that stimulates uterine contractions at the end of pregnancy and aids in the release of milk from the mammary gland. It may be a long stretch from vole to Dad, but biochemistry may yet be proven to play a role in the variation of nurturing drives felt and demonstrated by men.

Science still has far to go in understanding all the complexities of hormonal influence on the brain and behavior based solely on the presence or absence of the Y chromosome. *On average,* there are small differences in male and female competencies, though cognitive scientists speak of a few notable trends:

- Females show a slight preference toward language skills, rote memory, and discrete sensory/tactile discrimination.
- Males show a slight preference toward spatial perception, mathematical memory, and mechanical aptitude.

How critical any of these trends is to parental competence seems to me a moot point. Parental nurturance, warmth, and closeness are shown over and over again to be connected to healthy child development regardless of whether it is the mother or father at the helm. Besides, it is the child that turns us into parents, not genes or hormones.

It's instructive, even comforting, to review some of the many similarities between mothering and fathering before we head off into the lesser-known territory of their differences:*

- The attachment and closeness that mothers and fathers feel toward their newborn is not predicted by previous experience. University of Arizona nurses Sandra Ferketich and Ramona Mercer found that men and women do not differ in the depth of the love relationship they feel for each of their children. While experience may make the job of parenting a little less difficult and somewhat less depleting, each child is loved in a unique way by the father and the mother.

- Men and women are similarly predisposed emotionally to nurture their children in most ordinary circumstances, although they are usually not similarly prepared or supported by society or their own particular families to do so. Still, the nurturing inkling is there in both males and females as we see from the play of toddlers onward and, given half a chance, it becomes quite strong during the peak reproductive years.

- The desire to feel emotionally connected to one's children throughout life is the same for men and women, though it may find differing forms of expression.

- University of California psychologist Ross Parke found fathers and mothers equally able to interpret their child's behavioral cues indicating hunger, gastric distress, and fatigue and, importantly, equally able to respond "appropriately."

- Fathers and mothers have been found to be equally anxious about leaving their baby in the care of someone else. They plan ahead, hover, and double-check, showing behaviors that are more alike than not.

- Michael Lamb and his colleague Ann Frodi found no gender differences in heart rate, respiratory rate, or skin temperature in their study of the biological responsivity of men and women to infants in distress. They went on to investigate the psychophysiological responsiveness of eight- and fourteen-year-old males and females to videotapes of quiet, smiling, and crying infants; again they found no gender differences in responsiveness.

*I will emphasize throughout this chapter the interplay between parental behavior and the development of *young* children, since early development is when the impact of parenting matters most.

- Men and women appear to have a similar physiological capacity to differentiate their newborn from other newborns in the nursery. A team of Israeli psychologists led by Larry Katz at Hebrew University tested the ability of mothers and fathers to recognize their infant though sensory pathways other than sight, sound, and smell. They blindfolded parents and blocked their sense of smell with nose plugs. They found that both fathers and mothers were able to recognize their infant solely by touching the infant's hands.
- Single parenting is strikingly similar for men and women. In a study done of single dads in the air force, researchers listened to fathers discuss the problems they were having with discipline, loneliness, and the lack of adult support in parenting as well as their difficulty in finding and maintaining good child care arrangements, balancing work and family life, and finding personal time for themselves. These fathers' concerns couldn't be more familiar to single moms.

Since parenting is largely about solving problems as lovingly as possible for any given parent–child pair and since we acknowledge that men and women differ in the ways they solve problems, we can conclude that fathers and mothers have equal, if slightly different, parenting abilities. Similarly, there is no evidence that, given equal experience and support, parents of one gender necessarily excel as caretakers. Michael Lamb has written, "With the exception of lactation, there is no evidence that women are biologically predisposed to be better parents than men are. Social convention, not biological imperatives, underlie the traditional division of parental responsibilities." This most certainly doesn't presume that women exert little influence on the way that fathering emerges in men. On the contrary. Just as the personality of the child plays a role in the kind of fathering a man exhibits, so too do the character, experiences, and wishes of the mother (as we shall discuss in detail in Chapter 7). Marital experience and cultural background both play larger roles in sculpting the man as father than they do in shaping the woman as mother.

While we are at it, let's also discuss the effect of the child's gender on the way that mothers and fathers treat their children. For a quarter of a century, psychology's matriarchs, such as Eleanor Maccoby, have contributed to the debate over whether mothers and fathers treat sons differently from daughters. The latest contribution to the debate is a large meta-analysis by psychologists Hugh Lytton and David Romney of 172 studies, which resulted in this conclusion: the only consistent influence found was a very small tendency for parents to engage their child in play with sex-typed toys or games. Any trends favoring a difference in interaction caused by parental gender alone faded with time and age. Moms and dads apparently resemble each other more in parental style the older they and their children get. Lytton and Romney concluded, "The present analysis has demonstrated a virtual absence of sex-distinctive parental pressures on child development." Or, in my words: give it a rest. As we know, gender does not a parent make; a child does. Mothers and fathers share much more of the competent nurturing domain than they do not, and that is what matters to children.

Even as new research helps us free ourselves from past erroneous conclusions, we remain hampered in our core understanding of fathering's unique status by inadequate and insufficient science. One gaping hole is in the area of a man's transition to fatherhood. First of all, the information made available to men prior to and during pregnancy about becoming a father is, at the very least, embarrassingly inadequate for many young men, and destructive for some. To wit: when Marsha and I enthusiastically attended childbirth and parenting classes at Yale New Haven Hospital in giddy anticipation of our daughter Olivia's birth, fathers were largely the butt of the instructor's jokes about being breathing machines in labor, passing out during delivery, sleeping through the baby's cries, and generally bumbling their way into fatherhood. My heart ached as I watched the enthusiastic fathers-to-be (whether working class, professional, or unemployed, married or not, young or old, every father came every night) lower their eyes as if being chastised ("Take your place—and it's at the back of this bus"). Finally, I couldn't stand it any longer and spoke up. The nurse teacher, to her credit, apologized, unaware that this was anything other than humor. Later we found out that the expectant mothers, too, were uncomfortable about this not so subtle disenfranchisement of the fathers-to-be.

Meanwhile, science has not helped much either. The vast body of reputable research to date on the transition to parenthood has leaned toward the "matricentric," focusing either on the transition from womanhood to motherhood or on the transition from couplehood to parenthood. While these are important fields of inquiry, they cannot be understood as complete or compelling until the concomitant research is done on the transition from manhood to fatherhood. There is hope for new understanding, thanks to an important project headed by psychologists Bill Doherty and Marti Erikson at the University of Minnesota that is just now under way.

Given the limits of our current understanding, how do we know that involved fathering, as interesting as it is for a father to do, has any bearing on the well-being of his child? One place to start looking is evolutionary science, a perspective that prompts us to ask, Why would evolution or brain development itself have provided the early ability of infants to discriminate fathers from mothers if this ability had no survival value? *Would identification of this ability as a survival mechanism not prove once and for all that motherhood should not be used as the benchmark for standards by which we judge fatherhood?*

Sure enough, there are intriguing findings from child development studies that prove father care *is* necessary to the developing child from the first months of life. We already know that human development wastes little time or energy while promoting its own development, and the observable reality that infants only weeks old show interest in their father means that father care has its role in helping babies become fully human.

Here is what we know about the child's interest in the father, beginning from the first weeks and months of life:

- By six weeks of age, infants can distinguish their father's voice from their mother's voice. While a quiet and alert infant will attend more quickly to mother's voice, an upset or fretting infant will calm more readily to the father's voice.
- By eight weeks, infants can anticipate differences in maternal and paternal handling styles. Pediatrician and researcher Michael Yogman's split-screen video studies at Boston Children's Hospital of the responses of alert, comfortable infants to the approach of their mother and father are still disarming twenty years later. When infants were approached by their mother, they slowed and regulated their heart and respiratory rates, relaxed their shoulders, and lowered their eyelids (Ahh . . . Mom). When the father approached, the infant's heart and respiratory rates quickened, shoulders hunched up, and eyes widened and brightened (Dad's here . . . party time!).
- Toward the end of the first year, infants protest separations from mother or father less if they have an involved father. In fact, the infant's ability to connect with the father delays the onset of separation protest in general.

- Toddlers seek out and seem to join in the father's more playful, more robust, less predictable style of play. Boston psychoanalyst James Herzog finds children of this age seem attuned to and anticipate the disruptive, stimulating nature of such play.

From this intriguing list (which I will expand in Chapter 3), it appears that infants are born "pre-wired" or programmed to send certain behavioral cues (coos, gurgles, cries, smiles, knitted brows, and frowns) and that mothers *and* fathers are predisposed biologically to respond to those very cues. More importantly, even the youngest of our species seem predisposed to distinguish maternal from paternal responses to their cues. What is that competence to distinguish parental responses doing there, smack in the middle of development, if it serves no purpose? Why is the paternal response and presence of such interest to infants and young children, and why bother to look from so early in life for the things that only a father can give?

Rick loved being a father more than anything he had ever done in his life. In fact, it startled him to fall so deeply in love with his son, giving him a twinge of guilt that he'd never felt quite so head-over-heels about his wife. All his life he'd been a busy guy, playing every sport he could get near in school and during the summers. He worked as a welder for a structural renovation company so that he could be outside and stay active. It came as no surprise, then, to his wife that Rick also loved having an active little boy. When Rick got home from work in the evening, he would kick off his boots, wash his hands, and look for Damon, who was also usually looking for him. Rick learned to ask if Damon had just been fed, because too much postprandial activity had previously led to some "hurling." Says Damon's mother, "Rick seems to just like to get Damon turned on first, and *then* Rick gets involved with him." Fortunately for Rick, she appreciates this quality in her husband, pointing out that Damon tends to be a little on the passive side and feeling that his dad's "revving him up now and then" is probably good for him.

Rick's interaction with Damon is a classic example of what scientific observations have identified as a common paternal behavior: the predisposition in fathers to enjoy activating their children in order to interact with them. Fathers do this by entering the child's world in less predictable, somewhat more disruptive ways than do mothers. When this style of interaction is studied across several different time periods, we find that these interactions contain fewer and fewer repetitive patterns, giving this activation style a rather disruptive quality. This is especially obvious in infancy, when fathers and mothers approach their infant for care in such different ways. Mothers tend to pick up infants (usually to care for them) in the same way, time after time. They bend over the child, usually speaking softly and repeating the pattern similar to the previous pickup. Fathers, on the other hand, pick up their children to *do* something with them, and they pick them up in generally unpredictable ways, not repeating the patterns they used previously. They may want to surprise the child, for example, by picking the child up without warning or by approaching the child head first instead of feet first. Nine times out of ten, the father's approach will be unpredictable, unlike the mother's, which will be predictable in the same proportion. A possible reason for this difference may be that mothers typically pick up their children to physically care for them whereas fathers typically pick them up to "make something happen" with them. Mother care tends to be more rhythmic and repetitive, but father care tends to be less predictable and more playful—even when the father is providing full-time care.

What Rick likes to do most with ten-month-old Damon these days is play with him. Rick will lie down on the floor and prop Damon, sitting up, on his chest facing him, letting his son play with his hands, his shirt pockets and their contents, and his beard.

The father as play partner is one of the most enduring findings in the research on the role of the father in child development. Furthermore, the play between a father and his child has characteristics that are obvious even in the brief description here of Rick and Damon. For one thing, the play makes sparse use of toys. Toy-mediated play, in fact, is more characteristic of mother–child interaction, especially when there is an educational motive involved. The toy the father uses most often in his play with his young child is, in fact, always with him and rarely gets broken; it is his own body. Unlike the mother, whose body typically has already been well used by the child, especially if she has chosen to breast-feed, the father seems to appreciate the physical interaction with his child, having been so remote from the physical aspects of pregnancy, delivery, and lactation. Consequently, father-as-jungle-gym can be a pleasurable compensation for many men who felt frustrated by their physical disconnection from the fetus and newborn and are tired of being relegated to the cheap seats in the arena of physical intimacy.

Father play also tends to be qualitatively different from mother play in that it is frequently nonconventional. It relies less on traditional games and themes and more on the activation-exploration theme. Even the mundane chores of physical child care—bathing, diapering, dressing, brushing teeth—are often made more intensely physical and playful by dad than is necessary (in the opinion of many moms). Infants between the ages of seven and thirteen months actually respond more positively to being picked up by their father than by their mother precisely because Mom picks them up for maintenance whereas Dad picks them up in response to infant request or because *he* wants to play. French psychologist Florence Labrell has suggested that this nonconventional quality to father–child interaction has interesting implications for children's learning patterns and their faith in themselves to be creative and take intellectual risks (more on this in the next chapter).

Rough-and-tumble play makes up an important portion of father–child play, sometimes to the distress of anxious mothers. Still, most children have an appetite to reciprocate, especially as they master walking and running. Interestingly, some researches have suggested that this aspect of paternal behavior lessens as a father spends increasing amounts of time with his child. My own research into the development of children in intact families raised primarily by their fathers (Chapter 3), however, shows exactly the opposite: this more physical style of play is preserved even when the father has primary responsibility for the child's care. What does vary, however, is the amount of rough-and-tumble play across cultures: American fathers seem to use it liberally, whereas men in Sweden, for example, and in many preindustrial cultures do not.

Another deeply rooted idiosyncracy of father care is found through-out the mythology and cultural spirituality of indigenous American peoples. Pueblo and Plains Indians and tribes of the mountain, horse, and fish cultures are similar in that it is the father's task to take his chil-dren out of the village and show them the broader expanse of land, the world beyond the village. The same peoples typically assign the mother the roles of caregiving and instructing the child in self-control and self-care.

This same drive to show children the world around them may be at the root of another frequently observed father care characteristic: fathers, when carrying a small child, tend to hold the child face forward whereas mothers tend to hold the child facing inward or over their shoulder. The father position (called the "football position" in America)—buttocks in the father's upturned palm, body tucked between father's biceps and side of chest—gives the child the same view of the world the father has, that is, approaching it *en face*. One mother position, when the child faces inward, gives the child ready access to the mother's body and space; the other, when the child is placed over the shoulder, gives the child a view of the world the mother has just passed through. What the maternal and paternal carrying styles do have in common is the side on which the child is carried: 80 percent of the time both father and mother hold the child on their left side (even when left handed), next to their heart's side of the chest. None of these carrying positions is necessarily better than the others, just different.

Closely related to this behavior follows another trend in behavior father care researchers have watched for several decades now: the ten-dency in men to encourage and support novelty-seeking behavior in their children.

Ben is eighteen months old and is known in his family as Fear-less Fred because of his appetite for headlong forays into the un-known. More than just about anything, he loves to put on his "goat and butts" (coat and boots) and go to the park. Over the last few months, however, he has refused to go with his mother (and his baby sister, who is still nursing), crying only, "Daddy bark [park], Daddy bark." His mother explains, "Ben prefers his dad because he'll let him do anything. I'm not comfortable having him even on the little slide. Somehow he never gets hurt, but the odds are, that day will come."

___

Fathers *tend** to encourage their children, both sons and daughters, to explore the world about them a bit more vigorously than do mothers. There seems to be an invisible tether connecting mothers and fathers to their children, especially when they are in a new place. The tendency is for that tether to be shorter for the mother than for the father. Some children don't care about this tether, but to others it makes all the difference in the world. A longer tether means maybe your chances are better with Dad to get to touch that doggie, play with that new kid, try bike riding, go camping with your friend's family, or stay out late. In the next chapter, we'll explore the effect of this trend on the child's development.

The father care predisposition to support novelty-seeking behavior in the child may have a reciprocal template within the child. The father is himself a novelty from their first moments together. The mother, after all, has been part of the child's body since its conception, sharing tissue, body fluids, sounds, movement, illness, and food. But fathers are brand-new. And even though the infant's sensory apparatus remains immature for months, we know that infants attune themselves to their father's voice, handling style, and maybe even smells and textures from their first weeks and months of life. That these properties of the father are novel to the infant, that they are "not-mother" yet are nurturing and safe, seems to be both appealing and intriguing to infants. Consequently, novelty itself may be especially salient in the father–child connection because it is property both *of* the father himself and *felt with* him. I would not be surprised in the least to learn down the road that there is a biochemical component to this connection, probably in the prolactin hormone system of both father and child.

Related to the father's support of novelty-seeking behavior in the child is his tendency to help his offspring tolerate frustration when attempting something new. Again, this is only an observed *trend,* but its merits may prove interesting. When the child is struggling to find the

___

*Emphasis is added here to remind readers that I am only talking about trends here. We all know some mothers who sound like these men and vice versa.

last ring for the tower or a critical block for the bridge or to remember the shape of a newly learned letter, Mom and Dad tend to respond somewhat differently. Showing a strong educational motivation in their approach, mothers will more typically nudge the ring into the child's reach or start writing part of the letter before the child reaches a frustration level that might interfere with the ability to complete the task. Fathers in the same scenario, on the other hand, tend to hang back a bit longer, encouraging the child, verbally or with their physical presence alone, to bear the frustration and stick with the task, thus often enabling the child to pass the point at which help might have been offered by the mother. A classic example is the child learning to ride a bike without training wheels. Although there is huge individual variation here, dads are more likely to put the child back on the bicycle seat after a failed attempt than are moms. If the father withholds support for too long, the exercise falls apart, whether it's bike riding or letter writing, and nothing is learned. But when the timing is right, the feeling of mastery can be pretty gratifying for both father and child, and the experience is an interesting complement to what might be felt when the mother assists the child. My own speculation is that the goal of such paternal behavior is to encourage the child to master the frustration inherent in learning and not just to educate the child.

While a father's tendency to teach his child mastery of frustration is a topic in need of further study, it plays a supporting role in the development of an important trait many children feel is classically more related to father care than to mother care: the expectation of achievement. Firstborn children tend to feel this expectation more acutely, but their siblings also tend to attribute this one to Dad more than to Mom. Boston psychoanalyst Lora Tessman's study of the first undergraduate women to attend MIT found a disproportionately high number of close father–daughter relationships in the histories of these competent, achieving young women.

When Ben is with his mother outside the house these days, he tends to give her a run for her money. As a toddler just itching for more autonomy, he tests the limits on an hourly basis, running and darting away when he feels like taunting or throwing whatever he's done with, whether blocks or food. What bothers his dad about all this is that his mother "lets him get away with murder." He feels that "she should just make him mind. It's not that hard."

—— ●

What Ben's dad will find out with his daughter is that it actually *is* that hard with the child of the opposite gender (but more on that in due course). But it is true that there is another discriminating trend between mothering and fathering, and this one is found in the area of discipline and limit setting. Behavioral scientists studying the development of self-control and the conscience have long noted differences in the way mothers and fathers try to control a child's undesirable behavior. Mothers (who typically know their child better than the father does because of their larger role in child care) tend to discipline by emphasizing the relational and social costs of misbehavior. A common response by a mother to a toddler who has just thrown food is "Do you ever think about how much work it is for me to clean up the mess when you throw your cereal?" (Mom is thinking, "This is not good for our relationship for me to feel like your slave-charwoman.") Or she might say, "Now you've made us all be late because I have to clean up this mess and that's rude." (Mom is thinking, "It burdens the whole family when you act up.") Shame also tends to play a role when kids get a bit older: to a child who does not listen or obey, mothers now express their disappointment and feelings of being personally let down.

Fathers, on the other hand, tend to emphasize the mechanical or societal consequences of misbehavior, bringing more emotional distance to disciplining as a whole. This tends to give the impression that fathers are less manipulable and more functionary when they have drawn a line. Fathers tend to make comments like "Don't expect to have any friends if you're that selfish with your toys" and "Don't ask me for help if you aren't willing to do your share" and, later in life, "You'll never find a job if you are going to act like such a jerk with your teachers." The value to children of experiencing both a maternal and a paternal approach to discipline blended into the foundation of their conscience can't be overestimated.

The gender twist on this disciplinary trend, hinted at earlier in the example of Ben, is important to appreciate, because it may explain why his father feels Ben is easier to discipline than his mother does. Parents tend to feel more confident in, and less ambivalent about, their own authority when they are disciplining a child of the same gender. A child of the same gender simply feels more familiar to the parent; parents have the feeling of having "been there" themselves. Children sense this and, at least when young, tend to be more compliant with the same-gender parent. The back-and-forth nature of this phenomenon reinforces it over the years, fostering same-gender understandings and closeness.

The opposite holds true for the cross-gender parent–child duo. Boys feel more confident and able to say no to mothers, and girls are more comfortable saying no to fathers. That unfamiliarity parents feel in dealing with the opposite-gender child is sensed by them, and they exploit the advantage with vigor. In raising my own daughters, I remember well being startled at the power of their first refusals (they were not even two years old!) and the pleasure they took in my inability to make them mind. It was as though they were trying to teach me something about being female that was, simply because I was male, just beyond my reach.

Another common fathering quality is a style of communication that includes a tendency to use more complex speech with children, even young ones, than do mothers. When mothers talk to preschoolers, they tend to simplify and slow their speech, feeling this works better in getting and holding their child's attention. Fathers speaking to preschoolers use bigger words and longer sentences spoken in less rhythmic sequences. We can understand this as either the father's tendency to keep expectations high for the acquisition of language skills or his reluctance to baby his growing child in general. For infants, however, fathers adjust their speech patterns dramatically, speaking more slowly, in shorter phrases, and using multiple repetitions of a musical nature. Even in the newborn nursery, we find men speaking in high-pitched falsetto, a vocal range known to be effective in getting an infant's attention.

Over and over again in the science of father care, researchers point out that it is the quality of interaction between father and child—that is, whether the father is sensitive to the child's needs and reactions—that determines the overall value of his involvement in his child's life, not the quantity. Counting the minutes that child and father are in each other's company tells us very little about the ultimate influence of the father on the development of his child. What fathers do with their children, *how* they do it, and, probably most important, how they *are* with their kids matter more than how often or long they do it. This has profound implications for the changes in family structure that American culture is currently witness to and is of overwhelming significance in helping boys and men prepare for and maintain competent, sensitive parenting.

To bring this chapter back to the question of whether father care is distinct from mother care, I'll let a letter from Lois Barclay Murphy, one of the giants of child development study in this century, do the talking. Her words help tease out the answer to the earlier question of whether there are things only a father can do for his children. In October 1992, at the age of ninety, she wrote a letter to me expressing gratitude for my bringing my research on the contributions of the father to child development to the attention of child developmentalists. Murphy agreed with me that the "confidence-promoting quality of good relating fathers needs emphasis," adding, "I speak not only from a life of observations but also from personal experience." Her letter continues:

> While my mother tried to glamorize me and make me a "lady," my father always accepted me for the little booky girl that I was. I felt *safe* and adequate with him. My assurance in doing things that had not been done before owes everything to him and his parents and grandfather. And my relation with my father probably also has something to do with my freedom from a rigid commitment of being "feminine," *and* my ease with men, and, I guess, the endless support I've had from them. Thanks for reminding all of us about the contributions of fathers to the strengths of their children, in *all* families.
>
> Enthusiastically,
>
> Lois Barclay Murphy

Period.

2

The Dad Difference in Child Development

Two women in their thirties were ahead of me in the checkout line of our local food market, and their conversation, despite my respect for privacy, sucked me right in.

One woman, apparently referring to her husband, said, "He is so much closer to Abby because he stayed home for about two years between jobs and he essentially raised her. I was working and around a lot, but he was her chief cook and bottle washer. And it probably made her a different kid than Ben. And it's not just that they *know* each other better. He's close to Ben and loves him, too. I think men just raise them different than we do."

"What do you mean 'different'?" asked her companion, shuffling forward in the line.

"Well, he's rougher and softer at the same time. He's firmer about setting limits than I am, but a cream puff about hurting her feelings. I think it's been good for both of them. She would have whined me into an early grave. Somehow she made him sweeter, even to me. She's pretty cocky, thinks she's pretty smart in school, works hard, and will try almost anything. She believes in herself more than her brother does."

"Now that he's working again, are they still close?"

"He's more connected to both kids. Takes them to the doctor, school conferences, and he doesn't need to be asked!"

Their turn with the cashier had come, and I was disappointed that my eavesdropping had to end.

With my nameless consultant's testimony about her husband's impact on the development of her daughter, I am now changing our discussion from how fathers tend to be different from mothers with their children to what difference it makes that they are. We'll wade into the sometimes murky waters of what father care does to effect development in children and why we think it works the way it does. But don't be fooled. We have just begun to understand how this works, and every time we get an answer, we unearth more (and usually better) questions.

My strong suspicions regarding why we are just getting around to really investigating father care is that we have been stuck far too long on the tired old preoccupations of my discipline of developmental psychiatry: how mothers "go wrong" in their relationships with their kids and what the troubled outcomes for kids are. While some excellent science exists that helps us assist certain at-risk or impaired mothers in relating to their child's needs better than they might be able to do on their own, vast energies have been poured into the less than thoughtful practice of mother blaming. This practice has stalled and distracted us from better efforts to understand the impact of men on children's development. If the intent is mother blaming, what role could there possibly be for fathers to play in the development course of a child's life? If "bad enough" mothering is considered sufficient unto itself to foster trouble in a child's development, is father care more likely to be viewed as just another irrelevant variable?

Nowhere is this oversight more striking than in the circumstance of family violence. In a chapter titled "Fathers, the Missing Parent in Research on Family Violence," Kathleen Sternberg of the National Institute of Child and Human Development concludes that it is very worrisome that "a review of the literature on children's victimization and observation of violence in the family reveals a conspicuous lack of information from and about fathers in these families. Despite the fact that men are frequently portrayed as perpetrators on the nightly news and in television drama, little is actually known about the roles played by fathers and the other male figures in these families." A highly respected family court judge recently asked me to reevaluate a potential charge of paternal abuse. She had to throw out the previous three-month-long $15,000 evaluation because the assessment team had failed to even interview the father. Ignoring the effect of fathers in situations of family violence and failing to study it properly isn't just oversight, it's immoral.

This failure is made all the more poignant as other research continues to affirm that father care can promote healthy child development, albeit differently from mother care. Psychologist Larry Applewhite's comparison of maternally and paternally separated children in military families is definitive in this regard. He compared the emotional, cognitive, and behavioral functioning of 288 children, four-to-eight-year-olds, living with either mother or father on a military base during a leave by the other parent. No difference was found in the quality of the children's overall emotional or social functioning, whether they were experiencing a maternal or a paternal separation. Applewhite pointed out that while his findings in no way diminish the significance of maternal care, they do speak to the profound influence a father can exert on his child's well-being.

Before describing the unique and enduring effects of the paternal presence and care on children, I want to clarify my standards for calling a father present and capable of providing care. This matters because it is neither the amount of time nor the setting in which that time is spent with children (i.e., married or not) that ultimately matters but, rather, the quality of what the father and child do together—including nothing at all. All of our research proves that what matters most in influencing child outcomes, positively and negatively, is, in the words of Jason, an eight-year-old from my longitudinal study, "just the way my Dad and I *are* together."

Most of the effects we'll be discussing fall within the broad spectrum of fathering that occurs when a dad is reasonably involved or responsible. Even these adjectives carry different nuances, the former evoking physical and emotional presence in the routines of the child's life, the later implying a larger role in overseeing the child's well-being, making decisions, and embracing the parent–child conflicts inherent in setting limits. By responsible, I do not simply mean making children behave and act respectful or providing financial security or paying child support; I mean an emotional commitment sufficient to honor one's obligation to sustain the life and soul one helped create.

A curious overtone appears when we attempt to adapt British pediatrician and analyst Donald Winnicott's phrase "good enough mothering" for use in defining responsible or involved fathering. What is "good enough fathering"? Good enough for what? is, of course, the question. Good enough mothering means good enough for the child to feel secure, competent, and lovable (the implication in the phrase *good enough* is that mothering, while critically formative, is, like any human enterprise, forever imperfect). The phrase *good enough* is even more aptly applied to fathering, since this is a less encumbered and potentially more blameworthy pursuit, culturally and psychologically, than is mothering.

Average (moderately involved) father care is characterized by day-to-day emotional dialogue between father and child, allowing a back-and-forth shared attention—sometimes positive, sometimes negative—to resonate in their relationship. The content of the dialogue varies according to the fathering tasks required at different ages and developmental levels (e.g., a high level of physical caregiving is required during infancy while instruction in conflict management and problem-solving is more salient during adolescence).

University of Pennsylvania's Frank Furstenberg and Kathleen Harris fine-tuned our understanding of the father–child dialogue by showing that it is the closeness felt by the child to the father, not just his presence or even his living at home, that is most predictably associated with positive life outcomes for the child twenty-five years later. Children who feel a closeness to their father are twice as likely as those who do not to enter college or find stable employment after high school, 75 percent less likely to have a teen birth, 80 percent less likely to spend time in jail, and half as likely to experience multiple depression symptoms.

We are not talking about the intense or maximal involvement of the primary nurturing, or caretaking, stay-at-home fathers here (we'll discuss them more completely in Chapter 3). At the other end of the spectrum are the minimally involved, or simply present, fathers, that is, those who, though thin on responsibility, nonetheless participate in the family structure. Interestingly, their presence alone seems to have some impact on their children. University of Rhode Island's Henry Biller and University of Michigan's Norma Radin have conducted research showing that child development is positively affected in measurable ways by (1) the father's warmth, even when he's not especially involved, (2) his masculinity alone, and (3) his different-from-mother socialization and relationship behavior.

Behavior alone, of course, doesn't tell us much about why or how a father shapes his responsible behavior or closeness to his children.

Studies by Jay Belsky of the influence of women's and men's personality traits on their parenting behavior tell us that personality traits such as extroversion, agreeableness, neuroticism, and worry affect daily mood and parental behavior differently in men than in women. Fathering, for example, appears to be more consistently influenced by a man's extroversion, while mothering is better predicted by a woman's agreeableness.

Beyond personality effects are the ubiquitous and magnetic forces of culture. An almost unimaginable variation and variety in the amount of quality of father–child interaction is possible in any given culture in any given time in its history. And, of course, there is tremendous variation in parenting practices from one culture to another. Studies of mother–child and father–child contact in Belize, Nepal, Kenya, and American Samoa found vast differences in father presence and absence, in the amount of time spent by fathers in child care, in their degree of competence, and in maternal support for father involvement.

The first active force that father care brings to bear on child development is not direct behavior but, rather, the influence exerted by the father's expectations of who his child will be. Long before children begin to ply their considerable influence on father's behavior, fathers are forming mental and emotional images of who their child will be in their life together. Those images are heavily influenced by expectations drawn from the father's own emotional life.

● ───

David was a "total cellist" (performing, recording, composing), and music shaped everything that mattered to him in life. His wife was tone-deaf, but she had been instantly moved by her husband's playing; after eleven years of marriage, she begged him to play when she was in need of a certain comfort. During their pregnancy with Seth, David played to him through an amplifier fed to earphones yoked across his wife's swelling abdomen. He believed that Seth the fetus loved rhythmic passages, was distressed by "minimalist, New Age crap," and had a "hankering" for waltzes, Bach, and jigs. When Seth was four months old, David tested his theories in a brief recital he prepared for Seth, who responded with rave reviews by giggling to Bach, Strauss, and Celtic jigs; scowling at Philip Glass (minimalist, New Age); and remaining quietly riveted to Carl Orff (rhythmic par excellence). For David, Seth's response proved "beyond a shadow of a doubt that (1) the kid has a great ear and (2) he clearly remembers his dad's playing from his life as a fetus!"

Here we see a fine example of how paternal attachment to the fetus influences perceptions of the infant's actual temperament. What the expectant father thinks his child will be like has much to do with how he connects to the child in the first months and with how he will eventually assess his child's temperament. David was obviously thrilled that he felt known by his baby. This encouraged him to stay even closer and to do even more for and with this child whose appreciation of him and his music built a bridge that could now carry emotional traffic in both directions.

Paternal expectations tend to work to connect the father to his child emotionally, regardless of whether the father can say the child is "just as I expected" or "not at all what I expected." Either way, the father is actively engaging in internal dialogue emotionally or external (or both) dialogue with his partner or infant about who his child will be in relation to him, a dialogue that first catalyzes and then sustains their emotional connection and effect upon one another. David and Seth were developing their own tongue, and it would serve them especially well in the early preverbal years, reducing the confusion about what a baby wants when crying occurs, an event that marginalizes so many fathers unnecessarily. Fathers who don't or can't imagine who their child might, should, or could be tend to remain more aloof and noncommittal about who the child will be or actually is. Consequently, they usually find themselves stuck in the cheap seats of the theater as they watch their child's life play itself out from a distance.

EFFECTS OF FATHER CARE ON CHILD DEVELOPMENT

One of the most influential studies of paternal impact on the overall socioemotional development of children was done by developmental psychologists Ann Easterbrooks and Wendy Goldberg, who, after considering dozens of potential influences, such as social class, economic and marital circumstances, child's birth order and gender, concluded that the father's attitudes toward, and behavioral sensitivity to, the care of his children have more positive influence on the child's socioemotional development than the total amount of time spent in interaction with the child.

Bottom line: the closer the connection between father and child, the better off they both are now and in the future.

As we explore the ways that fathers directly affect their children's development, be assured that I am not imposing my personal top ten list. Some of these effects of paternal style may be more or less important to you as a parent, so make your own listing of desired effects and don't be unduly influenced by my somewhat random listing of the widest possible effects. For interest and convenience, I've grouped these effects into eight categories, arranged rather loosely in chronological order, listing the effects in the order in which they tend to appear in the child's life cycle. You'll also notice a slight tendency to emphasize how father care affects younger children. The science tends to be of better quality in this age group, and early childhood is the era of development that—given the brain's preference for such phenomenal growth in the first three years of life—tends, overall, to matter most in terms of ultimate healthy or less than healthy outcomes. As Rob Reiner states succinctly in his I Am Your Child campaign, "The first years last forever." Unfortunately, much of the science is skewed in the direction of middle- or working-class Caucasian families. Further, it seems that boys have been more thoroughly studied than girls in terms of father care impact. (Chapter 6 works at balancing our view, as more recent research has been much more concerned with multiple ethnic and cultural settings.)

ADAPTIVE AND PROBLEM-SOLVING ABILITIES

Infants who have been well fathered during the first eighteen to twenty-four months of life are more secure than those who were not in exploring the world around them, and they do so with vigor and interest. They tend to be more curious and less hesitant or fearful, especially in the face of novel or unusual stimuli. The combination of the father's more active play initiation and his somewhat less immediate support in the face of frustration promotes adaptive and problem-solving competencies in the child. This style is what the woman in the checkout line in the food market was describing when she said her daughter Abby was willing to try anything.

Helen, one of the children in my longitudinal study, had just begun to crawl at eight months. Though she periodically looked back over her shoulder to see that someone was still watching, she inched her way across every surface she could find, touching, scratching, and "talking" to everything in her path for long stretches of time. Loud noises or surprising textures were likely to distract her briefly, but she loved her "village walks," as her father called them. When Helen got stuck, she would push and pull at the obstacle and talk to it; if the obstacle wouldn't budge, she would back up and try another way. Only her last resort was to wail in frustration. Her father's style was to then unobtrusively nudge the obstruction out of the way or redirect her, rather than pick her up to comfort her. He preferred that his daughter have the experience of working her own way out of trouble. And Helen seemed to respond in kind; she gave a satisfied little giggle or coo and headed off to explore once again.

Research by Henry Biller and Frank Pederson explores these interesting predilections of fathers to show that by the time children of involved fathers are ready for school, they tend to have greater tolerance for stress and frustration, a quality that will stand them in good stead in a class with twenty-six other kids and one very busy teacher. These children are better able to wait their turn for the teacher's attention, remaining in their seats and maintaining enough interest in their work and confidence in their own abilities and thoughts to work on their own till the teacher can help. My mother, a veteran of fifty years in elementary education and still teaching at age eighty-four, tells me she can pick out the "well-fathered" kids in her classes by their self-confidence and willingness to try new things.

STRENGTHENED COGNITIVE CAPACITIES

In the early 1960s psychologist Ellen Bing initiated one of the first studies ever of the effect on children of time spent with their father. Its findings surprised even the author. Bing found that the amount of time fathers spend reading with their children is a strong predictor for many cognitive abilities, particularly of daughters' high verbal skills. Equally surprising is the finding that the amount of time mothers spend reading to children predicts neither daughters' nor sons' verbal ability, suggesting that there is something unique or characteristic about father–daughter reading time. Does the father's verbal style, combined with his penchant for activating and his attention-generating playful dialogue, energize and stimulate his young child's experience of words at some central neurological level in a way that the mother's verbal style does not?

Maisey was just two when I visited her home as part of my longitudinal study. Her father Caleb was reading *Goodnight Moon* in a rather vain attempt to get her to settle down for bed. Though he knew he was not helping his cause, he could not deny himself the pleasure he and his daughter took from his ritual production of particular noises generated to accompany each page's obligatory "goodnight" recitation. "Goodnight mush" was read with the anticipated deep guttural resonance that sent Maisey into peals of giggles. And so it went to the final page. Entertaining? Yes. Activating? Yes. But Maisey's dad was also reinforcing for her the notion that words can be symbols of important pleasurable emotions between men and children, that words can be learned and enjoyed at many sensory levels.

Another important investigation, by Norma Radin, compares preschool children of highly involved dads with preschoolers with less involved fathers. Radin found that both sons and daughters of the dad-involved group had higher levels of verbal skills. In an earlier study, she had already investigated the correlation between paternal childrearing practices and the intellectual functioning of their four-year-old sons. She found that the boys' IQ was positively associated with their father's nurturing, (appropriate emotional and behavioral response to child's needs) and, interestingly, *negatively* associated with their fathers' disciplinary restrictiveness. Boys with nurturing fathers scored higher than the boys whose fathers were less involved unless the father was a strict, authoritarian disciplinarian. So much for the desirability of boot camp fathering!

In a landmark study of the relationship between the behavior of school-age children and paternal influence, which expanded Radin's early findings, psychologists Jane Mosley and Elizabeth Thompson found strong parental control to be associated with more, not less, school problems, lower sociability, and less initiative. Authoritarian limit setting by a father clearly has its limitations and should be viewed with much suspicion when touted as a value.

Michael Lamb studied a group of preschool children of positively engaged fathers and recorded more cognitive competence on standardized intellectual assessments than for children of unengaged or negatively engaged fathers. Pediatrician Scott Nugent of Boston's Children's Hospital evaluated the degree of paternal engagement in the month following birth and at one-year follow-up and discovered strong positive effects of that paternal engagement on the strength of the infant's cognitive functioning. These findings take us beyond a shadow of a doubt here.

Let's return to the checkout line to continue our eavesdropping. Abby's mother had described her husband as doing something "different," and although whatever it was seemed "good for both of them," that is, for both Abby and her dad, it doesn't advance our understanding of the *how* by artificially measuring Abby's IQ in a vacuum. As Daniel Goleman's many discussions of emotional intelligence in *The New York Times* science section, 1994 to the present, have reminded us, it's a big mistake to assume that cognitive ability or intelligence is a simple, discrete measure of a child's capacity to think. No single test score will ever completely reflect or encompass the intellectual capacities of any individual child or adult. Standardized testing of a particular child may give us a fairly accurate prediction of his or her success in traditional academic domains on any given day, but that is all it tells us. Problem-solving and adaptive capacities, very important life skills, are rarely tapped by traditional cognitive assessments. Furthermore, IQ scores can vary widely for the same child as he or she develops over time. Creativity, original thinking or doing—whether in social, artistic, or spiritual pursuits—are not adequately assessed in traditional IQ testing.

Parental influences exert significant, but not exclusive, impact on how children maximize their intellectual assets. It is important to understand that general intelligence is but the final common pathway of many factors—genetic, environmental, nutritional, experiential, and biological. Harvard's Howard Gardner has tirelessly and convincingly argued for the existence of several separate domains of intelligence, including linguistic, spatial, logical-mathematical, musical, bodily-kinesthetic, social, personal awareness, and spiritual intelligence. We must look at IQ or cognitive outcome measures very conservatively. For example, families that support high involvement by fathers may themselves have cognition-promoting characteristics that are independent of the father factor; for example, the family may engage in lots of group discussion and open dialogue or have a great penchant for stimulation or enrichment experiences in general.

Mathematical skills have been another cognitive function of special interest in the father care literature. Henry Biller has repeatedly pointed out men's special interest in analytical skills in interacting with their children over time. Father-deprived children seem to have trouble solving the more complex mathematical and puzzle tasks. Biller found a trend among fathers to spend more energy and time stimulating mathematical thinking in their sons than in their daughters. Norma Radin found a positive association between father involvement and their preschool daughters' competence in mathematics. Interestingly, when a daughter shares an interest with her father in math and analytic thinking, as did those described in Lora Tessman's Massachusetts Institute of Technology study of the first undergraduate women to enroll there in the early 1970s, that shared interest seems to have special salience for her and a long-term impact on her continued interest and productivity in this domain.

Another wrinkle in understanding intellectual effects is the role played by children's perception of their own competence. Psychologists Wendy Grolnick and Maria Slowiaczek studied the connection between fathers' high involvement and how their adolescents think about their academic abilities and achievements. Not surprisingly, this in turn is associated with higher grades in high school. Yet another pair of research psychologists, Barry Wagner and Deborah Phillips, found that a father's warmth is itself positively related to third graders' *perceived* academic competence. Of course, the majority of these studies were carried out in two-parent homes, and therefore the mother's role must also be taken into account in the child's success.

What are some of the possible sources of this oft-measured positive effect of father care on children's thinking competencies? My own hunch is that the father's predilection for supporting his child's novelty-seeking behavior combines with his penchant for enriching and elaborating his child's more routine and passive states to play a strong supporting role in his child's measurable (and perceived) competence in problem solving and adaptation, a competence that is necessary for success in school and in the workplace.

It had been a very long, hot trip back from Sabba (grampa) and Safta's (gramma) house for four-year-old Sam, Eva and Michael's firstborn. As their car rounded the last corner of the trip home, Sam was "losing it," whining about spending his "whole life" driving back from Grandpa's. Eva suddenly hit the brakes hard to avoid the turtle crawling down the yellow line in the middle of the steaming asphalt. Sam was immediately distracted from his complaints and curious about the turtle, and Michael suggested that Eva pull over so that he could show their son, a budding herpetologist, this great specimen. Reluctantly, she complied and for the next twenty minutes father and son investigated this wondrous creature, after which they carefully placed it to the side of the road. For the next three years, every time they passed that spot Sam looked for the turtle. He eventually identified it in his nature book, learned its Latin name, assigned a pet name to it, drew pictures of it for school, had dreams about it, and wondered if it had any family or friends. Michael had used the turtle as an opportunity to encourage his son's sense of wonder, teach him responsibility for the well-being of creatures great and small, and extend his childish curiosity into a project that stimulated the exercise of a wide range of abilities.

SOCIAL COMPETENCIES

Social competence plays a major role in what makes our kids good citizens. Here, too, are intriguing effects of father care.

CAPACITY FOR ATTACHMENT

Fathers have ways of helping their young children feel securely attached to the important people in the world around them. Jay Belsky has studied many of the factors that influence father–infant attachment levels. After following 126 fathers and their sons through assessments of various attachment characteristics—such as how toddlers respond to brief separations from their dads or to the intrusion of a stranger in their play—Belsky found that fathers of securely attached infants (i.e., infants who can tolerate brief separations from their father without getting too upset or disorganized emotionally) tend to be more extroverted and agreeable in personality style and behavior than fathers of insecurely connected infants. A positive marriage and flexible connections between work and family also help these attachment-promoting fathers promote attachment in their child.

Frank Pedersen found that at one year of age infants whose fathers provided extensive care in the intermittent absence of the mother show higher rates of responding to their fathers and more frequent instances of exploratory and social behavior than children of less engaged fathers. These are babies who seem to enjoy initiating contact with their father by handing him a toy or by smiling and vocalizing; they then wait expectantly, confident that they will get a response from him. These infants smile more frequently at their father, show higher rates of face-to-face and general visual contact, and heightened exploratory behavior. Pedersen and his colleagues speculate that the enhanced relationship with the father contributes positively to the mother–infant relationship as well. Further benefits are seen in these infants' desire to approach individuals other than their parents and in their competence in doing so.

In related work, Michael Cox reviewed a large body of research to sort out the impact of variations in paternal behavior on infant attachment. He concluded that fathers who are affectionate, have positive attitudes, and spend more time with their three-month-olds, are more likely to have securely attached infants at twelve months than fathers who are more negative and distant. But, as usual, it was the quality of care, not the hours logged, that mattered more.

EMPATHY

An important long-term study of seventy-five children was started in the 1950s by psychologists Robert R. Sears, Eleanor Maccoby, and Harry Levin to explore the "tendency to experience feelings of sympathy and compassion for others." The milestone study contained unexpected positive news about the consequences of paternal involvement for both sons and daughters. When the children in the study were followed up thirty years later, it was found that of the various qualities of maternal and paternal behavior the children were exposed to at age five, the strongest predictor of a child's empathic concern for others in adult life was a high level of paternal child care. The original researchers had defined high paternal care as staying with the child when the mother was out and "taking care to do more for the child in that circumstance." Though this definition of "high paternal care" is pretty tame by today's standards, it apparently was sufficient to identify the fathers who were providing their infants with the level of father-support needed to enable them to become caring, empathic adults.

Developmental psychologist Susan Bernadette-Shapiro studied forty-seven first grade boys in intact families to explore the relationship of positive paternal involvement with the development of empathy in boys. Sons of fathers who took more responsibility for limit setting, discipline, and helping their child with personal problems and schoolwork had significantly higher empathy scores. Interestingly, this was true regardless of the father's own level of empathy as described by the father himself or by his wife. Apparently, "Do as I do, not as I say" is the lesson here.

ABSENCE OF GENDER ROLE STEREOTYPING

A friend of my daughter's had invited girls and boys to her ninth birthday party, and some of the parents were up in arms. Apparently it was, for them, way too soon to start boy–girl parties. Fine, except that this girl had never had any other kind. Her parents had shared an academic job at a nearby state university and had split child care from the time she was born. A feminine, athletic, and perky little girl, she had many friends, of whom a significant number were boys. She couldn't be bothered conforming her social world to the conventional gender role expectations among her peers of the third grade. It would be harder to find a more durable social competency then this absence in her of gender role stereotyping.

Another not too surprising outcome is related to the degree of gender stereotyping found in children who have experienced involved father care. Norma Radin's study of school behavior outcomes among preschool kids whose fathers performed 40 percent or more of the in-family child care showed less gender role stereotyping in the kids' choices of friends and in their overall social and behavioral expectations of their peers than children whose fathers were less involved in their care.

Finally, Edith Williams and Norma Radin looked at a group of adolescents who had positively involved dads either between the ages of three and five or seven and nine to see what effect that involvement had on later gender role expectations. As adolescents, these boys and girls held less traditional and less rigid views of and expectations for family life then adolescents with less engaged fathers. They expressed more open and flexible views about co-parenting and dual-earner marriage.

You've probably noticed that I've not chosen to segregate all the effects of father care on kids according to which effects are seen in boys and which ones are seen in girls. That would have given a false simplicity to the topic that the science does not support—and would have perpetuated a kind of gender role stereotyping in this field of research. The problem started when so much of the early research in the field of dads and kids focused on the preferential interest of fathers for sons, especially firstborns. This, of course, is a broadly supported cultural expectation, given millennia of preferential interest in patrilineal descent in most Eastern and Western cultures. But as the science has improved, we have seen that it is not that simple. Mothers, grandparents, and extended family in general support the overvaluation of the firstborn male, whose birth in many cultures is regarded as affirmation that their lineage will continue to be represented in name and in gene pool for generations to come.

Recent research continues to show there are some different effects on boys and girls of paternal engagement, at least insofar as the children develop attitudes and expectations about the role gender plays in their own lives. Constance Hardesty of Morehead State University looked at the relationship between father's involvement in family life during childhood (seven through eleven years of age) and young adults' gender role orientations (traditional male and female behavior) and their work- and parenthood-related gender attitudes. She surveyed two thousand 18- to 22-year-old men and women in order to understand the influence of the quality of earlier paternal involvement with them on their adult views on male and female sex-typical behavior and their expectations for ongoing relationships. Overall, she found that gender attitudes in both men and women are more strongly correlated with the nature and quality, rather than the presence or amount, of paternal involvement (sound familiar, bean counters?), although the effects were somewhat stronger for boys. Hardesty and her group found that high paternal involvement is associated with traditional gender role orientations in young men, although a close, nurturing, and ongoing paternal relationship is associated with nontraditional, more egalitarian orientations in young men. Gender role orientation and gender attitudes in young women were found to be shaped somewhat more by the father's personal characteristics and less by his style of fathering or the father–daughter relationship itself. The work of these researchers tells us that the way a man is as an involved father—the quality of his relationship and interaction with his child—affirms either the status quo or encourages broader horizons, especially for his sons. It tells us that dad's personality itself, when involved with his daughter, is at least as influential as the way he behaves or relates to her. Time will have to tell us more.

SELF-CONTROL

Hardly any behavioral trait in boys or girls is more valued by parents in these hectic, every-moment-accounted-for days than self-control. Psychologist Walter Mischel found young children with positively involved fathering displayed less impulsivity and more self-control, particularly in unfamiliar social situations than young children with negatively or uninvolved fathers. In a related study, psychologist Martin Hoffman looked at a group of seventh graders with regard to their development of internal controls over impulsive behavior, particularly in relation to degree of father identification. He found that boys with strong father identification scored higher on measures of internal control and conformity to rules; those with weaker feelings of paternal identification had more trouble with moral judgments and nonconformity.

Deprivation of fathering is especially toxic in this particular realm of child development for both boys and girls. The vast overrepresentation of father-absence literature that filled our journals until the last decade centered on this very finding, that is, that father deprivation is directly linked to difficulties in a child's self-control. This body of literature carried much more influence than it deserved to, because it rarely distinguished between nonresidential, abandoning, ejected, rejected, or even dead fathers. Both father presence and father absence exist on a continuum. *Why* the father is absent or present carries an influence all its own that has significant power.

Father-absent research still carries more influence today than it should as certain organizations call for a return to so-called responsible (using their definition, not mine) fatherhood and indict "fatherlessness" alone for the increased likelihood of a child's being suspended or expelled or dropping out of school, the increased risk of suicide in children, incarceration by the age of thirty, and the like. Of course, economic and other stress factors are probably equally influential in placing such children at risk. Hypo- and hypermasculinity have also been suggested as results of paternal deprivation. As for impulsivity itself, it can hardly be considered the sole outcome of any one factor, including father absence (but more on this in Chapter 5).

Educational psychologist Paul Amato evaluated the sense of self-control in elementary and high school children and found positive paternal engagement to be related to a whole cluster of healthy outcomes including life skills, self-esteem, and overall social competence. Apparently, self-control can be both a cause and a result of social competence, which itself is correlated with father care.

Related to the development of a sense of self-control in children is the fostering of an internal locus of control, which experts define as the belief that one's ability to affect one's own behavior and the outside world resides more inside than outside the individual. Many of Henry Biller's studies repeatedly reinforce the finding of a strong internal locus of control in children of involved fathers. This may not necessarily be measuring anything other than the superior problem-solving and adaptive skills that characterize many children of involved fathers, believing as they do that the world is their oyster.

MORAL SENSITIVITY

An awareness of the needs and rights of others is a highly valued quality in children and adults alike, and several studies have looked at the impact of positive paternal experiences on this quality in children.

Psychologists Eldred Rutherford and Paul Mussen tested this hypothesis by asking four-year-old boys to give two bags of candy to the two boys they "liked best" in their nursery school. Though some four-year-olds might not be able to share their cache with anyone, the boys who tended to be more generous were the same children who consistently saw their fathers as comforting, warm, and affectionate with them. What goes around, comes around, even at four.

In one of the more highly regarded, scientifically rigorous outcome studies of the correlation between moral behavior of children and paternal engagement, psychologists Mosley and Thompson found that positive paternal engagement, for boys and girls, is closely associated with (1) a lower incidence of acting out, disruptive behavior, depression, sadness, and lying; (2) higher sociability through complying with parents' wishes, getting along with others, and being responsible; (3) boys having fewer school behavior problems; and (4) girls having more cheerful and happy interchanges, greater capacity for positive self-involvement, and greater willingness to try new things. These results are especially compelling because it was statistically possible to isolate the father effects from mother effects with unusual clarity. Bottom line: positive father care is associated with more pro-social, and positive moral behavior overall in boys and girls.

PHYSICAL DEVELOPMENT

Even the way a newborn enters the world as a physical entity can be positively affected by the paternal presence. An important British study of at-home births in the 1970s found that the single most important birth circumstance that protected against birth complications and further illness or trauma in the newborn was the father's presence at delivery. This held true even when the father was less than enthusiastic about being present. A related study concluded that the father's presence reduced the mother's loneliness, fear, and confusion and even the average length of labor, thereby lowering the overall rate of birth complications (insurance underwriters, take note). When I was attending childbirth classes in preparation for the arrival of our last daughter, the nurse-midwife instructor was encouraging fathers to "be there, even if you're scared, queasy, ready to pass out, or just not ready—she and the baby will need you." Fathers said everything from "No problem" to "It's going to be hard to see her in that much pain," but everyone turned up when it mattered.

Ross Parke, a preeminent fatherhood researcher from California, studied how a child's physical development responds to involved fathering. Infants' scores on assessments of intellectual and motor, or physical, competencies are higher if fathers are actively involved during the first six months of their child's life. The father's tendency to activate his child in their interactions encourages and supports the child's pleasurable discovery of his own body.

INDIRECT EFFECTS

The father factor in child development may not always exert its influence directly, or, at least, in ways that have already been identified. Indirect effects also reinforce the positive developmental outcome for many children who have enjoyed engaged fathering. Maternal and paternal behaviors obviously affect one another, and three separate investigations by Jay Belsky, Ross Parke, and colleagues found that paternal involvement can affect the child indirectly through its effects on the mother herself. When a mother feels supported by the father, she is more patient, flexible, emotionally responsive, and available to their children. Interestingly, affectionate and facilitative fathering is also associated with more positive sibling interactions, indicating that paternal involvement has significant indirect effects for the entire family system.

●————————————————————————————

Siblings Cheryl and Brad were known in their school for their mutually supportive relationship. It stood in stark contrast to the more common rivalrous sister–brother duos among their peers. Cheryl was athletic, cute, smart, and perky. Brad, the older sibling, was shy and ungainly, but he was politically active and improbably popular. She came to his debating tournaments, and he came to her soccer matches. They were warm and affectionate with each other and were trusted confidants when things got complicated in the dating world of their high school. Teachers found them helpful in the classroom, but neither was considered a "suck-up." Both were consistently on the honor roll. Too good to be true? Nearly.

In an interview with the local paper after they shared a community service award for summer tutoring they'd done for special ed kids at the town summer camp, Cheryl explained to the reporter why she and her brother got along so well. "Our mother and father shared in raising us till Dad went back to college after I started first grade. It seems that we've pretty much had all the attention we needed from either one of them, so fighting just seemed like a waste of time after we tried it for a few years. They raised us to pass on what you have, so it's really no big deal."

This feeling in siblings with engaged fathers that parental attention is "always" available encourages in them a sense of responsibility for keeping the peace and lessens the need for them to test limits to assure themselves that someone is on duty. These conclusions are supported by research that addresses the relationship between father involvement and children's peer relationships.

SPECIAL CIRCUMSTANCES

Since life is never perfect, there is no shortage of opportunities to evaluate the effects of paternal involvement in special circumstances, for example, situations of medical risk, trauma, and mental illness.

PREMATURITY

The premature birth of an infant can be a risky moment in life for both child and family, and the outcome is influenced by both parents. Michael Yogman conducted an interesting study on the role of fathers in the cognitive and behavioral outcomes of prematurity. With a sample size of over a thousand fathers from Latino, African American, and other inner-city populations, he took a careful look at father involvement, ethnicity, and social class. Yogman wasn't satisfied with the conventional belief that a father who does not live in the home is uninvolved with his child, and he found that fathers could be categorized as having high or low involvement, irrespective of living arrangement. When his research group followed up the preemies at age three, they found a six-point difference in IQ between the two groups; that is, the children of fathers who were highly involved with them had higher cognitive scores than the children whose fathers had low involvement with them. These findings are especially convincing, because the strong design of the study adjusted for family income, paternal age, and stretched across high- and low-involved fathers as well.

MATERNAL ILLNESS

A significant research effort from several corners of psychology and child development has consistently shown that maternal illness or vulnerability can pull a father into a more vital role in the life of his children than he might otherwise have chosen, or than he might otherwise have been able to choose. However, the mechanisms by which this shift occurs have not been well studied; nor do we know how assumption of his new role affects the father or whether there are demonstrable benefits to the child. Common sense may affirm, but it does not unfailingly prove.

New Haven psychoanalyst Rosemary Balsam's small but elegant study of father's contributions to their adolescent daughter's development when the mother is significantly emotionally disturbed describes the heightened significance of the father in such a sad circumstance. These fathers involved themselves in their daughter's life, and the effects on the daughters were profound. The young women developed a kind of vital energy and interest in struggling with their problems in order to become fully functioning adults. They were determined, steadfast, and committed to friends, academic achievement, athletics, play, and extracurricular activities. They tended toward the driven at times. At the very least, Balsam's study show that the negative effects on child development of primary maternal vulnerability can be buffered by active paternal involvement and that this involvement can be sufficient to sustain development in daughters.

PATERNAL INFLUENCE ON CHILDHOOD EMOTIONAL VULNERABILITY

As mentioned earlier, we are just now being informed by studies that even attempt to evaluate the relationship, if any, between paternal emotional vulnerability and problems in the emotional growth of children and adolescents. Vicky Phares's thoughtful review of findings from research on paternal factors in child and adolescent mental illness indicates some beginning trends in formulating certain diagnostic categories. The researchers' message to date: "Keep an open mind." A few of the highlights from Phares's review are instructive:

> ATTENTION-DEFICIT HYPERACTIVITY DISORDER (ADHD): Fathers of ADHD children scored higher on nonclinical measures (better impulse control, and less distractibility than their kids) than comparison groups of fathers with undiagnosed children. Also, no difference was shown between the frequency of a history of either maternal or paternal emotional trouble.

> DEPRESSION: Stronger links were found between childhood depression and maternal depression than were found to paternal depression.

> ANXIETY: Fathers of children diagnosed with anxiety disorder showed higher rates of obsessive-compulsive disorder and general obsessional traits than did fathers of children who did not have this diagnosis.

> DELINQUENCY: There are consistent findings of links between emotional illness and adolescent delinquency (breaking laws, truancy, antisocial behavior). There are no studies yet that compare father's to mother's history of delinquency, despite evidence that high conflict between mothers and fathers has a stronger effect on daughters than sons.

SUMMARY

Enough bean counting. Fundamental assumptions about the emotional effects fathers have on their children have been accumulating throughout this chapter. I'd like to summarize them for the benefit of the woman in the checkout line at the food market (see first page of this chapter).

How does involved fatherhood actually go about shaping a child's growth and maturation, and what makes it so influential? Father influences may be especially important precisely because they are influences not of the mother. A dad begins to enhance his child's maturation and autonomy by balancing the powerful pull toward the mother; he does this merely by being an interesting non-mother partner in his own right. His very differentness from the mother as a physical being—his smells, textures, voice, rhythms, size—promote an awareness in his child that it is okay to be different and okay to desire and love the inherently different, the not-mother entities of the world. A father's separateness from the mother, in combination with his constancy, gives the child a safe haven in the storms over autonomy that blow up so fiercely in the second year of life. "My mother, myself" is hardly the whole story.

Dads offer intriguing and exciting imitative opportunities for safe and loving social interactions with a not-mother entity. This shores up self-regard and self-confidence when it matters most, in the early formation of personality. Fathers also offer older children an opportunity to explore and interact with the essence of maleness itself and to explore male–female differences. For boys it fascinates and comforts because the father's maleness is "the same as, but still of me," and for girls it intrigues and excites because it is "different than, but still of me."

Fathers promote children's acceptance of the real world by emotionally taking them to the mountain, teaching them to climb, showing them the world, and, over time, showing them the way through and around it. Even when men serve as primary caregivers, this role stays in their hands, and children seem to count on them to fulfill that emotional promise to get them, safe and whole, into the real world beyond their mother's arms.

In the end, an involved dad makes a difference in his child's life because of all the forces we discussed in the previous chapter and probably because the father's engagement itself fosters (and is probably fostered by) a family context in which parents can feel affirmed in their relationship to one another and committed to the ways in which they are with their children as parents. Somehow, this particular balance allows both parents to have what is emotionally valuable to them.

Had I followed them out the door of the food market—as I very nearly did—I would have told the two women whose conversation I overheard what I've just told you. I doubt, however, that Abby's mother would have been more than mildly interested, because, I suspect, Abby had already told her all about it.

3

Dad as the Primary Caregiver

FAMILIAR NOW with the tissue of fatherneed, we're ready to hear the fascinating stories of an intriguing group of families I've been following for over ten years where the father has been the primary caregiver to his children.

●————————————————————————

Haskell and his older brother, Audie, had been raised mostly by their dad ever since their mom went back to work when Audie was six weeks old. That hadn't been the original plan, but their grandmother had broken her hip ten days before she was to "take over the house." Then, a week before Mom's R-Day (return to work), their father, Chris, lost his job. As Chris puts it: "The writing was on the wall. We read it. I stayed home with the kids, she brought home the bacon, and the rest is history." That's how Chris and Amy came to qualify, over ten years ago, for my study of the impact on child development of primary nurturing by stay-at home fathers in intact families.

One day Haskell tried to explain to his kindergarten class at show-and-tell (or bring-and-brag, as Chris dubbed it) what his dad was doing at home raising him and Audie while his mom was at work. It was heavy going to get across to his peers what it's like having your dad "cook, clean house, change your nappies, and wash you when you're a baby, take you to the doctor, and pack your snack and lunch after-school days." Haskell summed it up this way: "He does mostly everything." Finally, Sally asked him if his mom worked because "she didn't like her children." Exasperated, Haskell raised a pleading hand and said, "It's like when your dad is your mom." Sally sat back on her heels with a small, comprehending "oh." Then, after a thoughtful pause, Haskell added, "Kinda." His teacher couldn't resist, so she asked him to explain "kinda." The little boy explained: "My mom goes to work to make money and sell people's houses. But she reads to us—and cooks and cleans sometimes like Dad, just not so much. Dad does the home work and Mom does all the other work. But she's still a mom and a lady, and Dad is still my dad and a man. It's just that they're raising us up different, kinda."

And so Haskell, in a succinct manifesto for children of primary nurturing fathers, explains his unique nurturing experience with some exasperation: ". . . it's when your Dad is your Mom, kinda." It is a fascinating group of intact families I've been learning from for years now as they each live out an experiment in which the fathers served as the primary nurturing figure during the critical early years of their children's lives. Although descriptions of the outcome for children at younger ages appear in my previous book, *The Nurturing Father,* this is the first look at what the children (and their families) are like at the threshold of adolescence, after a decade of this increasingly popular variation in nurturing style.

This study is an important exploration, because fathers who are the primary nurturer allow us our best shot at understanding the processes and effects of fatherneed in its purest form. Single fatherhood, though more common than primary nurturing fathering (as we'll see in Chapter 5), is as much a test of endurance, patience, and assets as is single motherhood; it depends as heavily as single motherhood does on support, economic and social, for many of its positive outcomes for kids. In Haskell's family, there is a limited role reversal between the parents that allows for her father and children, supported by mother, to explore their need for and attachment to each other—and Haskell's dad (and the researcher!) has an opportunity to explore his competence as a nurturer and the benefits to his children of father care. More accurately, we are seeing the effects on children and on family life that have been brought about by two role *creators*, not simply role changers or reversers. Gender itself becomes a wild card in this setting, allowing us to factor out role from gender effects in the nurturing domain. Which forces on child development are just part of the parenting job, and which are in the individual parent or child, the genes, or the culture?

The implications of these families' experiences are highly significant regarding what we can learn about the effect of fatherneed on children, men, and women. Although the latest census figures report two million stay-at-home dads (the numbers have been rising steeply over the past decade), it is unlikely that this arrangement will ever be used by a major proportion of American families, given societal, cultural, religious, and economic support for primary nurturing mothers as the norm.

A clear profile of at-home fathers in general has been emerging, thanks to several recent polls, especially the survey of the readership of the quarterly newsletter *At-Home Dad*. Robert Frank, an adjunct professor of psychology at DePaul University, reported data from 368 questionnaires filled out by dads of 650 children, dads who were the sole caretaker for their kids for more than thirty hours a week. The results were compared to a matched primary caregiving group of 490 women with 874 children. The following typical family profile emerged:

> There are two children, who have been at home with their 38-year-old father for at least three years. The parenting arrangement was chosen because the parents did not want to put their children in day care and because the mother made more money. The mother is "extremely satisfied" with the arrangement, as is the father. His parenting skills come from a mixture of his own experience with his kids and his intuition. The father plans, once the younger child is in grade school, to return to work, either working at home or outside the home.

These survey families describe fathers as "household managers," but that is as far as the role reversal goes. When the working mother comes home, she'll often pitch in with dinner and take over the child's bath or bedtime routine. This tends to lead to a more equal balance of parenting work and power in these households. Hurt or scared kids, day or night, will seek either Dad or Mom for comfort if they're both around. By comparison, traditionally reared kids go for Mom 80 percent of the time.

Speaking of traditional roles, even when the husband is the primary caregiver, he will still take the wheel 80 percent of the time when both parents are in the car and will still do the majority of home maintenance chores, inside or out—intriguing evidence of the durability of certain core gender roles. Women also show evidence of role durability: even in these untraditional family settings, mothers tend to do most of the bed and bathtime rituals. And they keep their children's schedules in their heads (traditional dads tend not to share this latter responsibility in particular). Finally, dads in the nontraditional setting feel more isolated than do primary caregiving moms, by almost two to one. Most feel, however, that the isolation is more than compensated for by the increased closeness they feel to their children.

THE LONGITUDINAL STUDY

Against this backdrop of the generic stay-at-home father, let me introduce the specific families from whom, apart from my own, I've learned the most about fatherneed. The eighteen families come from the large industrial and academic community that is the Greater New Haven area of New England. The parents are graduate students, hourly workers, artists, salespeople, professionals, and real estate brokers, representing an ethnic and economic mix of blue-collar, welfare, and professional families.

THE INITIAL ASSESSMENTS

When I first met the babies, their ages ranged from two to twelve months. Developmental assessment indicated that they were active, robust, and thriving children. They were competent and occasionally functioned above the expected norms on several of the standardized tests. The youngest group performed problem-solving tasks on the level of babies who were several months older. Personal and social skills were also ahead of schedule. An intriguing quality and style seemed to be emerging: these infants, all firstborn, seemed to be attracted to, especially interested in, and comfortable with stimulation from the external environment. They also anticipated that their diligence and curiosity would be tolerated and even appreciated by the adults in their environment. They seemed to expect that play would be rich, interesting, exciting, and reciprocal.

The rest of this early phase of these families' development, as described in *The Nurturing Father,* found the children comfortably dependent, assertive, and interested in mastery. The children at the four-year follow-up seemed to have a zest for life, tempered with the usual childhood worries. They were avid explorers of their backyards, bus stops, and grocery stores, confident that something interesting would always turn up. There were signs that these children as a group might be developing a resilience and flexibility in certain areas of their personality development, particularly in the ease with which they moved back and forth between feminine and masculine behavioral roles (not identities, but roles). While their peers were concentrating on joining the appropriate "gender gang," they were moving comfortably back and forth between gender groupings at day care, playgrounds, and birthday parties.

Their imaginary play was especially rich with images of fathers as a nurturing force. Several of the children employed a father doll with "seeds inside him" to show that, according to their worldview and experience, fathers "grew things." Clearly, having a father as a primary nurturing figure was stimulating in these children a curiosity and interest in father as a procreator, as a maker *and* a nurturer of human beings. All those "fatherisms," those father care benefits, mentioned in the previous chapter were finding their way into the tissue of the children's abilities and promise.

EIGHT-YEAR FOLLOW-UP

After eight years, the majority of families still had the father in a major nurturing role, either sharing child care equally with the mother or providing the majority of child care responsibilities. This was in stark contrast to the only characteristic shared by all families at the beginning of the study; at the time I originally met them, none of the couples considered their current parenting arrangement to be anything other than a temporary one, destined to last six to twelve months at most.

Ten families had new children born into them, and a second divorce was pending at the eight-year check-in. Interestingly, both marriages that foundered were from the group of six couples who had decided even before the first pregnancy that the father would do the bulk of the nurturing. What had seemed like a good idea at first had been given a good try. Both mothers felt that the nontraditional decision had played some role in the dissolution of the marriage. One said, "I still think it was the best thing for our kids, but Derek's being home and my working separated us as a couple in ways we could never get back from. I'm less warm and fuzzy, and I've loved the challenge and productivity of my career. Derek, no matter how hard he tried, could never make me feel as loved as he did our kids. I'm not sure it was really either of our faults, so we've stayed friends and close to our kids—maybe even closer for me, since I don't compete with Derek anymore when they're with me."

At eight to ten years of age, the children were old enough to reflect themselves on the experience of being reared in this way. They were now aware, through their encounters with friends' families and other social experiences at school and at after-school settings, that their family was unique, and they seemed to feel a certain uniqueness within themselves as a result. Eight-year-old Katelin explained, "I used to think everyone had a dad for a mom. I was just regular. My dad was just going to be there for the rest of my life. I'm used to this. I really like my dad. I feel 'specialer'—a little different. I learned from my friends' families, like I was a little different."

Did this bother her? "I mean, when you're growing up who cares? You're just a baby! But when I started to go visit other people's homes when I was two or three and I didn't see a dad around, it worried me and I'd ask them, "Why isn't your dad here? What happened to him?" Katelin continued:

> One time I felt kind of weird when my dad had to come to nursery school. He was the only man there, dancing around with the other mothers, playing with this chiffon thing. I knew he felt weird—looked weird, too! To tell the truth, it's not such a big deal now. Some of my friends used to tease me in kindergarten—"Your mother has a mustache"—and it hurt my feelings. They stopped teasing me when I told them it was really fun having a dad for a mom, because you have such a good time with a housedad.

I also saw a certain directness and confidence in the communication style of the children emerging from these nontraditional families. When ten-and-a-half-year-old Helen's younger sister was feeling somewhat excluded during the family interview in the living room, she simply got up, walked over to her father, leaned up against him, and said, "I feel left out; talk to me." This seemed to me to be more evidence of the self-awareness and self-regard that I had noted earlier in these children's social competencies.

A fascinating observation at the eight-year follow-up was how many of the children were involved in nurturing some form of life, as a childhood form of Erik Erikson's "generativity," a word he coined to describe the satisfactions of the mature years of having generated thriving and productive ideas and activities. Every one of the fourteen children had an ongoing commitment to growing, raising, breeding, or feeding something: plants (house and garden) were potted, watered, or propagated; pets were nurtured, fed, walked, even bred. Caretaking had become a valued activity of daily life. While each child's gender identity remained quite stable, a certain flexibility of *gender role* performance continued to make itself known. The kids' competence was now spiced with age-appropriate competitiveness with other propagators, a combination that spurred the development of new skills on behalf of and pride in their "progeny." As a possible companion to this kind of responsibility, all the study kids now had chores. It was as though a certain work ethic was being understood, if not actually embraced, by these children within nontraditional families.

The fruits of the children's labors were appreciated, and the actual products of their activities were in evidence throughout their homes. Katelin's artwork hung from walls and mantels, while Allen's pencil drawings of birds lined the hallways of his house. (As a five-year-old, Allen had been especially interested in birds with "big beaks who bite noses." Now he belonged to the Connecticut Audubon Society and had his own spotting scope and bird list.)

It occurred to me during the eight-year follow-up that having a father *and* a mother devoted to the nurturing of a child was such a pervasive culture in these families that children identified early with nurturing itself as a valued, powerful skill and role and wanted to explore their own competence in this domain. Also, fatherneed in these children was so uncompromisingly fulfilled that we can see the power of the now familiar fatherisms represented in their own behavior. Their confidence in their own style of learning and exploration was clearly linked to their father's support of their early novelty-seeking behavior. The children's use of humor and teasing seemed a repetition of their father's inherent interest in playful interaction, whether in disciplining or teaching. Their willingness to try the unconventional, such as maintaining friendships across gender gangs, seemed to reflect their father's willingness to ignore traditional gender role behaviors, and the readiness with which they accepted challenges recalled their father's early parenting tendency to withhold immediate help and give them the opportunity to learn to tolerate frustration in order to eventually succeed at a difficult task.

TEN-YEAR FOLLOW-UP

Now, ten years after the study began, fourteen families remained available for study. The children ranged from ten to twelve years of age, with six boys and eight girls.* The number of siblings ranged from three to none; the average was about one sibling per study child. Nine of the families still had fathers sharing in the child care or serving as the major caretaker in the family (cooking, transporting, helping with homework, disciplining, etc.). The other five families saw mothers at home either half- or full-time, with the father serving full-time in out-of-home work. There had been a second divorce, and that family chose not to continue participating in the study.

So, what is on the preadolescent's developmental plate? Imminent physical and biological change are the hallmarks of this stage. Emotional fragility alternates with great passions, personal mythologies, and dreams. In traditional families, girls start relating more ambivalently to their mothers, fearing the old regressive pulls of childhood and competing and bickering for an important female place in the household. Traditionally reared boys tease their mother but feel less competitive and rivalrous with her than with their father. Respect for parents is a frequent casualty, as increasingly autonomous offspring become suspicious of old intimacies and start to hunt for new ones.

●————————————————————————————

Helen, whom we've met before, now describes herself as a "soccer junkie" and was in her uniform and pads for her family inter-

---

*The reason the children are only 10 to 12 years and not 11 to 13 is that the families were divided into two groups, as there was only sufficient time to study half of the population per summer. In addition, it takes months to evaluate this kind of observational data.

view. Her father had been her coach up until this year. "We both thought we needed a break from each other. He thought he knew everything about soccer, and I did, too—till I went to soccer camp last summer and learned more than he could teach me. I miss having my dad at practice, but I'm playing great!" As for her friendships, she beamed as she reeled off a list of six "best" friends, three of them boys. She'd organized a mixed indoor soccer league in the off-season, and made up rules "to be fair to everyone." This league was a source of great joy for her.

How was Helen feeling about both of her parents these days? She felt close to both and felt they knew her well, even though they were "different—not better, not worse." She experienced her dad as easier to "hang out with" than her equally loving and loved mother. "My mom is neat, but she kind of nags. But my dad is cool."

Possibly, self-knowledge is reinforced twice as often when children are so in touch with both parents that they see themselves reflected in their two differing styles of caring and teaching and disciplining. Helen described the value of both parental styles: "Dad tolerates my confusing life better than Mom. When I changed my mind a thousand times about who was coming to my birthday, he just let me be nuts for a while and said, 'Let me know when you're done being crazy about this.' Mom would have gone crazy *with* me, and that's not the best way to handle my being nuts."

In the family interview with her younger sister, age eight, and her parents, Helen and her father teased each other vigorously and mercilessly about who knew more about soccer, the Red Sox, Pokemon, or the Spice Girls. Her mother and sister rolled their eyes, giving them a gentle "knock it off" sign, with little effect. Though Helen and her father communicated well and enjoyably, her nonverbal connection was more with her mother; Helen leaned back against her mother's chest as she lazily wove their fingers together. The father, when asked about any changes in the way the family was getting along these days, replied with mild but audible distress, "Helen doesn't tell me as much about what's going on in her life as she used to." To which Helen replied, "Oh Dad, stop complaining. I'm supposed to have a private life sometime." Her mother gave her a warm hug from behind, as though to reward Helen for her declaration of growing autonomy, while giving a reassuring glance to her husband across the room.

Helen's thirty-eight-year-old father, who now worked thirty hours outside the home in a job that was "just okay," was feeling a new remoteness, benign as it was, in his relationship with his older daughter. His wife had recently been promoted and was involving Helen in some office work (for which she got paid), lending lunch, travel, and social time to mother–daughter life. While Helen and her father remained affectionate and close, she was now confiding more in her mother (while also arguing more). Helen volunteered that she preferred to have her mom do the driving to the movies and the mall, because "Dad embarrasses me in public sometimes because, even though we're close, he acts like he thinks he knows me so well."

Later in the interview, we asked Helen to explain the word *embarrass*. She replied, "He likes to joke about stuff in public, like he wants my friends to know that we're close. But it feels kind of awkward, having him do that around my buddies, especially my girlfriends. He is my dad, but he is a guy—he can't help it!" It was as though Helen had discovered a "gendered" father, and his gender itself played a new and heightened salience in their relationship.

Allen, whom we've also met before, is now eleven. In the interview he had a lot to say about how his mom and dad differed in the way they "handled" him. He contrasted how his mom and dad gave him daily instruction: "Mom teaches like a teacher—remember this, remember that. Dad plays with me a lot and tries to sneak in the learning." His father corroborated this description: "While playing with him, I try to teach him words, math, even some values: to compete hard but fair (I don't let him cheat); how to deal with frustration and losing (we don't play for a while if he starts to whine and complain); how to reinforce new skills and how to handle power and aggression." Allen: "He doesn't use all his strength all the time, but I do!"

The oldest of three, Allen is especially proud of his responsibilities regarding his little sister. He taught her to "ride a bike, use the potty" and is starting to teach her to read. He winks as he says "read," indicating that he knows full well she's merely memorized what comes next in his dramatic readings of *Curious George*.

Allen's family interview was the longest interview of the follow-up, owing to the size of his family and their emphasis on everyone's getting a chance to finish what they wanted to say, an important value in the family. Allen's role as a caretaking older brother was valued by his younger siblings, who kept crawling up on him to whisper and "tell secrets" during he interview. When pressed to reveal their content during the interview by the mother, Allen said, "They're just us kids talking, Mom. Don't worry."

To the question about any recent changes in the way the family was getting along, the mother responded, "Allen seems to be giving me a pretty hard time these days, right, Buddy?" Allen fell silent for a moment, looking more thoughtful than wounded: "I think that's right, Mom. You bug me about my homework, my room, how long I'm in the shower or on the phone—you're all over me." The father broke in with a slight edge in his voice, leaning forward purposefully in his chair to cut off the angle of fire between his wife and son: "It's not quite that bad, but there is definitely more arguing than there used to be—with both of us. You don't listen the way you used to, especially to your mother." The younger sister, age seven, both excited and made anxious by this interchange, spontaneously yelled, "Fight! Fight!"—and thus brought the confrontation to a close with humor. Allen swept her up in his arms and lovingly called her "my troublemaker." She squealed in delight and queried, "Me? No! *You* troublemaker!"

In this family, the pattern of communication and closeness was transforming itself around Allen, and his parents were both reacting strongly. The mother felt that Allen was arguing with her more but that they still managed to feel loving toward one another. Allen's father appreciated Allen's beginning search for autonomy and felt less threatened by it, affectionately remembering his own efforts at the same age to "feel less close to Mommy." In the meeting, he closed his reflections on the interview by saying, "I could never imagine talking with my parents about myself and my feelings the way Allen did here today. I would have been too worried they'd be hurt, or that they wouldn't even get it. I'm proud of him for saying what he feels and of us for getting it."

In his individual interview, Allen described a dream that had been recurring for several months after the beginning of his sixth grade year: He is riding his new trick bike back and forth along a country road, with his mom at one end of the road and his dad at the other. He remembers a road sign that says ONE WAY, THIS WAY, but he ignores it and just keeps riding faster and faster, back and forth, until it starts to rain. After describing the dream, Allen commented that it was a "stupid" dream, because "I'd never ride my bike alone; my friends are always with me." He also remembered that he felt a little scared riding one way but not the other, but he couldn't recall which one.

Obviously, Allen was not on the couch when he told me this dream, but he'd known me for years, so I asked him what he thought of it. After a judicious pause, he said, "Mom and Dad had to work pretty hard to buy me that bike, because I could only put in fifty dollars from my chore money. I felt real happy to have it, but I don't go on bike rides with them anymore. So I guess I'm pretty confused in the dream about which way to go, and if it's okay with them." Not bad psychological dream interpretation for an eleven-year-old ornithologist! He described his guilt over getting his own needs met and his worry about hurting either his mom's or his dad's feelings as he pursues his own new competencies and developmental needs. Anxiety about favoritism buries the preferred route, consciously allowing him to preserve his closeness to both of them, ambivalent and uncertain though it may be. Clinically, one couldn't ask for a better harbor from which to take aboard provisions and set sail for the heavy weather that is adolescence.

———————————————————————————— ●

DISCUSSION

While I have focused only on two families in this chapter, my colleagues and I analyzed all the individual and family interview data for the study population and found that the children are still developing well in all relevant domains. Their families continue to handle their maturational needs reasonably well, despite the changes brought about by imminent adolescence. No statistically significant data can emerge from such a small pilot study, and a control group is not possible (given that you cannot clone these children and have their mothers raise the clones in identical circumstances). Consequently, we settle for reporting only the most obvious, common findings in this population, while being challenged to understand those things that surprise us. Several interesting trends have emerged in both the children as individuals and in the families' nurturing relationships.

The most robust finding in the families at this follow-up is this: the gender of the father now seems to be a far more significant aspect of his parental identity to his children than it ever was before. It seems that at earlier stages in his child's life his nurturing behavior, motivation, and overall parenting style outweighed the contribution his masculine gender made to his caregiving role; that is, from his child's point of view in the past, his capacity to be appropriately attuned to his or her needs had overshadowed any contribution his masculinity made to his fathering. But now, with the child on the threshold of adolescence, his masculinity itself is emerging as a central attribute in his ongoing relationship with his emerging adolescent. These children's new sensitivity to their father's masculinity is strikingly parallel to the ascendency of the issue of gender in their own life; puberty energizes a new focus on this previously more peripheral attribute of both of their identities.

By the same token, the mother's femininity now also assumes new importance, but at a slightly different level of meaning for the preteen. Her femininity was always an important attribute, because it was an important part of what defined her differentness from the primary caregiving father. This enhanced her power as the "important other," a term borrowed from the work of psychoanalyst Margaret Mahler and wonderfully expanded by another psychoanalyst, Ernst Abelin, to help describe the child's struggle for differentiation from the father (the traditional "other" parent, that is, the nonprimary caregiver), especially in the child's toddler and preschool years. Now, in the developmental stage when the child is no longer merely rehearsing psychological and sexual autonomy but is truly differentiating and becoming autonomous, the nonprimary caregiver mother's femininity is clarifying for her son, as it affirms his heterosexual interests, and simultaneously reassuring and challenging for her daughter. It's as if she can say to both her son and her daughter, "Trust me, I showed you before that it is okay to look beyond your father's love and to look for me—and with me—in a wider world." (This is the reverse of the Native American myths where fathers take their children to the mountain to show them the world.)

The overall consequence for the families in this study was that on the surface they looked more like traditional families than ever before as their firstborn children entered adolescence. Pubertal maturation, which had already begun for most of the kids, seemed to be increasing the incidence of conflict between the girls and their mother, but not their father. Maturation in the boys seemed connected to a slight chill in the relationship with the father, but less so with the mother. The fathers seemed aware that they were losing some of their power as a parent, though the mothers showed less concern.

The most vigorous observation in this group of fourteen preadolescent children: The children felt that their friendships and relationships with peers of both genders were very satisfying for them and that the gender of a friend, while an important attribute, seemed less important than the overall quality of the friendship. Gender polarization seemed a marginal, rather than central, issue for these youngsters on the threshold of their adolescence. Their equanimity concerning gender issues in their peer relations was striking because of the usual anxiety and conflict at this stage that typically suffuse previously comfortable and companionable peer relations. As gender differences become far more salient—as sexual and physiological reproductive readiness asserts itself in the obvious arrival of puberty in girls and in the assumed, if occasionally posed, arrival in boys—teasing, jokes, and sadistic humor are typically used by traditionally reared children to control the internal emotional conflict and anxiety that accompany this relational change. But for the children in this study, companionable humor and communication are surviving so far. The kids themselves are aware that, compared to their traditionally reared peers, they have a surprising number of friends of the opposite gender, friends who still come comfortably to their birthday parties and take in movies, community events, and occasional religious festivities with them as real friends and not, as Katelin put it, as "potential honeys." Furthermore, they are drawn to peers who share and respect their less restricted views of gender roles for men and women. Says Helen, "None of my girlfriends want to be housewives—you don't marry a house! None of my guy friends want nothing to do with their kids—they think kids are cool to teach things to."

While this cross-gender clustering of friendships resembles the findings we noted at the four-year follow-up, it seems to be a more significant observation now, because it is so counterintuitive a finding for a young adolescent population. My hunch: having your father serve as a primary nurturing figure for your early years while your mother worked outside the home but stayed very close (remember, most mothers continued to breast-feed after returning to work) affords you a bedrock trust and comfort with present and future male and female relationships so that the gendered aspects of those relationships may be less salient to you than their overall quality. How long this relative ease will endure and what role it may play in late adolescence, when sexual differentiation is more complete and the search for intimacy in a sexual context is more intense, awaits further study.

Many of my findings are supported in other descriptions of stay-at-home, primary caretaking fathers. In his study of such men and their families, Australian psychologist Graeme Russell, who has focused more on the effects on the marital coalition and less on the developmental consequences for the children, concluded that most families find that the overwhelming advantage of the father-as-primary-caregiver arrangement is an improved father–child relationship. The families themselves also note some increased tension and conflict in that relationship, despite its closeness, as a consequence of the demands on the father of being the full-time caregiver. Mothers see this increased tension as a kind of "deromanticizing" or correction toward a more realistic father–child relationship.

Norma Radin used four- and eleven-year follow-ups to focus on the stability of the father-as-primary-caregiver arrangement as well as on certain child outcomes. Studying the precedents of what she calls a "partial role reversal" in women (i.e., mothers whose husband is the primary caregiver for their children), she found that mothers who have good feelings about their own father, though perceiving them as having been less involved than their mother in child care, have husbands who are heavily involved in child care. On the other hand, Radin found little evidence of a link between the father's view of his own father and his own participation in childrearing.

As for the children, Radin found that children of fathers with heavy responsibility and participation are more likely to enjoy a more internal locus of control (recall that this is a psychological measure of the way in which responsibility is felt about life's events), indicating that such children enjoy a clearer and more trusting sense of how the world works in relation to their ability to affect change around them. Feeling in control allows one to make more creative, less fear-driven choices in life and to favor less rigidity as an adult. Teenagers who experience heavy father participation are more likely to approve of arrangements in which parents share child care equally or where there is greater father involvement, and they are less likely to approve of an arrangement where the mother's involvement is high and the father's is low.

In an Israeli study by psychologist Avi Sagi of sixty families near Haifa, the preschool children of primary caregiver fathers were found to be more empathetic and to have a more internal locus of control than peers in traditional families. As in the Radin study, the children were also found to have a more flexible, less sex-role-stereotyped attitude toward their future partner and life.

Radin also found an interesting Catch-22 for dads. For her four-year-old subjects, she found that boys' intelligence test scores were positively related to their father's nurturance. Seven years later, this was less the case. What had changed? What were the children responding to in the ongoing relationship with their fathers? Men who are very involved in childrearing pay a price in terms of their careers (sound familiar?). As such, a mixed message might be temporarily felt by older sons in particular, regarding grades and achievement, as they watch their father's career aspirations dwindle, or at best stall, as they increase their fathering time.

Are there Catch-22s for the mothers in such families? The research doesn't quite capture the complexity of the sacrifices they make and the uncertainties they endure to make this childrearing arrangement work for their children and husband. The women in my study families tolerated high levels of exhaustion, coming home at six or seven to sometimes help with dinner, supervise a project, give baths, and tuck kids in by 10 P.M. (Yes, by the usual standards that's a bit late for a preschooler, but many of the kids could sleep late in the morning and the extra evening time was pure gold to the mothers.)

The wives of the primary caregiver dads in my study also deeply appreciate that they do not have to worry about the quality, consistency, or devotion of their child's caregiver! They often feel their love and respect for their husbands grow to deeper levels. They are especially happy that they are showing their sons and daughters that they, too, will have options for raising their own kids. Listen to Helen's mother:

My husband is a pioneer crossing a new frontier. I think what he's doing will change the world that Helen and her sister will live in. I love and respect him for that. Sometimes its kind of a turn-on when I think about it [*nervous but coy laughter*]. Other times I feel jealous—sometimes very jealous—of the time they have together, their closeness, their little jokes that I have to get explained to me. But it was a choice we both made, and it was the right one. Those kids are so lucky to be his and mine together. I sometimes wonder if they'll ever know *how* lucky.

Helen's mother raises one tricky question in her reference to the "turn-on": does being heavily involved as a caretaker affect a man's masculinity or sensuality, and if so, how does his wife feel about it? Fortunately, psychologist Graeme Russell studied just that question and found that fathers classified as androgynous (mixing feminine and masculine traits) were more involved in day-to-day caretaking and play with their kids than those classified as strictly masculine. But, as we have seen, raising children changes men (and women) in unforeseen and powerful ways. Does the androgyny make possible, or result from, the reciprocal, intimate nurturing experiences of child care? Unable to separate the chicken from the egg, Russell concluded that taking care of children does not affect the masculinity of men; the instrumental masculine natures of caretaking fathers may simply be more balanced, rather than overshadowed, by the enhanced expressive and nurturing qualities called for in daily child care. Bem's research in the early 1980s showed us that a person's gender traits can be altered as a result of life situations. Taken together, these two conclusions effectively neuter the masculinity appeal question.

I will close the story (for now) on these remarkable families with a historical over-the-shoulder look at how far we have come in appreciating them. In 1988 I was sent an unsolicited transcript by an attorney in Detroit in which U.S. Circuit Judge Norman Lippitt was adjudicating a custody dispute over a twenty-two-month-old girl who had a "tighter relationship with the father than the mother." When expert testimony was offered to support a primary postdissolution relationship for the child with her father, given his primary caretaking role in her life up to that point, the judge cut off the attorney, saying, "I don't buy it. I don't buy it. I don't buy that the father is better for a twenty-two-month-old girl than the mother. And I can't swallow it. I'm going to vomit on it. I can't handle it . . . little girls belong with their mothers. I can't swallow what you are saying. I don't care how good a father [he is]."

Nauseating.

In a completely unrelated matter, eight years later I received a letter from a father in Watertown, South Dakota, thanking me for helping him negotiate joint custody for his three-and-a-half-year-old daughter and six-year-old son by writing *The Nurturing Father*. "We brought your book and entered it as evidence that men could do a good job of raising kids, and threatened to read it in its entirety into testimony . . . your thoughts and conclusions presented in your work helped me stay in my children's lives with custody. The lives of my children [and me] are now very much better, and I offer my profound thanks."

You're welcome.

4

Fatherneed Throughout Life

M Y FIRSTBORN daughter's toddlerhood was in full bloom with a fervent autonomy. After a few weeks of her "No! Me do!" and darting away just for the heck of it, I was struck by how very familiar her way of teasing—warm but slightly devious—seemed to me. Why it seemed so was just beyond my conscious grasp. A month later, during a holiday visit home to Indianapolis with my brothers, the epiphany occurred. My daughter's behavior was, glance for glance, nuance for nuance, exactly what used to drive my parents nuts about the way I used to tease my little brother, Peanut. Now it was my turn, almost 30 years later, to be irritated by behavior in my own child that I myself, to the exasperation of *my* parents, had once displayed.

How much of my fathering—or, better yet, of me—was in my daughter? How much of my father's fathering, or of him, might be in me? And how much of the "me" in my daughter, good or bad, was out there in the world already, or might yet be revealed over the course of her (and my) growing up? If it could irk me that she was so much like me in this way, where might this end? Well, it doesn't actually end; it just gets passed on down the line. I saw my father tease *his* brothers, and warm and clever though he was in the doing of it, it wasn't much appreciated by them, or by their parents.

My thoughts about this familial teasing raised the wider question of what happens to a father's need for his children and to the reciprocal need in his children for him over the course of life, over the time it takes for children to grow and fathers to age. It has always felt to me that the development of men and women into parents and their children's maturation into adults work together like an ornate version of the simple "push me, pull you" toys of the turn of the century. The transactions between family members—involving their individual and separate strengths, weaknesses, creativity, fears, and passions—push/pull them all forward in life in an infinite variety of rhythms. Furthermore, no parent is skilled or inept at every one of the stages through which children grow and develop, any more than any one child masters all of life's stages with the same aplomb or ineptitude. Instead, the continual transactions between parent and child fuel the development of each and drive them both forward in life. As a result, they probably get further than either of them could have alone. In this chapter we'll look at how the "push me, pull you" of a father's and his child's development fulfills fatherneed over the life span.

But first a word about raising kids in general these days. Yes, Cicero felt that Roman youth in the first century B.C. were going to hell in a handbasket, calling them unruly, dissolute, lazy, heavy drinking, arrogant, disrespectful of elders, self-absorbed, and rude. His orations bear a remarkable resemblance to the urgent warnings of any number of fretting television evangelists. Still, raising children today is probably harder than it was when you were a child. The social environment that laps at our kids' heels is more toxic than the one you probably knew. This puts heavy demands on parents to increase their effectiveness beyond basic nurturer to savvy agent of socialization. At the same time, it puts the heat on schools to take on a more competence-promoting role. To many of us our neighborhood feels at least a little menacing, and for a lot of us it's downright dangerous. In today's culture, money, as opposed to enduring friendship, peace, safety, and sense of well-being, seems the only thing worth having. Television fans our baser interests in aggression, envy, erotica, and acquisition—no small achievement for a small appliance. Its influence is helped considerably by the twenty-eight hours a week the average preschooler watches. And to boot, a lot of you are feeling pretty lonely out there, having moved away from your hometown and family in pursuit of . . .

The families from my longitudinal study remind me that fathering, like mothering, changes across the years. Experience, adult developmental stages themselves, aging—all interact (with varying degrees of success) with the changes imposed on them by the developmental changes of the growing child. Babies, toddlers, and preschoolers, although small, require a wide variety of skills: emotional and physical stamina and the sensitivities of selflessness. The sensual intimacies of the physical care and feeding of tiny offspring are part of what makes many men fall so completely in love, so fast, with their babies. Yet we see men responding differently from women to their child's growing autonomy; for example, they show less ambivalence than women toward their toddler's need for separateness—and the kids love it.

The challenges of parenting a school-age child can be particularly interesting to fathers because of the interests they share with the child in skill building and being competent in groups such as teams. Boys' groups led by men are culturally supported, because it is recognized that young boys (like young girls) prefer to hone new skills with peers of the same gender, whether those skills are in athletics, the arts, or religious practice. Adolescence worries and confuses fathers of daughters and typically challenges fathers of sons (fourteen-year-old Aaron: "My dad freaked out when I started to wear his shoe size. He's working out and losing weight—it's like he has to prove he was here first, and I'm never going to pass him up, or something").

The way a father feels about aging and the increasing distance from his own youth plays a major role in how comfortable or competent he feels in fulfilling fatherneed in his children at different stages. Also, what he remembers of and what he feels about being fathered at different stages of growth strongly shapes the efforts he makes with his own children at those stages. Loving or hating school or work, being an athlete or not, feeling secure with girls or not—all mold his experience with his own children when these issues arrive in their lives.

In the real world it is crystal-clear that the role of the father evolves as his children age, necessitating changes in the specific nature of his involvement in their lives. Yet much of the current research indicates that, despite the changes in the outside world, there is a certain consistency in a father's interactions with his children through time owing to the stability of his own goals, values, and attitudes. The father who reads to his child as a toddler will later encourage academic achievement in grade school and also tends to encourage it in his teenager as well. The actual *form* that that encouragement takes will change with the age and developmental needs of the child, but the father's overall intent and its impact on the child tend to stay the same.

Hidden in this linear scenario is an assumption that bears scrutiny. Culturally, mothering behavior is assumed to kick in automatically in a timely fashion (roughly synchronous with the delivery of the placenta). Once on, it's on. There are no such assumptions about fathering behavior. This is a blessing and a curse: a blessing in that it gives the child and the mother a chance to participate in the conversion of the man to a father and a curse in that if fathering behaviors don't appear, the impatient question "If not now, when?" arises.

As a clinical exercise after the writing of my first book, I began to ask men who had become fathers and were consulting me (for whatever reason) this question: "At what moment in time did you begin to really feel like your child's father?" I had been tipped off during my research that the critical moment doesn't, by any means, always occur in the delivery room. But most men can tell you what direction the wind was blowing in and the length of the shadows when that moment occurred for them. It is a moment unique to each father–child pair. While it is probably related to the total amount of time they have been in each other's company, more togetherness would not necessarily make it happen sooner, nor would frequent absence necessarily always delay its onset. And the mother is rarely in the picture at the critical juncture. When the "Aha!" happens, when every detail of the child—the expression on the face, the feel of the skin, the sound of the voice, the smell of the breath, the absolute, unique essence—registers in the father as *mine,* all gets etched in memory stone.

I call it an "Aha!" because it strikes as a sudden and perturbing awareness of something perceived as both absolutely novel and yet somehow previously half known. Others have struggled with what to call "it." San Diego psychiatrist Martin Greenberg, in his classic primer on fatherhood, used the word *engrossment* to describe the father's intense awareness of the baby's attractiveness and helplessness. The exhilaration the father feels, mixed with his strong desire to touch and be with the baby, simultaneously enhances the father's self-evaluation. Researchers Pamela Daniels and Kathy Weingarten called it the fatherhood "click." It is the feeling a man has when he just knows he's a fully realized father, a feeling whose emergence is often distinct from the timing of the birth of the child.

The beginning of true fatherhood is probably also affected by the closeness a father feels to a particular child at a particular time in their shared development. The temperamental fit between father and child, the competence a man feels as a result of his child's positive response to him, the man's perception of his own father's competence with *him* and the man's age(s) when he perceived it—all probably play a part in the timing of when a man claims his fatherhood emotionally. Too many men simply mark time until the moment comes, hanging back to avoid bathing, diapering, and feeding the baby, running too quickly to always man the camera instead of the child.

Once the "Aha!" happens, however, there is no guarantee it will persevere. For one man, it may always be there with him. For another, it may appear only to later disappear, perhaps to reappear again according to certain stresses in his life or the developmental challenges he faces in raising a particular son or daughter through a certain stage. We've all heard fathers make remarks like these:

"I'm not a baby guy."
"Give me a toddler to mix it up with any day—my favorite time of life."
"They have to talk before I think they are real."
"I can't wait for them to be teenagers. They're so alive at that age! I loved my adolescence, I'm sure I'll love theirs."

In these frank avowals, we hear that men, like women, experience the transitions between their children's developmental stages as emotionally complex, and none of us can be all things to our children all the time.

The intimacy needed by children may be more easily tolerated or expressed by men through action, shared activities, and what some experts call "instrumental behaviors." These include daily activities like play or sports, running errands, and home maintenance, as opposed to the sharing or expressing of feeling and emotion. This predilection for action fits some developmental stages better than others and sometimes leaves a man who connects well with his child at one stage feeling a bit bereft or less competent or comfortable at another. In fact, the leaving of one stage of their child's development and the entry into another is often tinged with sadness for both men and women. When such transitions coincide with developmental stress in the man himself, with job dissatisfaction, midlife anxieties, or generativity disappointments, fathering a difficult, challenging child can understandably make a man feel depleted or discouraged. If, however, the child has a less challenging personality and is thriving, he or she can actually reaffirm and encourage a father facing those same stressors.

THE STAGES OF FATHERNEED

By firmly placing ourselves in the real world of slowly aging men and rapidly growing kids, we can create a rough chronology of how fatherneed evolves over the stages of development our children go through. This chronology will force us to more honestly assess the changes that fatherneed—the need in men to provide fathering and the need in their children to experience it—undergoes over time.

INFANCY

Fathering an infant requires a huge array of skills, many of which we've already discussed. The infant–father connection was explored extensively in Chapter 2, because it makes such a powerful difference in the life of the child—and in the father's life. Suffice it to say that what children at this stage need and require of their father and mother is in inverse proportion to their mass. Diminutive beings require massive infusions of selflessness, attentiveness, and patience. The required amounts of physical and emotional stamina and control, if universally known prior to conception, would make a formidable contraceptive (this may be precisely why this information *can't* be known prenatally—the species would end in one generation).

And formidable, frightening, fabulous creatures they are. Infants evoke the most powerful sensual intimacies outside of sex. Their helplessness draws men and women in like light into a black hole. Fathers need the vitality and affirmation an infant brings to their lives, and infants need their father's power and separateness to affirm their right to their own life (and fathers of infants are good at that; they are less ambivalent than infants' mothers about autonomy and independence, two powerful Western virtues).

In the paragraphs that follow are some ways expectant fathers have successfully prepared themselves for the arrival of an infant. (The rest of this chapter will be addressed directly to men. Women: keep reading.

This chapter will give you a little insight into what it often feels like to be a man in a birthing or parenting class.)

Prepare your emotions:

- Talk to your spouse about your and her expectations of you as a father.
- Discuss fathering with your father or an older man you esteem.
- Get ready to feel some intense emotions (some you may never have experienced before), both positive and negative.
- Wrap up unfinished business with your own father. This should get settled before too long, or it begins to gum up the works in your fathering.

Prepare your nest (you've probably been talking with your partner about what to expect financially. If not, now is a good time):

- Make sure your living space is safe and ready.
- Think about finances, insurance, college funds (compounded interest works best when you start at zero time).
- Review your career aspirations.
- *Seriously* consider paternity leave. It's the law and it changes your life permanently as a father.

Prepare your skills:

- Read a good book or magazine on infancy and discuss what you learn with your partner.
- Learn how to diaper, feed, bathe, carry, play with, and massage an infant.
- Rehearse with a live child if you can.
- Take birthing and parenting classes and *speak up* in class. No one is likely to ask you much or put much effort into hearing your opinions (with the possible exception of another guy).
- Visit your library. Libraries are loaded with good videos and books on how to care for an infant. There are wonderful resources and how-to advice for expectant mothers; there are also some good, solid choices for new dads (take a look at the appendices at the back of these books). And check the Internet.

Prepare your marriage:

- Interview and line up competent child care (family members can be great, but remember it's your kid, not your mother-in-law's) to occasionally help you remember your marriage.
- Prepare to feel marginalized for a while (it's not called the "fourth trimester" for nothing). Learn how to give (and take) a decent massage. Sex will eventually return.
- Learn as much as you possibly can about what your baby's mother will be going through. Postpartum depression hits women *and* men in large numbers. Be prepared for it, because it's easily treatable and can make things tough on her, you, and the baby for a long time if it goes undetected (see Chapter 8).

TODDLERHOOD

Unlike infancy, toddlerhood is not the fastest stage of human development, but it is, for my money, the most exhilarating. Consequently, I recently wrote a book about it, called *Me, Myself, and I,* to describe how during this period, unlike any other in human development, the body and mind work so well together in the service of pleasure, competence, sensuality, and growth. The experiences toddlers have with the important people in their life are so vital that they actually affect the eventual shape and power of their brain, since the brain is incredibly busy developing permanent connections during toddlerhood. Temperament is clearly defined by now, and there is no doubt how important you and your toddler are to each other.

It's also the first time many of us parents get rocked back on our heels by the power of our child's push for separation and autonomy from us. We often feel uncertain about how to encourage individuality in light of the need to set appropriate limits on new impulses never before seen in our little darlings—hitting, biting, kicking, spitting. Simply shocking!

It is in the toddler years, from 1½ to about 3½, that fathers play one of the most critical roles they ever play in the life of their child: helping the child safely and securely separate from the intense maternal dependency of infancy. Healthy though dependency on their mother is for children at the beginning of their life, they will not experience, let alone practice, their own competence and mastery skills if they do not strike off in search of their own physical and emotional autonomy. And in this world, you, the father, are the expert guide. You, after all, have already figured out how to be separate from Mom and lived to tell about it, so you *must* know the way, or so your toddler believes. And that is why he or she comes looking for you in earnest. Many dads who have not found it easy, or sometimes even possible, to be actively physically engaged in the life of their infant, are stunned to feel the powerful bid of a toddler for their attention and time.

Toddlers, unlike infants, *can* come looking for you, demand your attention, and make your day with their unconditional love and affection. They can also drive you nuts with their oppositional tendencies, stubbornness, and "in your face" communication style and attitude. But that is precisely the way they are supposed to be in order to prepare for the world beyond Mom. And for so many kids, the world beyond Mom begins with Dad (as we saw in Chapter 1). Dad's skills, his very differentness-from-Mom, make him the undisputed expert on this matter. A recent child-oriented animated television series about a dinosaur family scripts the toddler-like character to call her father "not-the-momma." It's all in a name.

Although this stage provides a golden opportunity to satisfy the fatherneed, it also harbors some potential hazards. Michael Lamb has cautioned that fathers tend to pour more energy into their relationship with a toddler son than a daughter, reinforcing gender-stereotyped behavior in children by talking more to a daughter but playing and roughhousing more with a son. As I saw in my own research with stay-at-home dads, this tendency fades when a father is deeply involved in the care of his child, suggesting that this differential treatment is not an innate property of the father–child relationship and is therefore subject to change with education, experience, and support. Although I suspect that the inclination to treat little boys and girls differently is starting to soften, it will probably never disappear entirely, given the tenacity of cultural expectations. So, fathers, consider yourselves informed, and watch out for this tendency. As we've seen previously, daughters strongly supported by fathers early in life wind up with greater strengths—and opportunities.

Here is some practical advice for fathers on raising toddlers:

Prepare your nest:

- Remove or elevate treasured or dangerous breakables. This is not spoiling, it's safety. You'll be putting these items back in a few years when they can be more safely handled.

- Do a thirty-six-inches-and-under walk-through (crawl-through?) of your home, looking for potential dangers and safety-plugging electric outlets, gating stairs, and child-locking kitchen and cleaning cabinets (kits are available in hardware or toy stores).
- Make sure the shelves for your toddler's books and toys are low and safe enough for the child to access.

These suggestions tip the management of your toddler's world, and his or her need to safely explore in it, in your favor. These preparations are not responses to overweening efforts on the part of your child to remake *your* world to conform to his or her every whim. Struggling over control of everything doesn't build character at this age, only frustration.

Prepare your skills:

- Read a good book, magazine, or Web site on toddlerhood and discuss what you learn with your spouse.
- Practice "toddlerese"—short, clear instructions ("Let's do [one thing]." "It's time for . . ."). Forget metaphor, sarcasm, figures of speech. No one is more concrete or literal than a toddler.
- Learn to offer choices but limit them, usually to two acceptable options ("Which of these two books before your nap?" or "Will it be juice or milk with lunch?). If you want toddlers to comply, *never* ask a question like "Do you want to go to bed now?" No is their only choice.
- Rehearse limit setting. Toddlers are busy mapping your world, so show them the boundaries: "We don't throw food" or "I won't let you hurt [the dog, baby, me]." Then redirect your toddler's efforts or offer an acceptable substitute for the current object of interest (e.g., give your child modeling clay to replace the dog food being played with). These strategies work better than a screamed "No!" or a "How many times do I have to tell you . . ." (apparently too many). Do *not* leave this all up to your spouse. It's not fair and it doesn't satisfy the fatherneed in you or your toddler.

Prepare your emotions:

- Practice being calm and gentle when you feel exactly the opposite. Toddlers mimic *everything,* including your meltdowns.

Prepare your calendar:

- Establish routines. They're lifesavers. Toddlers have no sense of time, especially yours. So bath, bed, and nap times should all be ritualized with whatever reading, dressing, and singing routines you use. Do your best to begin a ritual at the same time and follow its steps in the same sequence every day. Predictable is helpful and pleasant, not anal.
- Anticipate the near future for your toddler. Transitions can feel chaotic to a toddler, especially if they're unanticipated. Give five-minute warnings ("We'll need to get coats on to go home in a few minutes"). For older toddlers, try something like "When you wake up in the morning, we get to go . . ." This promotes more mastery and less resistance.
- Limit television and video watching to one or two hours a day. More interferes with engaging the real world, stimulates an appetite for junk, and can frighten and fascinate with its violence. These objections also hold for news programs. You'll just have to watch them at a later hour.
- Schedule daily vigorous activities. Body mastery is one of your specialties, so enjoy playing outside with your toddler and going for walks (or runs and chases). If the weather or your neighborhood is bad, find physical activities indoors: build furniture-and-pillow castles, use the stairs to burn energy, play hide-and-seek. Passively watching stimulating TV programs can activate energy that has to get used somehow, making indoor confinement worse not better after a few hours of TV.

Prepare your marriage:

- Your child can tolerate slightly longer separations now, so do an overnight away from home with your partner and spend some money. This will prove an excellent investment—a short- and a long-term gainer.

PRESCHOOL YEARS

By age three, the human brain has completed 98 percent of its growth. It will spend the next six to seven years shaping, refining, and pruning itself, finalizing its architecture through the late adolescence and young adulthood, in dynamic dialogue between its genetic blue-print and environmental experiences, beginning with preschool. It's daunting, I know, to think that experience with us human beings is still so important to the development of a kid's brain after hundreds of thousands of years of evolution, but what can I say? Don't be fooled by the fact that most of us have no memory of our life before our third or fourth birthday. It matters plenty. Our experiences during these early years may be what ultimately sets us up here, currently atop the evolutionary tree.

Having largely mastered control of bodily functions and some self-care skills, preschoolers turn their considerable (and, thankfully, more organized) abilities and enthusiasms to other things. At this stage the innately fascinating difference between boys and girls gets a lot of attention, and when preschoolers figure out that Mom and Dad are different in some of the same intriguing ways, the plot thickens. Gender clarification is a major theme, and Dad is not just not-the-mother anymore. Instead, he is the grinding stone on which his son sharpens his emerging masculinity and the appreciative audience to which his daughter plays out her femininity. Although puerile enthusiasms for Dad's and Mom's attention can amuse, don't be fooled. Preschoolers are not just being cute. These are serious games in which gender is being refined and defined in the triangle formed by two same-sex sides against the hypotenuse of the opposite gender. Even the strongest marriage can feel the strain of a determined preschooler. Kids actually make comments like the following: (daughter to mother) "Mom, you can sleep on the couch now; this bed belongs to me and Daddy in the mornings" and (son to father) "Daddy, stay at work; Mommy and I are having quiet time tonight." Fathers usually rise to the occasion by helping their preschool-age son displace and discharge his aggression and anxious rivalry by engaging him in physical play (significantly more than do mothers, who seem to be busier with instructional activities, according to the work of Ross Parke and his colleagues).

Dads seem to have a slight proclivity to encourage their preschoolers of both sexes to play with sex-typed toys, unless they are made aware of this potentially unhelpful tendency. Dads home in on their preschoolers' needs by periodically modifying their own speech and language patterns to communicate more predictably with them. They do not adapt fully, however, and continue to use slightly more sophisticated speech than a child this age can always make use of.

Henry's father, one of the big talkers in my study of stay-at-home dads, was fond of telling his preschooler, "No more baby talk, Henry. Use the words you just learned, and I can hear them better." When I asked him to explain what he was doing, he said, "Henry can be a lazy talker, using his old 'googletalk.' It's better for him to use bigger and clearer words so people won't treat him so much like a baby—something he really hates these days, because he's so busy being a big boy." It appears that fathers like to stretch their kids' communicative skills in preparation for more worldly dialogue.

New developmental sociological research from Carol Gilligan and her colleagues, who first directed our attention to the worrisomely self-effacing behavior of preteen girls in our current school culture, has begun to identify a crisis for male preschool development. I've seen this also taking shape in my role as diagnostician and consultant to the Child Development Unit of the Yale Child Study over the last twenty years. Up until six or seven years ago, our most common reason for referral of children under age five was language delay, and the ratio of boys to girls was roughly the same. Now the most common visitor to our clinic is a boy under five with a behavior or conduct problem, often a moderately serious one.

It seems that as schools have focused on correcting our serious oversight of the needs of girls over the past decade, boys are finding themselves in increasing trouble early on. Now, it seems, preschool boys are in somewhat of a crisis of their own. When normal male traits, such as excess energy with a drive to conquer, are stimulated by excessive TV and video watching and improperly channeled by mediocre day care, they can snowball into outbreaks of symptoms like impulsivity, aggression, bed-wetting, separation anxiety, and conduct problems. Boys have innately higher levels of testosterone and inherently lower levels of hormones like serotonin, which mutes impulsivity and the expression of aggression.

Thus, when he is preschool-age, a boy needs his father's help more than ever to manage this heavy load of excitement and agitation—especially in the face of age-old social pressures that "macho up" little boys in day-care settings during free play, where it's not rare to hear four-year-old boys calling each other sissies or girls for being scared to do something daring or foolhardy. Positive emotions in little boys like warmth, affection, sympathy, and mutual supportiveness especially need a father's help to survive and flourish in such environments. The stress on little boys can be further exacerbated by their tendency to lag behind girls in the skills that preschool and pre-kindergarten curricula value and reward, that is, verbal and social skills. Beyond the preschool's block corner, gross motor skills and visuospatial abilities—what boys excel in—don't get valued nearly as much as a little girl's calm demeanor or her desire to be the teacher's helper.

Enter Dad. His affirmation of positive emotions and his clarification of boundaries and expectations, both social and academic (especially in the women's world that is preschool and pre-K), can powerfully support his daughter to be more active and assertive and his son to stick with the mastery of verbal skills and friend-making a little longer. The teachers and day-care workers who worked with the children of the families in my study were often highly complimentary and supportive of the boys in their classes for their thoughtfulness, social awareness, and rare use of aggression and of the girls for their competitive will and ability to tolerate frustration when mastering new skills.

As for dealing with your preschool daughter's desire to "marry Daddy someday," you can enjoy the attention but affirm that she'll enjoy finding someone of her own, maybe someone *like* you (surprisingly, that's often just what happens), when she's older. You can point out that you are already married or partnered, and (hopefully) happily so, and that, in fact, it is from just such a happy union that she herself has come. Don't ridicule or mock your daughter's declarations of love for you. Her affections are real, and it is essential that little girls have the experience of feeling and mastering the power of their worth and appeal to their father, the first object of their love for the opposite sex. Of course, mothers must deal as gently with a small son's declarations of love.

Here is practical advice to help fill fatherneed in the preschool years:

Prepare your nest:

- You can replace some of those breakables now.
- Some of the safety barriers can be relaxed. Replace them with instructions and rehearsal about what to do if there's trouble, calmly teaching your preschooler what to do if a fire alarm goes off or there is a loss of power, etc., if your child isn't too prone to worry.

Prepare your skills:

- Review your disciplinary style and check for gentleness. Discipline means to *teach,* not punish; consequently, discipline and anger are best put in play separately. Your child is now big enough that he or she can hurt someone else if the impulse arises to enact one of your meltdowns at someone else's expense.
- Read a book on preschoolers that includes dads and discuss it with your partner.

Prepare your calendar:

- Make time to read with your preschooler, and make it a more interactive venture now. ("Tell me what you think happens next." "Did that surprise you?").
- Make time to transport your preschooler to the doctor or to the daycare center. Make time to talk to teachers and other parents, and get to know your child's friends.
- Take your child to work and show him or her your world, your friends, where you eat lunch, the photo you keep of him or her on your desk, in your locker, at your workstation.
- Take your preschooler on errands with you or have him or her with you when you do chores—and expect it to take twice the time. Enjoy your kid's company. He or she won't care this much about being with you forever.

Prepare your emotions:

- Be on the lookout for private jokes at Mom's expense from a son; they'll backfire.
- Be on the lookout for special affection from a daughter. Appreciate, but don't inflate. She needs to feel her mother's strength and competence, too.

GRADE SCHOOL YEARS

Even the most reluctant fathers usually cave to the intense desire of their school-age children to have them in their life. Learning how to *do* stuff starts to matter as much as having relationships—sometimes more. Gender gangs take shape, and belonging to one is everything for some children. Fathers can usually now remember being a son of this age to *their* father, so if fathering has been hard for you to fathom up to now, such recollections can play a catalytic role for you. Depending on the nature of the memory, of course, things can go either way. John Snarey found that when men with positive memories of being fathered face an impasse with their school-age child, they are guided and supported by those memories. On the other hand, when the memories are negative, such impasses are often seen as opportunities to rework one's father's inadequacy (even competitively) and find a better solution.

At this stage, father involvement now has special salience for helping build a child's self-regard and overall sense of competence, since that father specialty of instrumentality is now so much more likely to be rewarded in school, both academically and socially. Ross Parke discovered that children (daughters in particular) who are exposed to high levels of paternal play and attention at this stage are more popular and assertive with their peers in later adolescence. Conversely, authoritarian and intrusive fathering (of sons in particular) is associated with reduced creativity in children and poorer academic and social performance in adolescence.

Engaged fathering, as my own research so clearly bears out, endows children with the skills they need to handle the social demands of this stage with relative grace and ease. The sexual stereotyping that so rigidly and inaccurately stratifies and categorizes boys and girls as opposites of one another was significantly softened for the father-involved kids in my study. This is especially helpful at this stage, where the air is thick with bigoted epithets. To be a real guy, in the opinion of many of one's peers, one must reinforce homophobia and eschew caring, creativity, and compassion; to be a real girl, one must reinforce homophobia, eschew strenuous physical activity and random acts of kindness, and be willing to trash your friends on conference calls and in Internet chat rooms. Children who have experienced father care are less easily seduced by these powerful forces and are more likely to maintain friendships and respect across gender lines, especially in these critical years.

Some research suggests that school-age children perceive pronounced differences in their dealings with mom versus dad and may exploit those differences as a way of getting ready for the tsunami that is puberty. Fourth and fifth grade children were studied by the psychology team of Herman and McHale with regard to their perceptions and coping strategies in dealing with parental negativity. These researchers found that boys are more likely to cope by "forgetting" their father's and mother's negativity while girls are more likely to talk about such negativity with their mother than with their father. For both mothers and fathers, parental warmth was related to the child's likelihood of talking to them about their worries. This reminds us that both children and parents are growing at this time in terms of finding new communication strategies.

Fatherneed in general, but in this stage in particular, shouldn't be seen as an isolated phenomenon unaffected by other forces. A large study by psychologist Grolnick of the effect on a child's performance of parental involvement in the child's schooling found that children do better when their fathers *perceive* them as doing better. This held true even when objective data did not confirm positive academic performance. Fathers perceived their child as academically successful when they felt more involved with their child and the school. And they were more involved when their spouse was more involved.

But fathers aren't the only ones whose behavior is shaped by what they perceive. A companion study of seventy-five high-achieving third graders by Wagner found that when children work separately with their mother and father on preordained tasks—some solvable, some not—their perceived competence is positively related to their father's warmth and involvement, even when the tasks are unsolvable. If it feels good, it gets good.

Interestingly, the power of perception alone to shape behavior toward a child may also hold for teachers. Educational psychologist Ann Epstein found that when parents of kids who run into academic trouble are already known to teachers, the school takes interest sooner in intervening. Likewise, parents who know their child's teacher are more likely to be supportive of the child's attempts to fix a behavioral or academic problem if one arises.

Here is some advice on fatherneed in the school years:

Prepare your nest:

- Do not allow a television in your children's bedrooms unless you never want to see them or know what they are dumping into their minds.

Prepare your calendar:

- Things will shift now, and you will start joining your child's life more than your child will be joining yours. The pace of your child's life will accelerate. Schedule lessons and games so that you can drive, watch, or participate. Don't expect endless appreciation; it's your job.
- Copy the school calendar into yours so that you can make open houses, teacher conferences, and performances. Kids know that if *you* value school enough to do this stuff, they'd better value it, too. Also, if trouble arises, knowing the players helps hugely.
- Schedule in volunteer time for class and field trips. You'll be amazed at what you can learn about your kids and their school world when you're a volunteer. Do *not* embarrass them. It's their world now, not yours, and it's not funny at this stage, especially from the bleachers.
- When you have to be away, stay close: call home lots and leave notes in book bags, but go easy on the gifts (they set a bad precedent—guilt gets expensive—and complicates reunions).

Prepare your skills:

- Read a good book or visit a Web site on development in school-age kids and discuss what you've learned with your spouse.
- Read one of your child's books and get some idea of what piques his or her imagination these days.
- Tell your child more about your work life in terms that parallel the school experience, that is, projects, hard work, research, deadlines, teamwork, memorization, neatness, friends, being bossed around.
- Focus your energy on what now interests your child, and follow up with library visits, Internet time, or field trips. Don't compete, but acquire a skill yourself so you can join in. When you show you care, your child will do more.
- Start teaching your child about money—earning, spending (the child's own money), saving, and sharing it.

Prepare your emotions:

- Be aware that this is increasingly your child's world, so go easy on driving your child emotionally to develop skills. Childhood should be savored, not accelerated. Adulthood isn't all *that* great.

- Pride and shame in what our kids do is now more complex, because we feel implicated in both, now that the whole world is watching them (us). Measure and dispense praise and blame according to your child's needs, not yours.
- Get ready for questions about sex, drugs, and rock and roll. Tough as they are, these issues are easier to manage now than when gonads awaken and information and reason drown in impulse. Good books abound.

ADOLESCENCE

You're not in Kansas anymore. Puberty has arrived, and the possibility emerges that you and your partner are no longer the sole reproductively competent people in the family. Open doors snap shut, the breezy chats come to an abrupt halt, the shampoo and deodorant disappear—all replaced by "attitude." Who *is* this person and where did she come from? What did he do with my sweet boy? It is a brave new world for you, but much more so for your child. Biology, not psychology, has pulled them aside and said, "Childhood is over. It's time to stop rehearsing. This is real now." It's fabulously exciting and frighteningly real for your child, as it is for you.

Sons awash in testosterone find themselves changing shoe sizes monthly and, when crossed, facing down previously cherished parents. Dads get challenged, while moms get teased, even ridiculed. Daughters, now menstruating, begin to compete with Mom, devaluing her taste while borrowing her clothes; they struggle to pull away from the old closeness and security with their father, yet, at the same time, they want his appreciation of their emerging autonomy, attractiveness, competence, and femininity. Fathers strive to find their footing on this slippery slope, setting limits without disparaging individual striving in daughters or sons or abdicating their own masculinity in the process.

Involved fathering affects the development of both sons and daughters, but in distinctly different ways. John Snarey's research informs us again: a strong father–daughter relationship within the context of a strong marital and parenting relationship predicts the daughter's later academic and career success. In particular, a father's support of his daughter's physical/athletic development during childhood and adolescence alleviates sex role rigidity in the daughter, promotes her social independence, and encourages upward mobility in educational and occupational levels in her early adulthood. Adolescent sons of involved fathers, however, differ from daughters in that they enjoy more work success and educational competency but fewer of the social gains shown by their sisters.

Fathering during adolescence has a lesser, though still significant, impact on sons than on daughters. Adolescent sons face the task of separating somewhat from their father and challenging his authority while still needing and appreciating his support from the sidelines. Adolescent daughters, however, appreciate their father's active emotional support while they negotiate the task of separating more emotionally from their mothers without losing their identity as females. Paternal support for an adolescent daughter is especially important because of the burden so many young teenage girls feel. Innovative researcher and author Carol Gilligan documented the crisis of self-worth experienced by so many eleven-to-thirteen-year-old girls who begin to blunt their emotions and insights. The bottom line, documented over and over again, is that the degree of involvement of fathers with sons and daughters is solidly associated with positive self-esteem measures in older adolescents.

As for the effect on men of fathering adolescents, positive father–adolescent relationships are found to be consistently related to lower paternal midlife stress, greater paternal emotional expressiveness, and lower levels of testosterone (maybe less is needed).

Practical advice for fathers of adolescents:

Prepare your emotions:

- This stage will see your lowest and highest feelings of satisfaction, so expect a bumpy ride and hang on.
- Your feelings are going to get hurt, a lot. Remember it's business, not personal. Expect to be challenged, but stay in control. Somebody should.

Prepare your calendar:

- Chase your children down occasionally, buy them lunch, and listen. Don't wait for them to always come to you. They can't. And, yes, do *not* preach, lecture, or begin any sentence with "when I was a kid" (you didn't appreciate unsolicited advice when you were their age either).

- Periodically give each of your kids a day or half day of your time, and tell them to find something you can do together. Don't be upset if they want to bring along a friend. This might be the only way to make such a day possible (you'll learn a lot about your child from that friendship, anyway).
- Think *very* carefully about family vacations.

Prepare your skills:

- Read a good book for fathers about teenagers and discuss it with your partner.
- Practice talking about your beliefs and experience without lecturing (this is particularly a father problem).
- Listen to what your teenagers are thinking about and believing; ask them for some advice and listen some more.
- Talk occasionally about your world—work, friends, the news—and engage your teenagers respectfully about theirs.
- Watch for radical changes in your teen's friends, sleep habits, or money usage. Calmly and respectfully inquire, but don't endlessly interrogate. Kids in trouble need your love, help, and support sooner rather than later.
- Stay in touch with your kid's school life by talking to teachers, coaches, counselors. Kids notice if there's follow-up on your part.
- Don't avoid discussions about sexual behavior and interpersonal ethics. Otherwise, they think you don't care or know much about what's happening in their life. These conversations are supposed to feel uncomfortable, but have them anyway.

Prepare your partner and/or marriage:

- Now your kids are *happy* to have you go away, so do it. But leave somebody trustworthy and adult in charge (the whole high school will know in hours).
- Your kids are watching the way you and your partner treat each other with special interest, now that they are starting the hunt for relationships themselves.

YOUNG ADULTHOOD

> When I was a boy of 14, my father was so ignorant I could hardly stand to have the man around. But when I got to be 21, I was astounded at how much the old man had learned in just 7 years.
>
> —SAMUEL CLEMENS

Mark Twain's pithy insight is from the perspective of an aging adolescent. His father's perception of *him*, as he moved from hopeless to noteworthy across the same seven years, might have been identical.

Fatherneed gets satisfied in a wholly new way during this stage. The father's reaction to the incredible maturation of his child, maturation that has brought him to the threshold of his own generation, is profoundly shaped by what he sees through the lens of his *own* aging. Some parts of fatherneed don't even appear until now, and the ones that do are intriguing. Psychologist Betsy Speicher-Dubin's landmark study of the impact of a father's above-average standing in moral development, emotional warmth, and nurturance on his child's moral maturity found that such paternal traits do not predict a child's moral maturity in late childhood or early adolescence, but that they do significantly predict it in adulthood.

Two highly contrasting images from our culture come to my mind that portray fatherneed in the relationship between a father and an adult child. One relationship is healthy, the other not. In both Spencer Tracy's and Steve Martin's portrayal of the father in the film *Father of the Bride,* a warm, concerned George Banks must prepare for his daughter's marriage. Feeling terror, rage, and competitiveness internally, he nevertheless expresses support and empathy externally to his daughter and future son-in-law. He wants his daughter to be happy, but he craves his life back with his little girl. For much of the film he is shown in humorous but painful ambivalence. Ultimately, father lets daughter go, with his blessings, to share the love of a man of her own choosing.

The second image is of failed fatherneed, as portrayed in the distorted allegiance between father and daughter in *King Lear.* Lear is devastated and enraged when his daughter Cordelia, in response to his query regarding how much she loves him, says, "I love your majesty according to my bond; no more no less." Lear is blind to the understanding that real paternal love of an adult daughter prepares her to give and receive love in the context of her relationship with her chosen mate.

With this Shakespearean illustration of fatherneed gone wrong, we come to the end of this chronology, knowing that fatherneed never actually ends but merely recycles, just in time for grandfatherhood. I am not implying that there aren't still some especially critical opportunities to express and fulfill fatherneed during one's child's young adulthood. In fact, the birth of grandchildren, their entry into school, and times of illness and stress in the young family are tailor-made to get a dad's (or granddad's) attention, just at the moment when any man's learning curve is about to head straight up a sleep slope indeed.

Practical advice about fatherneed when your child has reached young adulthood:

Prepare your nest:

- Don't rent out rooms just yet. You may have liftoff but have not yet achieved orbit. Gravity is formidable, and leaving is hard these days.
- Money is often an issue. Talk about it calmly, as kids feel guilty when they need it—and you feel guilty that you do, too. Your goal should be to help start-up; fostering dependency fosters trouble, not love.

Prepare your emotions:

- Make room for a new sense of partnership with your kids. They can teach *you* a few things now, and you should listen—you're still fathering.
- Be ready for a few bumps. It's hard for young adults to establish a new life, so prepare to support, not rescue—unless there are no other seaworthy craft available. It's their life now.

Prepare your calendar:

- Establish communication routines when your kids do leave. You may have to come to them occasionally if they are working especially hard at independence. But reconnect on the early, rather than the late, side.

CONCLUSION

A little reminder: no parent is gifted at, or even happy at, every single one of the stages of child development. Our children learn early that we each have our strengths and weakness, our sweet and sour buttons. Somehow, it usually works out that Mom and Dad are rarely especially good or particularly terrible at exactly the same periods of their child's development, so children are spared that kind of double jeopardy. This discussion has been written to help you keep your balance as you hang on for dear life to your child's developmental adventure—and remember to accentuate the positive.

5

Divorce: Challenge to Fatherneed

●───────────────────────────────

For one hundred and four weeks now, Bret has picked up Edith and Susanna, his five- and seven-year-old daughters, every Wednesday from after-school and has taken them first to his parents' deli for a snack and then home to his small condo. It is three blocks away from, but in the same complex as, his old home, now their mother's condo. Bret cooks the girls dinner (with which they enthusiastically "help,") gives them a bath, reads to them after they play a game of Old Maid, helps them call their mom, and puts them to bed. The weekends alternate between one and two overnights for the girls at Bret's, according to the schedule he has worked out in mediation with their mother. Bret has never missed a child support or alimony payment. He loves his kids "more than life," and he's so depressed on Thursday and Monday mornings that he's come to consult me about reducing visitation.

Bret thought that by now, after two years, it would feel "less like brain surgery with a dull knife" to leave his daughters after each and every visit. "But it's getting harder, not easier," he says. "It's not that the ex and I are fighting. If we'd cooperated like this before the divorce, I'm not sure it would have ever happened." Bret is in psychotherapy, on antidepressants, and exquisitely aware that his boss is not amused whenever he's late for faculty meetings on Wednesday mornings, which he always is if there's the slightest glitch getting the girls to school. He has read all the books and knows not to be a Disney Dad any more than he can help it. Bret also knows that his girls love him. They call him frequently from their mom's and want him and Mommy to be "always friends," which Bret and his ex earnestly try to do.

What is killing Bret now is his perception of an increasing drift away from real life with his children. He has frequent dreams (daydreams, too) about running away. He simply can't find the closeness he used to feel with his daughters anymore.

"I don't think I ever will," he tells me, "and it's breaking my heart. Seeing them makes it worse. It's perpetual walking out, like Sisyphus—only it's leaving my kids instead of pushing a stone."

"So why stop trying now?" I ask.

"I wonder if it'd be better for them to be with me less when I'm like this. I turn into this plastic dad the mornings I have to take them back. I'm bloodless—efficient but bloodless—and they have *got* to sense it. There's always a fight or a meltdown about some dumb thing—and I know it's me. My five-year-old was really upset last week just before leaving for school, because she needed to find me to get her shoe tied. She was heaving with sobs when she told me she *knew* where I was—she just couldn't *find* me. God, is that the truth! I can't find me either. It can't be good for them to be going through this with me."

Divorce has become the single greatest challenge to fulfilling fatherneed. Bret is a perfect example of the paralyzed dad with kids who need and love him but can't find him. In divorce, we see the greatest threat to a father's fulfilling his simultaneous responsibility and need for his child in his life. Divorce likewise threatens the fulfillment of the child's need for the father. Culturally, marriage—when the father lives with the family and has a good relationship with his wife—has typically been the domain chosen for the gratification, protection, and maintenance of fatherneed. But when marriage falls on hard times, it is reduced to its contractual bones. And as a contract, marriage falls under the jaundiced eye of the law to uphold or destroy. But in applying the law—in dissolving the contract, dispersing property, and determining parental rights of reasonable visitation—havoc is wreaked on fatherneed and on the skeletal remains of a marriage, even when the law insists in its heart of hearts it is doing exactly the opposite.

> Marriage is a contract, and in most societies of the world you can rescind it, but parenthood is not a contract and you cannot break it. The law's attempt to achieve the civil death of a noncustodial parent is foolish and destructive.
>
> —MARGARET MEAD

Bret understood the meaning of "civil death" instantly. Lots of families experience divorce—a vast number, in fact—but the relationship between divorce and trouble is as complex and idiosyncratic as the relationship between marriage and happiness. As a young medical student, I was taught that children would thrive best when raised in an "average expectable environment." Gone are the days. You know the numbers: U.S. Census tallies tell us marriages ended in divorce four times as often in 1996 as they did in 1970; between 40 and 50 percent of marriages will end in divorce, though the rate in 1998 was the lowest in twenty-five years. Just 34 percent of all children born in the last three years of the twentieth century will reach the age of eighteen living with both biological parents, a minority by anybody's count. The most important number for our purposes: of those divorcing, 54 percent had at least one child, meaning that over one million kids a year are affected by divorce. Twenty million American kids live with only one parent, and a third of these children are younger than six years of age.

Here are the postdivorce numbers that illuminate the tricky relationship between fathers and children: According to the U.S. Census, a little less than half of fathers continue to support their children financially after divorce. And the visitation numbers are wild, depending on whom you believe and how they interpret the data. Frank Furstenberg, who surveyed nationwide in the mid-1980s by using self-report questionnaires, reported that only one-sixth of kids saw their fathers once a week or more and one-third to one-half had no contact the previous year. If, however, you choose numbers from Berkeley's Robert Mnookin and his colleagues, 64 percent of children in their large, compelling 1992 California sample were reported to have seen their father (separated from their mother for 3 or more years), in the previous month. The samples are different, the eras are different, the research methods are different, and the numbers games played by experts and the media don't always help the children we purport to help by studying their families.

Indeed, these numbers should not distract us from the fact that it is not simply family shape and schedules that change after divorce. They preoccupy us because they are the simplest dimension to measure of an event that we know is seismic. What changes most profoundly after divorce is hardest to measure, even one family at a time—the balance of needs, emotions, dreams, support, and gifts that parents and children bring to one another, which changes forever.

We all know that the quality of a marriage affects the quality of parent–child relationships. Likewise, the quality of a divorce affects the quality of parent–child relations after the divorce. And vice versa, of course. When the daily bond of parent–child life is stretched and distorted by divorce (as process and event), the sadness, anger, envy, and resentment that follow, not to mention the unhappiness that precedes it, can drown child and parent in such anxiety that the relationship may not endure without continued effort on both their parts. What makes this extra tough is that most parents' capacity to parent during divorce is considerably reduced, just as most kids' ability to be loving, trusting, and receptive to both parents is itself diminished.

Statistically, fathers and children lose each other most; consequently, fatherneed is where the gangrene sets in all too often. Though some of the data is overblown, many fathers do renounce their responsibilities to their kids postdivorce, though the reasons are as varied as the desertions. The ebbing of responsible fathering postdivorce is easy to oversimplify, and fathers have their own ideas about how they get treated in contemporary divorce. Once they move beyond the idea of divorce into the emotional realm, they struggle their way through layers of remorse, guilt, loss, sense of failure, and vulnerability. This alone can place the fatherneed at risk. The important research of psychologist John Gottman in Seattle shows us that men in an unsatisfying marriage are more likely to withdraw from their wife and children, with or without divorce, than men in a satisfying marriage. Does this affect the kids? Of course. Even babies know an unhappy father from a happy one. Eleven-month-olds are less likely to look to their father for help in novel learning situations (e.g., the approach of a stranger) when their father is in a distressed marriage. It's as though they already know it's every man for himself here.

The lack of a clearly sanctioned societal role for fathers in the lives of their children in general shows up in spades, highlighted in lacerating detail, in divorce. Fathers after divorce are known to feel even more uncertain about how to relate to and behave with their children, especially when they no longer live together. Some research has strongly supported the notion that fathering postdivorce is more complicated than fathering in general. The meaning of fatherhood itself, not to mention the fatherneed, becomes more ambiguous, making it harder for a man to sustain active involved fathering with his children. In a study of seventy-five divorced men, Terry Arendell, a professor of social work, found many role changes and increased ambivalence about parenting in his subjects, but the men were not hopeless about their job as father. Even nonresidential dads find their role interesting, appreciated, and socially valued, though complex and a lot less manageable than it was inside the marriage. This tension between finding parenting important but barely doable drives much of the disengagement process between fathers and children after divorce, a process we caught a glimpse of in Bret's story.

The conflicting emotional stress and tension between a father's need to stay close to his child out of devotion, love, and legal obligation, on the one hand, and his desire to escape the shame of a failed marriage, on the other, entangles many a decent man. These are some of the reasons why we see, for the majority of men, father–child contact initially increasing soon after the divorce, only to start declining the next year, and often to some degree every year thereafter. What complicates this seemingly inexorable drift is that with the passage of time alone both children and fathers, especially noncustodial ones, develop new relationships that are no longer common to both father and child. Changing economic and emotional circumstances and the degree of encouragement or discouragement from friends and extended family can either strengthen or weaken the father's resolve and involvement with his child. Combined with the inevitable desire of each spouse to limit the contact that must be endured with the other after a painful divorce, drift becomes severance without much notice. We will look at these vulnerabilities later in this chapter, but here we focus on the primary damage to the father's end of fatherneed: the painful loss of a satisfying and meaningful relationship with his child in the real world of his child's life.

Even the majority of fathers know that, hurt as they are, their pain is not paramount here, and that what needs to be addressed in the process of divorce is the well-being of his child. Children hunger for their now absent father once he leaves their day-to-day life. Whether young or almost grown, children can feel discarded, divorced, or as though they have become a burden.

Sondra was eight when her parents divorced ("Because they didn't want to be friends anymore," she explained). Although she feels bad ("Because I cost so much money when I go to dance class, and I like computer games"), she thinks her parents should not fight over who gets more time with her: "Because they both made me and own me. I belong to both of them, don't I?" What a clear statement that children are a relational asset to both their parents and that they should share and protect this resource even after divorce.

Children react to marital distress, especially fighting, even when it neither involves nor concerns them directly. Mark Cummings and Patrick Davies' important research into marital conflict shows us that conflict causes distress in children, although the effects of that conflict are not always mediated solely through parenting behaviors. Parental depression and withdrawal can also be correlated with marital conflict, can distress children independent of the conflict, and can undermine parenting and the parent's self-regard. Children can be so distressed by marital conflict and its ripple effects that they try to be mediators and take responsibility for managing their parents' damaged relationship.

How sensitive are kids to their parents' marital conflict? Although sensitivity varies according to a child's innate level of awareness about things occurring in the world around him in general, most divorcing parents would be very surprised to know how much their children notice. Subtle changes in mood, schedule, habits, attitudes, friendships, attire, cooking and cleaning routines, disciplinary practices and limit setting—kids notice it all. However, they tend to say very little until these changes begin to coalesce into something that threatens them or their relationship to their parents or their family as a whole. Their vigilance is understandable, given that their family is their port in the storm that can be their outer world. Their ability to cope with marital conflict, however, varies with their own temperament and overall sensitivity to relationships, and children of divorced parents often have a long history of exposure to and awareness of parental conflict. Jean and Jack Block found children exhibiting heightened emotional problems such as aggression, impulsivity, anxiety, and hyperactivity eleven years before parental divorce. Consequently, it's not surprising that one reputable study, by senior divorce researcher and psychologist Mavis Hetherington and her colleagues, found that 66 percent of parental interaction postdivorce is characterized by anger and conflict and that a fair number of those fights are about kids' issues such as visitation and rearing.

How adults fight matters more to children than what they fight about, whether they are still in or already out of their marriage. Children are more distressed by conflict that is angry, physical, and unresolved. Even frightening displays of anger can be less toxic if the parents end the conflict by somehow managing the process toward resolution. In seven-year-old Darren's words: "When my mom and dad argue at night, I don't sleep until it's quiet for a long, long time. But it's okay in the morning if they're being nice to each other. It's like medicine for my feelings." In fact, parental fighting has emerged as a better forecaster of children's functioning than changes in the parents' marital status; in other words, researchers have found that high levels of marital conflict are more accurate predictors of children's behavior problems than is the family structure itself. This means that anger management and conflict resolution skills, which men with tempers can profit from, would probably go a long way toward ultimately satisfying fatherneed.

If our goal here is to learn how to preserve the child's welfare, with particular regard to protecting the child–father connection postdivorce, it would help if we knew which kids were especially vulnerable to divorce's negative effects. The eruption of divorce-related anxiety places the parent–child connection in a completely different world, one in which the child can be either hypervigilant or blind to the parent for years.

Sophie, the oldest of three daughters, explained: "I was nine when my mom and dad told me they would be getting another apartment where dad could live and we could visit him. I didn't sleep for weeks, because, till Daddy left, I sneaked into their bedroom every night to watch that he was there sleeping. I cried so hard at school my teacher let me call him at work two or three times a day to hear his voice. I thought he was going to disappear if I didn't watch him." Divorce, however, is such a complex event that it's usually futile to predict exactly which child–father pair will be damaged by divorce itself and which might even improve.

Disruption of fatherneed in children of divorce can stir up plenty of trouble across the child's developmental landscape. Academic and cognitive deficits have been described in an important longitudinal study headed by James Guidabaldi, who went into homes to study intact and divorced families with first, third, and fifth graders. In a follow-up study two years later, he found that children's math and spelling grades are predicted by the quality of the child's postdivorce relationship with the noncustodial father: the better the relationship, the better the grades and testing, especially for boys. For girls during these years, reading is the skill more affected by the father–daughter connection, but social skills and emotionality are also affected. For first grade boys, a better postdivorce relationship with their father is associated with better peer interactions and social communication. For the girls, sibling relationships showed positive effects from satisfied fatherneed in the years following the divorce.

Boys seem to take the biggest hit postdivorce when relationships and events don't go well. Self-control, sleep, and motivation seem to suffer, especially when boys remain with their mothers following contentious custody battles. Even six years down the road, according to Shirley Hanson's research on divorcing families, boys experience reactive depressions, social incompetence, and acting-out behaviors. These effects are often ameliorated, however, if a good joint custody arrangement allows the boy ample time in a good quality connection with his father. Intriguingly, boys in such effective joint custody arrangements do not differ significantly from sons of happily married couples.

Through the divorce research runs an interesting trend about same-sex custody of children. Hanson's important work shows us that boys with fathers, and girls with mothers, tend to do better in terms of social competency, maturation, and conscience formation than similar children raised in cross-gender households. According to the work of Richard Warshak and John Santrock, boys who live with father postdivorce tend to be warmer and more mature and independent and to have a higher degree of self-esteem than boys who live with their mother. We, as always, need to be careful about research methods that rely too heavily on one-time-only snapshots at the expense of the long view. According to pioneering researcher and author Judith Wallerstein, girls seem to show sleeper effects (subtle effects that lay dormant at one stage of data collection only to awaken and be measurable at a later stage) into late adolescence and young adulthood, particularly in terms of their relationship with their mother.

Wallerstein's finding raises a critical point regarding the differences between fathering and mothering across the life span of the child: it seems that it takes time for the father's deeper influences to show up in the life of his child. My own belief is that fathering is a more interactive socially and relationally determined phenomenon than is mothering in our society and its effects coalesce over time into the intricate quilt that is fatherneed. Mothering, because of its biological components, has neither the luxury nor the obligation to take its time. With motherneed, what you see is what you get whereas fathering, in its more traditional forms and in spite of its easily recognized not-the-mother behaviors, takes years to show its cumulative effect in the lives of children. It's a long underground river that surfaces occasionally at critical transitions—the child's birth, the first days at school, illness, dating—before it finally spills into his child's estuary sometime in young adulthood.

How this particular quality of fathering might affect fatherneed postdivorce is explained by Andrew, divorced father of three teenagers. "Before we divorced, I knew my kids' lives superficially. Sometimes I was intensely connected to them, like when they were born, or sick, or had just learned to read or ride a bike. But a lot of the time, I didn't feel much responsibility for them emotionally. Materially, yes; emotionally, no. I'd forget their friends' or teachers' names. I worry what the effect of those gaps might be down the road. For now, though, we have figured how to be connected with each other weekend to weekend. It took us years, but we did it."

The age of the child at the time of separation turns out to be an important consideration in assessing children and fatherneed postdivorce. Psychologist Nicholas Zill looked carefully at the data from the National Survey of Children in order to understand the long-term effects of divorce on parent–child relationships. He uncovered informative and sobering trends when findings were extended to include outcomes for young adults. In subjects aged eighteen to twenty-two whose parents had divorced when they were school-age or younger, two-thirds had a poor relationship with their father, one-third had a poor relationship with their mother, one-quarter had dropped out of school, and 40 percent had received psychological help. Factoring out income and demographic differences, young adults from intact families had troubles only half as often. Mother–child problems, less obvious in childhood and adolescence, emerged in young adulthood, especially for girls.

Companion research from Denmark adds an intriguing twist to the dual roles of children's gender and age and their relation to preservation of self-esteem and closeness to parents. Over 1,600 Danish urban dwellers, ages sixteen to twenty-two, were evaluated regarding the relationship between family structure, depression, and self-esteem. For girls, the fatherneed equation is very relevant in this study: girls who feel distant from their fathers were found to have lower self-esteem and to be at greater risk for depression than girls who remain close with their fathers. It is fascinating to me that no correlations were found for boys. My hunch: if researchers look at delinquent or behavioral symptoms, they will find plenty. In another study, by Nord and Zill, joint custody arrangements allowing teenage boys to be close to their fathers correlate with better overall health outcomes.

Trish, now nineteen, explains how her closeness to her father sustained her self-esteem during a hard period with her mother: "My father was my lifeline when I started high school. Before then, I thought he was dependable and boring. You know, every Wednesday for dinner, every other weekend, two weeks in the summer with his brother and parents—the usual. I'd beg, even bribe, my friends to come with me so it wasn't so *boring*. But after high school started, my friends changed and so did my mother—such a bitch—from nowhere! I'd crash at my dad's place all the time—no hassles—as long as I did my homework and chores. And I don't think my mom minded much; I was being a bitch to her, too. I knew I was going through a mother–daughter thing, and I'm so glad I had my dad's life to borrow for a while. He helped me keep myself sane and self-confident through that time. What do kids do who don't have that chance?"

We often assume that earlier is better if there's got to be trouble in a child's life. That way, kids have longer to get over it and youth is on their side. Right? Wrong. Most experts believe that kids who experience the disruption of their parents' marriage before the age of six show poorer adaptation overall, more uncontrolled, antisocial behavior, and a particularly degraded relationship with their father. Surprisingly, remarriage doesn't have the protective effect on children's adjustment that we might hope for, unless it is early and stable.

Beyond the child's age and gender, the postdivorce arrangements themselves affect children and fathers and their relationship. We have long known that separated and divorced fathers feel better about themselves in general and about their relationship with their children specifically when they have regularly scheduled, shared childrearing responsibilities. Half-time and quarter-time fathers express more satisfaction and feel more competent than either fathers who have limited visitation with their children, those who have the traditional schedule of one weeknight and every other weekend, or those with sole childrearing responsibility. In the traditional arrangement, fathers suffer from the double-edged sword of the pain of always having to leave their kids and the pressure to endlessly entertain them. How does this wind up being so unsatisfactory for so many men and their kids?

As I've witnessed patients, colleagues, friends, and family members first consider and then experience divorce, I've watched loving and competent fathers get incredibly confused and lost as soon as the issue of child custody raises its head, let alone gets decided. It is an issue around which very powerful emotions swirl for women and men. Fathers who genuinely and even appropriately believe that they should have at least joint physical or even sole custody of their kids often agree to maternal custody because they feel they might lose even more if they dispute the claim of maternal presumption. The study of 1,100 families that Eleanor Maccoby and Robert Mnookin have conducted since the mid-1980s involved interviewing parents throughout the divorcing process and determining their preference for custody just after the petition filing. The researchers found that 82 percent of mothers want sole physical custody—and most of them prevail. In contrast, fathers initially seek a range of custody arrangements—paternal, maternal, and joint—in roughly equal proportions, but over a third of them wind up asking for less physical custody than they really want. Mothers are much more likely to act on their stated desires than fathers. The reason? Fathers have reason to believe their more generous request for time with their kids will falter—and possibly even come back to haunt or penalize them. When parents make competing claims for custody, the mother's wishes are granted twice as often as the father's. More worrisome, however, is that even when both parents *agree* that fathers should have primary custody of the offspring, judges contravene the often hard-won parental agreement in at least a quarter of the cases! Whose family is this anyway, your honor?

When the gravity of occasional parenting finally hits a father, it's like getting broadsided from a blind spot. Constantly playing hello–goodbye, feeling more grief than they bargained for, dealing with anxious, demanding, and sometimes hurt and surly kids, these fathers privately begin to wonder if their children really miss or even need them in their life. The typical noncustodial pattern—every other weekend and an additional few hours on a weekday, some holidays, and maybe a month in the summer—is hopelessly inadequate in terms of preserving a close relationship with another human being, especially one who happens to be growing and maturing at a dizzying rate. It makes critical day-to-day shared experiences, such as school involvement, a crucial benefit to a child and a sign of a father's interest in his life, a sad joke. And so fathers drift further and further out of the loop. God forbid that anything untoward should happen between a noncustodial father and his child, because it will take a month to work out a twenty-minute misunderstanding even with just an averagely mulish kid. Planned fun risks becoming the only relational currency, devaluing all others, since no other memorable human interaction can be crammed into such a schedule.

That "reasonable visitation" always works for kids and dads is one of several myths about custodial fathers. There are five other myths that center on men who have custody of their children: (1) there are few single fathers, (2) most divorced fathers remarry, (3) many single fathers are widowed and few are never-marrieds, (4) they are economically very well-off, and (5) divorced fathers receive custody mostly of older boys. But the facts expose these myths for what they are: outdated, unsubstantiated, and anti-fatherhood. The facts are that (1) the number of single fathers has increased fivefold from 1959 to the present, making them the fastest-growing family type in America today, (2) 59 percent of divorced fathers remain unmarried, (3) the number of children living with never-married fathers increased fifteenfold from 1970 to the present, (4) although the incomes of single fathers are higher than those of most mother-only families, fully 20 percent live in poverty and many more are near poor, and (5) while the trend is for slightly older children to live with custodial fathers, 17.5 percent of single-father households are families with girls under three and 20 percent are with boys.

If custodial fathers are having a hard time being understood, other varieties, such as co-parenting dads, aren't faring much better. Strong parental relationships with kids have the best chance when they are woven into a pattern of frequent, responsible interaction around real-life issues in the here and now. Joint physical custody, which typically includes joint legal status, or co-parenting, has the best crack at sustaining this possibility. Former couples who share physical custody this way, assuming their kids are old enough to manage it, are happier with their custodial arrangement than are couples who don't. Kids themselves seem to feel more secure in such arrangements, since it allows real time with both parents and, as such, can accommodate more flexibility when things come up in their lives that they want to take advantage of. Judges find it a welcome alternative, since postjudgment disputes come back to courts only half as often in co-parenting than in other custodial arrangements. Finally, it practically eliminates default on child support, according to census numbers: 90 percent of fathers with joint physical custody pay up on time, compared to 56 percent for visitation-only fathers. In fact, it is only when custody *and* visitation are consistently denied that fathers' child support payments fall below the 50 percent line. True, it requires cooperation with the ex to co-parent successfully.

SPECIFIC CHALLENGES TO FATHERNEED DURING DIVORCE

A brief divorce primer: No divorce is like any other. Boys face more adjustment problems postdivorce while they are growing up whereas girls tend to look better growing up but show problems in young adulthood. For the vast majority of children, these problems are eventually manageable, though quality of life is affected for most. It may be that marital conflict itself, both before and after divorce, more than the divorce itself, is the true culprit much of the time. Mothers who share custody are typically more satisfied with the custodial arrangement than are those with sole custody and periodic contact with fathers. Sole-custody mothers with no contact with the father are the most unhappy, as are their kids. Divorce is the most serious threat to a child's relationship with his father and vice versa. Quality of time with either parent matters more than total time. Voluntary agreement by parents on custody is far superior to any court-ordered arrangement. Ongoing, meaningful contact with their father protects children against many of the negative consequences of any divorce.

Since divorce is here to stay, what's to be done to soften its predisposition for menacing the fatherneed? To begin with the obvious, *men can inoculate themselves, their child, and the relationship that connects them from the malignant effects of divorce as process and event by participating physically and emotionally in the whole life of their child from conception on.*

It works best when we begin at the beginning, but it's not the only or last place to board the bullet train that is your child's development. Wherever you are is as good a place as any to begin. But if you are reading this chapter carefully because divorce is or has been a part of your life (including in your family of origin) or because it threatens to be in your life, then some practical advice follows, based on all that has gone before in this book.

MONEY AND FATHERNEED: TWO PEAS IN A POD, OR STRANGE BEDFELLOWS?

Child support is the court's way of ensuring that children are provided for materially, regardless of how father and mother may feel about each other, now or ever. Theoretically, the law, though not necessarily the judge, recognizes the responsibility of both parents to provide for the financial needs of their children. But in the real world that responsibility rests more heavily on the father's shoulders.

Food, clothing, education, health care, and maintaining the family's lifestyle are the things fathers think about from the delivery room on as being in their column of responsibilities. So when this column changes headings during divorce, fathers struggle with how it now feels to be mandated, or ordered, to give what was previously an expression of devotion and commitment, even an expression of fathering itself. It serves kids best when their divorced father makes his child support payments in full, on time, and by check and keeps meticulous records. Many kids feel a little abandoned every time a father departs from that expectation.

TELLING

Do whatever you can to ensure that you and your child's mother tell your kids about the divorce together. Practice or consult with a professional about how, but try to do it together. Most of you made the kids together, so they deserve your best effort here to explain together that you must now come apart—but without divorcing *them*. Hard as it may be for you, this joint effort will reassure your kids that you both believe in helping them stay in both your lives. The wording obviously depends on the age of the child and on what the child may have already experienced of your marital distress.

Children under five need to hear that they are not losing their family because Mom and Dad can't live in the same house together anymore. Cover only the basics, keep it short, and don't expect much reaction until the kids see the effects in the real world (suitcases, missing furniture, an empty bed and closet).

Children over five need some details about what happened to the friendship between their parents. A simple definition about divorce such as "stopping being married to be happier" will do for a while. You'll get many cracks at this. Don't even think of blaming your child's mother. Blaming each other burdens your child terribly with fear and shame. Children will watch the way separating parents treat each other like hawks, so honest, respectful answers will lessen their fears that their "family is dying," as Greg, five and a half years old, explained to his buddy in the block corner. One of a child's major worries will be whether the parents will stop being mommy and daddy because they stop being husband and wife.

Kids eight and over will want to know if you "tried really hard to be nice and stay married," as nine-year-old Serena asked her father. Furthermore, they may want to know if they now behave, pick up their room, brush their teeth without being asked, and stop teasing their younger sibling, will you feel happier enough to want to be nice to each other and get married to each other again someday? Obviously, they need to hear from both of you that there is *nothing* they can now do, or ever could have done to fix the problems that are leading to the divorce.

As you've noticed, this advice is aimed at your child's well-being here, because, as upset as you may feel about the changes pending in your life, they are peanuts compared to what your child must cope with over the coming years. Serving your child's needs in this way serves to gratify the fatherneed best.

LEAVING

Set up a temporary custody and visitation arrangement before you leave home if you are doing the leaving. The sooner the kids and you figure out you can still be together regularly, they and you will start to settle down, usually after some grief and sadness, and remember that fatherneed is alive, if a little nervous. Time is very important here, in terms of protecting the relationship you already have, and presumably want to continue having, with your kids. Practically speaking, setting up this temporary arrangement also gives the message to whoever cares to hear it that you want an involved parenting plan, and your behavior, not your words, proves it.

Good evidence tells us that the first postseparation year is especially salient in reorganizing your relationship with your child. If it's established as positive within the first year, you'll have a better chance of working things out. Otherwise, time passes, you settle for less of each other, adjusting to the hole that used to be your relationship. Increased involvement becomes much less likely, and your importance to each other wastes away like a paralyzed muscle. So instead of decreasing the time you have with your kids during this crazed time, increase it. This will help the healing and reassuring process. Eventually you'll have to detail this agreement, but for now certify your presence in each other's life with this witness to intent.

COMPETENCE

Are you ready to cook, discipline, comfort, visit school and volunteer there, skip work, ask for help? Fast food has its place as a supplement but not as the mainstay for growing children. And cooking together is an interesting way to get your kid and you headed in some good directions, postseparation. It nurtures both of you metaphorically and realistically: "No one's going to starve here for food, affection, trust, or connectedness. We shall endure."

Parenting alone whether it's custodial or "visitation" is like moving to a different country, one where the language, culture, and tax structure are completely different from what you're used to. Don't be proud. Seek out parenting education classes, videos, books, tapes, all the tools to help—anything to get you thinking meaningfully about what you are doing with your child that works (and what doesn't). Parenting is always on-the-job training, for everyone, and retooling is essential to staying competitive in the marketplace. Many fathers find marital conflict-resolution strategies especially helpful. The more competent you are, the more satisfied you'll feel as a noncustodial father. But the less you know how to do with your kid, the less you'll do, and the less your kid will want to be with you. Your very identity as a father is directly linked to your involvement beyond biology, to your emotional and physical involvement in your child's life.

Some practical advice:

- Periodically refresh yourself on the developing abilities and expected trouble spots of your child's particular age group through reading or the Internet. Forewarned is forearmed.
- Don't do the Disney Dad: guilty, cut off, competitive, and afraid of losing your child's love. This is a recipe for defensive fathering on a cosmic scale. Deal with the emotional stuff first, and then take a searing look at your behavior. Doing the Disney Dad is a dead end. You can't afford it. Even if you can, it erodes your child's innate interest in and (sometimes) respect for you as a father, man, and partner in fatherneed.
- Plan ahead with your kid what your time together will be like. Don't simply offer menus or catalogues of decisions (goodies) from which to choose. If you have more than one child, time together should be divided between group and individual, with some private time for everyone included. Eating, play, and downtime all should be figured in. Ask to see a list of their options, add your own, and then pick a few. Keep it varied.
- Don't try to make up to your kids, whether it's lost time (impossible), hurt feelings (accept these and move on), or your own guilt (it's yours. Don't ask them to help you get over it; they have their own).
- Treat your kids like they're family and live with you, and they'll feel reassured in the long run that they are and do. Make them do their homework (with help), practice the piano, and feed the dog. Chores regularly done at your place encourage the kids to feel they are valued and needed by you in your life and home. Don't let their whin-

ing dissuade you. It's their job. Ask their help if emergencies arise; we all love feeling useful to the people we care about.

Long-distance fathering can be menacing to the fatherneed in many ways. Because of the distance, you must work consistently without much reward and without many clues on how you're doing as you try to nurture your child across distance and time. Promises must be kept about visits, letters, and birthdays with an obsessional zeal. Awareness of your child's life must rely on collateral sources—school, coaches, religious leaders, extended family members—and your ex if she and you can communicate. So stay nosy, but not intrusive.

ATTITUDE

The way you decide to divorce is strongly influenced by the way you were married throughout your marriage. A cynical truism: what makes a good divorce is a good marriage. Implied here is that if there was any trust, respect, or cooperation around raising the kids before, there (eventually) will be later as well.

The way you chose to deal with the divorcing process told your child a lot about what you hope will happen to the family. A contentious, adversarial divorce reduces kids to piles of anxious, often smoldering rubble, because self-centered bitterness and pride got more attention from their parents than did their threatened and shaky well-being. As one of nine-year-old twins, an articulate veteran of a vicious $350,000 (legal fees to date) custody battle, said, "It only *looks* like they're fighting over us, but it's *way* over us—like on another planet. It's not about being good parents anymore, it's about who's going to *win* us. What a joke."

Your job, the one that will benefit your children most and hence your relationship with them, is to help your ex be the best kind of mother she can be to *your* children. That is a great benefit to them, and will enhance her ability to mother. Be civil and circumspect in your dealing with their mother. Machiavelli is not a good theoretician on which to rely as you reason out how to preserve your life with your children. One of the little mental tricks to help you accomplish the necessary attitude correction is to use as a guide a simple assumption about parental behavior (within or outside marriage): *Most of us at any given time are doing the best we can with our kids.*

Departing from this maxim usually breeds suspicion and trouble, and simpleminded as it sounds, it's precisely the way you want her to be thinking about *your* parenting of *her* kids. What goes around comes around.

Most of us lose something in divorce. In our relationship with our kids, it can range from influencing their growing up to the privilege of sharing the details of everyday life. Divorced fathers lose the sweet daily nonsense that a more leisurely, shared, and intimate life together grants. Grieve for this. It's gone and it's sad, and it most assuredly is not the child's fault. Furthermore, the inconveniences that flow from this truth are yours to bear, not your child's.

You will, undoubtedly and eventually, face the ridiculous impossibilities of meaningful life as a visiting father. But there it is; it is what it is. Choose your cliché. Your kids feel some of the same futility. But endure. Choose a friend and rail and rage, run a few miles, meditate, do what you must. But endure. Nonvisitation will not work.

I ran the Ocean State Marathon in Rhode Island a few years ago with my brother. At the "wall"—22.5 miles *exactly*—I simply had to stop as he ran on. I looked down at my legs, tremulous and awash in lactic acid and agony, and realized that stopping was no better. I realized that my legs would scream at me no matter what I did now and so I decided that I might as well avoid further humiliation, stay in, and finish the damn race.

In fact, not finishing, or complete nonvisitation, leads to even more stress. In the research of Mavis Hetherington and M. and R. Cox, 100 percent of the fathers who had been involved with their kids before the divorce and had no contact with them after it showed a high level of anger and metal health problems. They reported a sense of deprivation and a "shocking sense of isolation" that lasted for years after the divorce. We know that the conditions of visitation itself make it feel periodically impossible—the artificiality, the sustained potential for conflict with the ex, the inherent emotional strain, and the pull from the child's and father's new lives. No wonder it "sucks," as so many kids succinctly explain.

THE BIG PICTURE

As postdivorce fathering gets further understood, we see small changes in the ways parents are trying to work together to keep from divorcing their kids. There is a divorce industry that can make this better or worse, depending on how and when it interfaces with the fatherneed. Clearly, divorce is less destructive to the fatherneed when men and women figure out a way for fathers to assume real responsibility for their kids, emotionally and domestically, a way to support the father's willingness to invest materially and relationally in his children. Paternity, more than maternity, is continually being redefined by human experience. Public policy must focus on incentives and supports that keep postdivorce fathers as an integral part of their children's lives beyond (and in some cases in spite of) child support, that sustain meaningful parenting functions, that erode deterrents to the resolution of disputes around parenting plans and child support, and that require former spouses to structure their commitments to their children and to one another.

My advice to Bret: trust your children and your relationship with them. Right now, time is on your side, where it belongs. If you cut back on being in their lives, time moves way out in front, where it does not belong, and will be called as a witness when the petition to revise is filed by your kids. Do not quit. Quitting doesn't work. It hurts your kids, hurts you, and drains the soul, heart, and life out of fatherneed.

6

Expressions of Fatherneed

THE TALL, thin Native American with a long braid and the toddler on his shoulders had been standing off to the side of the auditorium, skillfully attending to his child most of the morning. I was giving two lectures and leading a discussion with an audience of about 350 men and women regarding recent changes in the role of the American father. This was my second trip to Phoenix in three years, and I remembered him from the last time I was here, when I addressed a smaller but similar audience. Finally, he approached me as I tried to sneak out the side door to grab a solitary lunch before resuming the afternoon workshop. He spoke softly with only occasional eye contact: "Doc, I wanted you to meet my son, Small Hawk. He was too young to come hear you last year, but he wanted to meet you after I told him about the story you told about the Hopi father's job—the one about taking his child to the mountaintop to show him the world beyond the village. I told my father about it, and he cried to hear the story was still being told somewhere. We picked a short mountain so both of us could go, and we took Small Hawk together. The women didn't like it much, so we told them you said it was our job and they left us alone. It was a strong spirit time for all three of us, one we won't forget." He shook my hand and simply walked away, his beautiful, dark-eyed boy faintly smiling over his father's broad shoulder at this deeply moved doc.

Though I am about one thirty-second watered-down Choctaw, I certainly didn't feel that I was an authority on the Hopi, or any other tribe for that matter, especially regarding legend or culture. I was just passing on what I had learned about this particular version of fathers showing their children the world outside their mother's intimate domain. And who was this toddler "wanting" to meet me? This encounter was a wonderful lesson into the fathomless variety of the expression of fatherneed.

The image of the modern father—reliable provider, male role model, warm companion, mother supporter—has been shaped by an uneasy alliance of economic and cultural forces: mothers in the workforce, feminist advances, egalitarian societal expectations, and changes in the workplace itself. But the molding hand of culture has not been seen in the research until very recently. Its absence has created an artificial emphasis on Euro-American, Caucasian, biological, heterosexual paternity, depriving us of a deeper understanding and appreciation of the more diverse expressions of fatherneed that our children know so well. As the more homogeneous Caucasian piece of our multiethnic pie further shrinks to minority status over the next century, it is especially critical that we understand more fully what shapes fatherneed in *all* the homes in our neighborhood, literally and figuratively, because change changes us all.

Investigators across the board have now uncovered trends in African American, Hispanic, Native American, and Asian father–child interaction patterns that lead to strong cautions against using Euro-American family functioning as a basis for understanding all child–parent relationships. Bill Cosby is no Ernest Hemingway (thank God) when it comes to fathering. Indeed, we have much to learn about fathering fom our neighbors. Several groups of investigators have studied how role flexibility and concern for children create opportunities for African American men to engage in surrogate father relationships with kids who don't experience day-to-day interaction with their biological fathers. Norma Radin and her colleagues, in studying Michigan's Ojibwa families and their children's school performance, found that better grades correlate with larger amounts of time spent with fathers as primary caregivers. But high paternal nurturance by Ojibwa fathers seems to increase the tension of cross-cultural integration in the Anglo schools their kids attend, causing some performance problems, especially for sons. The researchers concluded that it is unwise to "generalize from white samples to other ethnic groups."

While comparing and contrasting the vast richness of ethnic differences may be interesting, it's hardly the only way to understand the various expressions of fatherneed in our culture today. What we need to do more of is try to understand what accounts for the variations in the father–child relationships within particular ethnic groups. This allows us to further our understanding when the differences are less ethnically and more culturally shaped in America, as in the case of teenage fathering, stepfathering, gay fathering, incarcerated fathering, low-income fathering, fathering of kids with special needs, even grandfathering. In this chapter we'll learn from the groups that have been better studied, keeping in mind our goal of understanding how fathers and children need and affect each other across their life span.

AFRICAN AMERICAN FATHERS

African American fathers have gradually emerged from the research to challenge many restrictive stereotypes, thanks to several creative investigations by the psychology team of Ahmeduzzaman and Roopnarine. They carefully documented that (1) black men are more likely to share household work and child care than their white counterparts, (2) there is more egalitarianism among black couples in sharing household work and responsibilities, and (3) the greater the economic security, the more involved they are with their children, regardless of income, employment, or sex role attitudes. John Lewis McAdoo expanded these findings by showing that black men share equally with their wives in decisions on childrearing and that male nurturance is spread equally between sons and daughters. With other colleagues, Roopnarine affirmed that both the black father's ability to communicate effectively within the family and his commitment to the family are significantly associated with his degree of involvement in feeding and comforting his infant. Like so many other researchers, Roopnarine, too, found that fathers tend to spend more of their time with their infants in play rather than in providing physical care.

All these encouraging reports pose a serious challenge to the notion of the detached, inaccessible black father. They indicate instead that black men, and black fathers in particular, endorse the significance of their role in the family and in their specific cultural context, a context shaped by migration, slavery, segregation, and through "kin and friend" networks. The reliance on and trust in one another within these networks endures and heavily shapes communication between a caregiver father and those who are involved in the child care domain, for example, those who provide educational and health-related services for his child. McAdoo's research suggests that the viability of the kin and friend network may be more true for disadvantaged black families than for those from the middle class. Still, the effects remain strong across class. When *Zero to Three* conducted a series of focus groups to assess what parents of children in the first three years of life felt they knew, didn't know, and wanted to know about the developmental needs of their children, the African American fathers focus group indicated that if the information is important and reliable, they prefer to get it from a brother.

One of the most misunderstood aspects of African American paternal influence is the confusion between nonresidential fathering and nonexistent fathering. Marc Zimmerman and colleagues have shown in their study of the relationship between family structure and emotional and social functioning in African American families that in many families the father's absence from the home as a resident does not necessarily mean that he is either psychologically or physically absent from his child's life.

Baba was eleven when he wound up in the emergency room after a bad wipeout on his skateboard as he was boarding down the steps of the library. A broken ankle and a compound wrist fracture meant he'd have to stay in the hospital overnight. When the admitting nurse filled out his paperwork, Baba heard his mother reply to one of the nurse's questions with the comment "There is no father." Baba protested heartily: "Just because he don't live with you, Mama, don't mean I don't have one. I got one and I know where he is right now and I want him to come see me." His mother told him to "hush up, and now." We found out later that she was on welfare support and that paternal contact or reunion meant less support; that is, official documentation of Baba's father's presence in his life could bring questions and further hardship for mother and son.

And Baba's mother has reason to worry. Several court decisions have upheld that two-parent families are not eligible for Aid to Families with Dependent Children (AFDC) even when the parents are not living together. This leads many men, regardless of ethnicity, to the conclusion that the best way to assure AFDC eligibility for their children is to limit contact with them and their mother. Baba's father explains: "The least I can do is not be around to risk their eligibility for welfare [such as it was]. I just stay out of the way because I don't want to mess up her payments. I can't replace them yet, so it's the least I can do."

But staying out of the way does not always mean being out of a child's life. Most African American kids know where their father is and how to get in touch with him and feel emotionally connected to him in important ways, regardless of what the state knows. Over and over again, the research on black fathers shows us that nonresidential does not mean absent or uninvolved.

Expert psychologists have coined a rather cold term, the "family deficit model," to explain why children in a home where the father is absent are apt to have more psychological and behavioral problems. But such a model may simply not be applicable to black families. The over-reliance on mother report, that is, mothers' responses to interviewers asking them to explain "father–child interactions," has left gaping holes in our understanding of what actually happens when a father is in a child's life, especially from school age on, but not in the home. In fact, I have often thought of suggesting to journal and book editors that a boxed warning label be placed at the bottom of the title page of every appropriate article or chapter dealing with fatherneed research that reads WARNING: MATERNAL REPORT ONLY.

Kids see it differently. When researchers ask children about their family, they are more likely than their mother to include their father in their description of their family network; in fact, in their stories about their family they mention their father more frequently than their siblings or grandparents. From the children we hear loud and clear that "the presence of supportive fathers, *whether or not they live in the home,* and parental support in general, may be more significant for urban African American male development than family structure" (emphasis added). As Norma Radin and her colleagues found in their investigation of young African American fathers' interactions with their infants and children, "absent does not mean uninvolved," especially compared to Caucasian families of similar structure. In the latter families, paternal absence from the home really does appear to mean less paternal contact overall; in African American father–child pairings, this simply is not the case.

Another intriguing aspect of African American fathering concerns attitudes toward abortion. A black male is more likely than a white male to encourage his sexual partner to avoid abortion; consequently, he is more likely to become a father as a result of unplanned pregnancy. Whether such an event occurs in his adolescence or young adulthood is significant, given the shame that often accompanies a man's inability to provide for his young family. We do know that the vast majority of teenage males of all ethnicities are, despite the realities of their life and their relationship with the baby's mother and her family, very moved about becoming a father and that they at least *begin* life as a father with high hopes. (We'll specifically examine teenage fatherhood and its distinct developmental realities later in this chapter.)

HISPANIC FATHERS

Latino families in the United States labor under their own stereotypes. The classic is a familiar one: strong gender-differentiated roles, with women primarily responsible for caregiving and domestic work and men occupied with outside-of-home responsibilities. As in the case of African American families, when we take a closer look at what children and men actually have to do with each other, these stereotypes begin to fragment. Some recent investigations by ethnic sociologist Mirande reveal instead that the traditional macho authoritarian image is being replaced by the image of a more companionable, nurturing father.

Roopnarine and Ahmeduzzaman looked at father involvement with preschoolers in middle- and lower-middle-class Puerto Rican families in a northeastern American city. They found that the fathers spend about a third as much time as their wife in primary caregiving and that the more involved they are with their children, the more committed to and less authoritarian they are with their families. Very importantly, they also feel more competent in that commitment. Although support from his spouse matters, neither family income nor educational level is significantly associated with paternal involvement. The researchers conclude that the more child-centered Puerto Rican men in their study simply "do not fit the stereotypes" of a man who exhibits distancing, traditional authoritarianism toward his children. They speculate that these families do not use the strong extrafamilial and extended family supports typical of their island homeland culture and have instead adopted a lifestyle that is more like that of most mainland U.S. families.

Perloff, another ethnic behavioral researcher, studied a less advantaged Hispanic population, a mixed ethnic population of welfare recipient families, and looked at the impact of welfare fathers on their children's well-being. The largest ethnic minority in this study was Puerto Rican, and the portrait that emerges here, too, is a stereotype buster: although 71 percent of the fathers were reported to have a high school education, none was married to the mother of his children. Perloff found that those who pay child support are more likely to be employed (no kidding), to have a high school degree, and to telephone their children regularly and that nonpaying fathers have much less contact and tend to have substance abuse and legal troubles. Interestingly, marital status did not differentiate fathers who pay from those who do not, warning reformers not to get too carried away about the power of marriage itself to promote responsible fathering in this population. Again, the children themselves (and not their mothers), when asked about their father's place in their life, reported that they felt loved by their father and saw him as someone who makes them feel better and as someone they could turn to for help; in their social network ratings the children ranked their father ahead of siblings and grandparents. Over half of the kids in the study had contact with their father, regardless of his child support payment history. This especially holds when the children are younger.

ASIAN FATHERS

Asian families figure increasingly in the growing diversity of our country. Understanding fatherneed in their cultures, in addition to the ones we've already discussed, affirms that fatherneed is clearly universal.

Studies of Asian father-child interactions are rare, but they are beginning to appear in the literature with greater frequency. On a recent trip to mainland China, where my wife and I visited child care facilities as an adjunct to a cultural exchange, we noticed large numbers of grandfathers and fathers very involved in the daily care of their offspring, in both urban and rural settings, a fact corroborated by the owner of several for-profit day-care centers based in X'ian. A shirt factory owner, Hubert Li, developed an interest with his wife, Gao Xiao Li, a television executive, in establishing "English Kindergartens," group care facilities where some English is spoken every day by at least one of the three or four 19-to-21-year-old women who care for twelve to fourteen children, ages 4 to 6, in a five-day-a-week boarding arrangement. The couple has noticed a significant male presence from the day they opened their centers, something that surprises them. Given the one-child-per-family policy in China, which is more honored in urban than rural settings, many children are cared for by grandfathers and fathers even when their mother is home and not working for pay.

As the capitalization of the Chinese economy rages on, women are increasingly pulled away from home and men are being pressed into services as caregivers. Although there are few statistics available, some interesting trends are noted in the nature of the advice parents seek from the teachers and owners of the English Kindergartens. Many families are complaining that their children are spoiled, acting like "little emperors," refusing to obey, and being aggressive and disrespectful to their parents, teachers, and other adults ("Even the girls are bad," said one exasperated young teacher of the four-year-olds). This behavior is especially painful, as many of these parents had, and continue to have, a relationship with their own parents that was very different indeed, where spoiling rarely was a problem.

In a rare study of relationships between young Chinese adults and their family of origin, Lau, Lew, Hua, and Cheung in 1990 studied nine hundred young adults and found that they experienced paternal dominating control and warmth to be inversely related: the greater the family harmony, the less severely parental control was practiced. A generation later, a very short time by any cultural measure but especially so compared to the longevity of Chinese culture, parents are very worried about raising a spoiled generation. Their theories center around the fact that six adults dote on every child ("How can it be avoided?" asks Gao Xiao Li of the English Kindergartens mentioned earlier). "Should the fathers be more strict? How can you motivate children to behave when they do not want to?" Sound familiar? To us, yes; to the Chinese, no.

In Japan, family structure changes have followed economic growth, and concern there, too, is rising about paternal involvement and perceptions of the father's role. In an intriguing cultural comparison involving face-to-face interviews with nearly 1,200 Japanese and American father–child pairs, Japanese boys were found to spend only half as much time as American boys spend with their father whereas Japanese daughters enjoy more time with their father, who is much more protective of them than an American dad is with his daughter. Breakfast time is child time for Japanese fathers, as compared to American fathers, who see their kid more at night and on weekends. Sports, hobbies, and homework are more commonly shared father–child activities in America. Interestingly, this study found that increased paternal involvement has a more direct effect on fathers than on their offspring. Hints also emerge that recent social and demographic changes in Japan are encouraging a slow transition from workaholic absent fathers to more nurturing fathers, possibly encouraged by the frightening incidence of *karoshi* (death by fatigue) in the 1990s.

ADOLESCENT FATHERS

Teenage fathering certainly crosses ethnic boundaries, but it's a universally shaky transition to adulthood. About 10 percent of adolescent girls get pregnant each year, and males under twenty account for over 80 percent of the fathers. About 40 percent of the girls overall (a smaller percentage for African American girls) terminate the pregnancy. For the other 60 percent, the father-to-be tends to play an important role in the decision to complete the pregnancy. Unfinished adults, the prospective parents have hardly completed separation from their family of origin; by procreating so prematurely they are complicating emotional with economic immaturity and achieving only fledgling autonomy. Andre Derdeyn and colleagues profiled teenage fathers and found that they were significantly more likely than teenage males who were not fathers to have suffered academically in elementary and middle school; they were seen more negatively by their teachers, their parents were less interested in their education, and they typically wanted to quit high school. At a time of lust for independence, the dependence that follows the birth of offspring hobbles many teenage parents and compromises their dreams, relationships, and promise as an adult.

Because of the concern regarding teenage pregnancy and parenting, much of the research has focused on populations that tend to share certain risk factors such as low income and undereducation. Allen and Doherty's interviews of African American teenagers tell a complex story of young men trying to navigate their transition into adulthood at the same time they are negotiating their relationship with their child's mother but living elsewhere; they are faced with the task of sorting out not only their own developmental needs but those of a child as well.

The portrait that emerges is another stereotype buster. The majority of these men, ages fifteen to nineteen, see their child at least every other day. A closer relationship with the child's mother means a closer relationship with the child. Of course, since this was a volunteer study, these self-selected fathers are somewhat motivated young men (in this study the voices of teenage fathers who do not seek involvement with their child remain silent). Most of the young fathers reported that they feel they are being a better father to their child than their father is, or was, to them (although their life as a father was only beginning). They thought it very important to be there for the birth, feeling that "that's where everything starts."

A teenage father told me, regarding his son's two-month checkup, "I felt like all my hopes were so fresh, and my life was just going to work out because of this baby coming to me and her right now. Maybe like those old Wild West frontier days—everything new ahead."

Some teenage fathers tell me of the deep convictions they feel about being the father to their child that they themselves desperately needed but never had. Noting that their own mother could have used more help raising them, they often comment that it is the dad who "keeps a family together." They complain about the lack of powerful paternal role models in the media, saying that the "only place you hear about good men as fathers is in church."

The teenage fathers described in Allen and Doherty's interviews bitterly complain about the obstacles that an uncooperative attitude in their child's mother or the mother's family places in their way, and eventually the strain shows up in an increasing reticence about the nature of their connection to their child. They express special resentment toward the staff of schools, hospitals, clinics, and social service agencies that hinder, rather than help, their efforts to stay involved with, provide for, and look after their child, speaking of the combination of such institutions as "a deck stacked against me." The authors conclude that the conflict between these teenage fathers' strong convictions about responsibility to the family they have helped create and their virtual inability to fulfill those responsibilities drives many of them out of the relationship with their child's mother and away from their child. Voluntarily establishing paternity clearly facilitates father involvement and can be seen as a sign of a young man's desire for a committed relationship with the child and possibly even with the mother as a co-parent.

There is a trend noted in much of the black teenage father research of a decline in the father's involvement with his child over the years. Involvement with the child tends to start reasonably well, if it's going to start at all, with more playing on the father's part than anything else, partly because, like teenage moms, teenage dads have little preparation for doing anything else with a baby. Then involvement declines as the child gets older. Some researchers believe that the decline may be more related to deterioration over time in the young man's relationship with the child's mother than with disaffection with fathering this particular child. Deterioration of the relationship between the young parents adds to the higher resistance encountered from these boys' own parents, as compared to white parents, making fatherhood an uphill climb for them indeed, but not uniformly impossible.

Damion was seventeen, Kyesha was sixteen, and their baby girl, Jasmine, was twenty-five months old when I met them. Damion's parents had thrown him out of the house when he told them he was going to be a father, and his uncle had taken him in, promising that as "long as he intended to finish high school there would be no rent." Kyesha and he had "dated" since they were twelve and eleven and "really loved" each other. At their high school, Jasmine was in day care, and both Kyesha and Damion were in a group of same-gender teenage parents. Damion described how "talking with a few brothers" helped him get from being a "biological father" to a "legal father" (i.e., by establishing paternity). "And now I feel like a real father—a dad," he told me. Groups like the ones Damion and Kyesha belonged to in their high school have teen co-leaders and offer sex education, legal consultation, job training, and information on child development, along with instruction in anger management and conflict resolution.

Damion admitted that his excitement about being a father had, even before Jasmine was born, turned to "feeling shame" because he couldn't provide for her. "I had no clue I'd feel that way," he said, "but I did, big time. Now, because I give her forty bucks a week on the 'DL' from my Wendy's job for Jasmine, I can hold my head up around her, her family, and myself." Kyesha felt that Damion's interest in Jasmine made her family nervous: "My grandmother thinks he just wants to be in my face, not Jasmine's, but I know different. He loves her and she's real bonded to him." This last statement by Kyesha presaged research by Susan Brunelli that indicates that the mother's perception of paternal emotional support predicts positive maternal childrearing attitudes more than does grandmother support of her daughter's mothering. The future is better for Jasmine than it is for most babies of teenage parents, because of the support Damion and Kyesha are getting at school and from his extended family. They are lucky and they know it. Maybe they'll tell Jasmine someday.

STEPFATHERS

As we soften teenage dad stereotypes with new truths, I wonder if the same will ever be said of the most durable of all negative stereotypes—the stepfather. In Spanish the word for stepfather is *padrastro,* which can also mean hangnail. Pejoratively described, there are twenty-three million of them in America, most of them making it up as they go along. A stepfather neighbor of mine once called stepfathering the "black hole of all black holes." Do *you* know of any great stepfather role models?

Two-thirds of the women and three-quarters of the men from the 60 percent of first marriages that end in divorce will remarry (most of them within three years). *One-third of all American children will spend some time in a stepfamily before the age of eighteen.* That's a lot of kids spending a lot of time with men who are making it up as they go along.

Remarriage is no walk in the park. How hard it is depends on how things worked out in the first marriage, the economics of the transition, the number and ages of kids, and the way they feel about remarriage in general, not to mention these particular remarrieds. It's easy to see why it is so hard to add family members. Such complexities make stepfathering at once one of the riskiest and yet most rewarding forms of fatherhood. It seems to be a work in perpetual progress. Consequently, it makes sense to ease into this one.

Cindy's first marriage ended after the birth of her third child, when her husband confirmed a long-term suspicion that he was gay. They parted amicably and he continues to be in her life and in the children's through a mutually agreed-upon parenting plan. A few years after the divorce, Cindy married Hank, whom she'd known for years as her older boys' soccer coach. They'd been happy when their mother told them, ages seven and nine at the time, of the marriage plans and the news that Hank would be coming to live with them so they wouldn't have to leave their beloved neighborhood. Hank knew their father, and the two of them collaborated well about the children's needs. Seven months after the wedding, Gabe, the oldest, asked, "Mom, when's Hank moving back to his house?" Cindy later told me her heart sank when she heard that question—even though it had occurred to her earlier that things had been going a little *too* well. Cindy, Hank and the kids used the occasion to talk through what the kids and adults were feeling and reminded one another that this would take time—a lot of time—but would be worth it.

In general, men, given half a chance, have a better shot at making stepparenting work than women do. Mavis Hetherington has shown that in the absence of conflict between the biological parents, noncustodial fathers don't typically interfere with a positive relationship between a stepfather and their kids (this is not the case between biological mothers and stepmothers). However, an important variable in the equation is the age of the child. When remarriage occurs in a child's early adolescence, good quality stepfather–child relationships are the exception, not the rule.

An important study comparing stepfamilies with nondivorced families by James Santrock and colleagues found that stepfathers commonly experience (1) problems in feeling sufficiently prepared for the task of integrating themselves into a new family structure and role, (2) tension over leaving children from a previous marriage, (3) uncertainty regarding the amount of authority in their role as stepfather, (4) painful loyalty conflicts, and (5) confusion about appropriate affectionate interaction with their stepchildren, stepdaughters in particular. Their research found that prospective stepfathers are quite sensitive to their potential stepchildren's acceptance of their marriage, with over 50 percent saying that in the face of opposition they would reconsider or postpone the decision to marry. The researchers also heard frequently about showdowns with stepchildren after the marriage that involved the assertion of authority for the first time. Often these showdowns had the effect of settling down and deepening the relationship. The overwhelming advice from the men in the study regarding "how much to be a parent" was that it takes a long time to develop a relationship with a stepchild. Or, in their words: "Be patient," "Keep your cool," "Give it three times the time you think it needs," "Move slowly, slow and steady." So let the tortoise be your guide.

So while Santrock found that stepfathers often stay more distant in the first years for this very reason, stepchildren fare as well as children living with both biological parents on measures of self-esteem, competence, peer relations, and behavior. Most children express positive feelings about their stepfathers, hinting that there are compensations for the family as a whole that offset the relative distance that stepfathers keep in the early years of remarriage. Stepfathering is a work in perpetual progress.

GAY FATHERS

An especially egregious lack in the scientific study of the varieties of expression of fatherneed hampers our appreciation of gay fathering and its effects on children. In the past, this role may have seemed self-contradictory to some, but no more. Although there is a worrisome absence of well-controlled, long-term studies of gay fathers' interactions with their children, what we do know tells us repeatedly that being a parent presents no measurable limitation to providing competent and meaningful care to children. If anything, the 10 percent of gay men who are fathers often talk of feeling a special urgency to be proficient, given their desire to discredit widespread negative stereotypes. Furthermore, their reasons for becoming fathers in the first place are not dissimilar from, or are at least as varied as, heterosexual men's reasons. Charlotte Patterson, a psychologist from the University of Virginia, points out that gay fathers are likely to have higher self-esteem than gay men who are not parents and that the numbers of gay fathers is substantial. If the one to two million gay fathers in the United States have the average of two kids, then two to four million American children have gay fathers; their visibility in the media is certainly on the rise.

The vast majority of those who are close to their homosexual fathers grow up to be heterosexual adults. Furthermore, in an important study of sexual orientation among male offspring of gay fathers, psychologists Bailey and Bobrow found that the fathers rated 9 percent of their children as gay or bisexual, which is the same number that is frequently reported in the general population, suggesting that homosexual parenting is no more likely to predispose children to a homosexual orientation than heterosexual parenting is. This number was unrelated to the number of years spent living in a gay household or to the frequency of contact. As Patterson rightly concludes, we need to learn far more about how gay men and their children relate to one another over time and how the fatherneed expresses itself in these families.

What we do know is that there is no reason for concern about the developmental or psychological competence of children living with gay fathers. Still, children can have a difficult time coming to terms with having two dads (or two moms), and being unusual in this way can leave a child open to being harshly judged by less enlightened peers.

Most gay fathers encourage a certain openness and honesty from the beginning with their children. Shame is the twin of secrecy, and it is hard to dislodge once rooted. Furthermore, it is love that binds relationships, not sex. Consequently, the particular details of the physical aspect of the parents' relationship are as irrelevant an issue for the children of gay couples as for the children of heterosexual couples, though gay fathers know to brace themselves for questions from their children's friends, given America's penchant for homophobia.

Children are, in general, accepting of their gay fathers. In listening to the children of gay fathers, researcher Frederick Bozett has found that many are taught to accept social and personal variance in others. These fathers and their children read together about homosexuality, meet family friends, and develop a wider, less prejudicial view of the world. In his report Bozett includes a letter written to Anita Bryant by the nine-year-old daughter of a gay father: "If God did not like gays, he would not have created them."

Bozett's investigations into the perspectives of children, ages four-teen to thirty-five, on having a gay father give us important insights into this variation of fatherneed. He found that children whose fathers were more open with them about their homosexuality tend to feel closer and more genuine with their fathers than do children of more "closeted" fa-thers. The more open fathers, however, also have children who share the concern that they, too, might be seen as gay by their network of peers. Consequently, they devise ways to control the interface between their fa-thers, whom they love, and their peers. Most of these fathers are quite aware of their children's concerns and often adapt accordingly. When the children reported the advantages of having a gay father, they cited the fact that he was less judgmental and more open-minded about everything than the straight fathers of their friends.

Seth was talking as one of the straight members of his high school's Gay–Straight Alliance meeting, describing what he liked about his gay father: "Of course, I wouldn't know what he was like if he wasn't gay, because he is, and I suppose that affects everything he does—but the way he is, is just cool. He never disses my friends—or anybody, for that matter. We'll be watching the news and he'll say something that makes me understand there are lots of ways to look at what goes on in the world besides your own tiny lit-tle ideas."

A companion study comparing gay fathers with single-custody heterosexual fathers (all the children were twelve-year-olds and younger) found that they did not differ significantly in teaching their children problem-solving strategies, encouraging their children's auton-omy, or interactive recreation; the gay fathers placed comparatively er emphasis on nurturance, felt more positively about themselves as parents, and placed less emphasis on their role as economic provider.

The children's only negative concerns in Bozett's study about their father's homosexuality was its role in the breakup of their parents' marriage and the subsequent absence of a feminine presence in their new household. Kids routinely indicated that the marital breakup was far more painful to them than their father's (or mother's) homosexuality. A study by Bigner and Jacobsen challenges the last myths about the competence of gay men as fathers by comparing their parenting characteristics to those of straight fathers. The study found that gay fathers in general

- Tend to place greater emphasis on verbal communication
- Show more consistency in enforcing limits
- Are generally more strict and authoritative disciplinarians
- Explain more cause-and-effect correlations in the world around them, thus promoting understanding of social rules
- Respond more reliably to the perceived needs of their children

ADOPTIVE FATHERS

Adoption has been surfing a rising wave over the last quarter century, as many couples encounter fertility troubles, having put off childbearing until their higher-risk later years. The conscious decision of many coupled and single adults, heterosexual and gay, to open home and heart to a nonbiological child has contributed to a pool of about 2.25 million adoptive adults. This is a committed population that is often more knowledgeable about child development than biological parents are. Statistics show that married adoptive parents are less likely than biological parents to divorce. They make a major contribution to the well-being, even survival, of countless children who might otherwise live high-risk lives indeed. Researchers Scarr and Weinberg found that couples who adopt provide lasting relationships for their children and a supportive environment. Their children are more successful academically and socially than children of the same social class raised by their biological parents, who remain behind in less stable and less socially enriching environments.

The single greatest challenge that adoptive fathers (and mothers) face is the critical task of informing their children of their adoption. If the reason happens to be the adoptive father's infertility, it will be especially important for the father to sort this out emotionally before he discusses this with his child, because the potential for shame about this in our culture is huge. The best approach is to tell children in small bits that fit their developmental and cognitive appetite for understanding in general. Toddlers should hear the word frequently enough to know that it is not a loaded term. Preschoolers will be more interested in facts but will forget a lot of them. Kindergartners will want to hear the story over and over again, especially the part about being chosen and loved by you with a love that's permanent. As the facts of life are grasped by adopted children, they will request more information until finally the issue of why *their* birth parents didn't want them arises. This question needs serious attention. If you know the answer—and I hope you do, because it will be easier on both of you—then tell your child in age-appropriate detail.

Fathers definitely need to be part of these discussions *whenever* they occur, because their absence raises the child's anxiety, marginalizes them in the child's adoption story, and adds more bewilderment than intimacy. This is especially true if it is the mother's infertility that is the reason for adoption, as her potential for remorse and guilt can compromise her ability to understand what the child needs to know. Both parents need to understand that adoptive kids do feel different, though by no means pathologically so, in many ways. So, heads up around Mother's Day, Father's Day, and birthdays. These celebrations are not simple for them. Respond with opportunities, not obligations, to talk. It's hard to get the balance between overdoing and underdoing the adoption thing. Best advice I ever heard was from an eleven-year-old girl who told her parents after one too many where-you-came-from discussions: "Being adopted by you is *not* the most important thing in my life—being *loved* is! So now shut up about it till *I* want to talk about it next time—puhleeze!"

Adoptive fathers in my clinical practice seem to carry a special vulnerability, and it has to do with feeling lonely and uncertain about their inadequacies—the regular ones that come with trying to raise children. Biological dads never have to go through any kind of qualification test to become a parent (although it's an idea with more than a few merits), but having been approved to adopt a child sets adoptive dads up as though they have some seal of approval against which their performance as a father will always be judged—and we know that performance anxiety in men is far from a simple thing. And when they fall short, as they surely must, adoptive fathers feel hurt, distant, and lonely. So my advice to you if you're an adoptive dad: talk to another adoptive father—they're around, and they're just like you—and keep these emotions from accumulating in your soul.

FATHERS OF CHILDREN WITH SPECIAL NEEDS

Fathers of children with special needs have only recently been "discovered," and they are an interesting lot. They are not terribly different from other fathers, but they respond to their child's needs in intriguing ways that distinguish their parenting approach from their wife's. They differ from mothers of disabled children in that they tend to be more concerned about the long-term implications of their child's handicaps. Consequently, they tend to respond to the birth as more of a crisis than do mothers. Mothers, meanwhile, feel more sadness and guilt, as though the child's biological defect flowed more directly from their body to the child's.

The one study to date investigating this father–child connection directly was done in Kansas. Vicki Turbeville from the University of Kansas studied eighty-six fathers of specials needs children, and drew this profile: The father of a disabled child spends more time at home with his child than do fathers of nondisabled kids. He is more inclined to hold and engage the child nonverbally and watches a lot of TV. He follows his own, as well as prescribed, agendas for his child's rehabilitation in part because of his own perceived problem-solving competencies and in part because of deep resentment at the exclusion he experiences at the hands of the institutions and caregivers that he consults to help his child. Many fathers feel such exasperation from these exclusionary experiences that the withdrawal they are already flirting with becomes a *fait accompli*. The tendency for fathers of disabled children to withdraw is especially destructive to the men, their children, and their marriages, and interventions need to target this above all. Interestingly, programs that expect participation from these fathers get it, and those who don't, don't—to the degradation of the program, its participants, and the long-term value of its intervention.

Amanda, a consulting physical therapist to a cerebral palsy clinic at a large urban hospital for sixteen years, sums up her own experience with fathers of a disabled child: "After my son's daughter was born with spina bifida and I watched him try over and over again [and fail] to even get his name on his daughter's treatment plans, let alone be included in instruction by the male *or* female staff, I regretted the hundreds of fathers I'd left standing at the periphery of my vision, my clinic, my consultation, and my compassion. Eventually, they would stop coming, and I felt this weird relief, as if I'd been bothered by what to *do* with them. They *do* need different things, but they are usually there and want to work. What a waste. Now I'm so converted I'm obnoxious about it. I wish I could find every one of them and apologize."

When fathers of children with special needs are included in their care, things change for the better. Michael Yogman's study of father involvement and the cognitive and behavioral outcomes of nearly a thousand low-birth-weight preterm infants showed that high father involvement compared to low involvement meant a 6-point or higher rise in IQ measured at age three, regardless of income, paternal age, or neonatal health. Special needs make special dads.

INCARCERATED FATHERS

Talk about your frustrations of fatherneed! Try understanding what happens to fatherneed in men who are incarcerated and to the children who lose them. Seven million American children have a parent in jail, prison, or recently released on parole or probation. The father is the parent in 93 percent of the cases in which a parent is behind bars. Three-fourths of these fathers are unmarried, and two-thirds of them are never visited by their families. But even these are probably shaky numbers: in most cities when police make an arrest, they don't ask if the offender is a father. The fathers rarely speak up out of fear that it will damage their ability to keep fathering by threatening their right to custody, visitation, or their children's welfare benefits.

Is it a good thing to sustain contact between a child and an incarcerated father? Nobody really knows yet. There is so little research on the topic that science is essentially mute on this subject. Some hints are forming, however, that men who maintain family ties while in prison have lower rates of recidivism and that their kids show some moderately positive outcomes, but these findings have not yet been replicated.

We know that there is a discouragingly high percentage of entire families—fathers, mothers, daughters, sons, grandparents—moving through prison, parole, and probation in both the white and black populations. We also know that addressing an inmate's identity, needs, and skills as a father can positively affect his behavior while in jail, thanks to an innovative program in San Antonio. This is a vital opportunity to at least begin addressing the meaning and effect of the complete absence of consistent male caretaking figures found in the vast majority of these inmate's lives. How vast? Michael Murphy, psychologist for the Massachusetts Department of Corrections, estimates we are talking about 70 to 80 percent of the entire inmate population. Yes, these are huge and worrisome numbers.

Seventy of the 3,200 San Antonio inmates who volunteered for a five-day-a-week one-hour parenting class to learn anger management, child discipline techniques, and attachment theory have "changed the jail culture among their group. They express emotion more appropriately, there are no racial cliques or fights, and they have made no attempts to smuggle drugs. Of course outside it's different." Very different indeed.

OLDER FATHERS

Late-time fathering, or having your first kid after age thirty-five, appears to be on the rise. Since census records list births to women and not to men, it is hard to express in numbers exactly how many first-time fathers over the age of thirty-five are in our midst. But since births in our species tend to involve couples within the same age range, we can assume that the 19 to 37 percent increase of first births to women in their thirties from 1976 to 1998 reflects similarly upon men. "Mature" fathers differ from young ones in interesting ways: they are often spared the twin agonies of financial and time strain, having simultaneously both a more established career and schedule flexibility. Furthermore, their marriage (or partnership) is better established, adding a certain consistency to parenthood instead of detracting from it. They can count on more support from their non-kin social networks, according to intriguing research by Ross Parke and his colleagues. The marriage of a mature father may have longevity but not necessarily perpetual happiness. The effect of that stability, however, has no impact on the father–child relationship, a very different finding from the direct relationship found between marital satisfaction and father–child involvement in younger fathers. Fatherneed, it appears, is age sensitive. A nationally representative sample of mature fathers studied by Cooney found them to be more likely than younger fathers to be highly involved and feeling positive emotion regarding their paternal role.

Jonathan became a father for the first time at the age of forty, after he'd sold his second small business. "It's a good thing I made a little money early in my life before I had kids," he says. "I'm having such a fabulous time with my little girl, I doubt I'd keep my mind on what I was supposed to be doing at work. My energies are focused on her, being with her, making her mother secure and comfortable as a mother, making sure there are plenty of diapers, wipes, whatever. I forget appointments and don't return about a third of my calls. And, to be brutally honest, I'm having a hard time caring much about it. I think they call it babybrain."

Further qualitative differences between young and mature fathers were reported by Ross Parke and his colleagues: the older the father, the less frequent is physical play and the more frequent are reading sessions and pretend play. As men age, they depend less on their spouse to mediate their relationship with their child but tend more to resemble their spouse in her interactions with their child. Jay Belsky's research group extended these findings for mature fathers, finding them relying less on physical arousal and more on cognitive mechanisms to engage their child. We currently have no clue what the long-term effects on children are of these age-related differences in the expression of fatherneed.

Heath investigated the impact of delayed fatherhood on father–child relationships and found fathering by mature men to be significantly different from that of younger men in both the quantity and quality of their time with their children. Mature fathers spend more away-from-home time with their kids as well as more time in reading and playing with them. They place greater weight on their children's positive and productive behaviors in athletics and creative activities and show significantly more nurturing behavior such as praising and hugging. Finally, they have fewer offspring. If the best is saved till last, then maybe fewer offspring are needed.

GRANDFATHERS

True, to be orthodox, grandfathering falls outside the purview of fatherneed. But when grandfathers describe what their relationships are like with their grandchildren, it is clear that the fulfillment of fatherneed is often present. So many things hoped for in fathering one's children seem finally realized in grandfathering one's children's children.

This bumper sticker pasted on so many slow-moving large white sedans is amusing and also profound: IF I'D KNOWN THEY WERE SO MUCH FUN, I'D HAVE HAD MY GRANDCHILDREN FIRST. (Try explaining that one to a six-year-old!) I was amused when I saw this the first time, but it also gave me a little twinge right in my fatherhood and made me wonder, "Well, then, what about those of us in between?" Margaret Mead nailed this one, too: "The tag that grandparents and grandchildren have a common enemy is explicitly faced in many societies. In our own, the point is most often made that grandparents can enjoy their grandchildren because they have no responsibility for them—do not have to discipline them and they lack the guilt of parenthood."

Every birth instantly creates four grandparents, emotionally and physically. It awakens in grandfathers and grandmothers the old wish for the child that will make them feel like the parent they have always longed to be. The vitality of new life and the hint of immortality that is seeded in every child join to replenish the grandparent's spirit, promising relief from past disillusionments and assuaging the fear of dying with "nothing of real value to survive me." Stanley Cath, a longtime champion of the study of this stage of life explains: "Of all loving relationships, the grands may possess the greatest overall potential for late-life emotional refueling."

This may be particularly true for grandparents who are able to grandparent on time (somewhere between fifty and fifty-seven years of age), when they are able to invest time and energy in this developmental stage of their own life. If grandparenthood comes too early, they are still entangled in building their own career and in childrearing; if it comes too late, their energies are diverted internally, making involvement much harder.

Grandfatherhood's direct effects can be powerful and unique in the lives of their grandchildren. Given that 7 percent of children in America live with at least one grandparent and that a third of these children have no biological parent present, these influences are not inconsequential. Increased life expectancy, more closely spaced families, and remarriage rates have all increased contact between these generations. Because of the greater opportunity for "life overlaps" in our society today, three or four generations of parents and children often coexist.

Grandfathering shows interesting characteristics in a variety of studies. A life span perspective on maternal and paternal behaviors shows us that as women become more instrumental over the life span, taking over more administrative duties in the family, men become more affective and interpersonally oriented as they age. In fact, psychologist Feldman found that grandfathers are more behaviorally responsive to infants in waiting room settings than all other men except fathers of young children. The arrival of grandfatherhood seems to catalyze much greater interest in infants in men in particular. The gender of the grandchild, the age, and the child's accessibility to the grandfather will affect the degree of involvement eventually established with the grandchild. If the parent of your grandchild is your son, if he lives nearby and cooperates with your efforts to establish a strong relationship with your grandchild, and grandfatherhood came to you when you generally expected it, and if you are frequently available to nurture that relationship, then all three relationships are maximized.

Of course, when circumstances place grandparents in the role of primary caregiver, all bets are off. The energy demands of parenting, the resentments for being pulled out of one's golden years, the catastrophic reason for the change of roles itself—all place tremendous burdens on grandparents. Group and peer support and community resources can make the difference between life and death here.

Sociological studies of typical grandparent–grandchild interaction indicate that although over a third of the interviewed grandparents had taken a grandchild on a day trip within the last year, many of them did not feel a very close emotional bond with the child. In a study by sociologist Kornhaber of attitudes toward grandparents, only 5 percent of the thirty-three school-age children interviewed said they felt a very close, positive relationship with a grandparent. The ones who felt close to their grandparents found it easier to relate to people of all ages and were less anxious about illness, aging, and death-related issues. Grandfathers are especially important in families where there has been some kind of paternal absence or deprivation, even temporarily. In a study of adolescent mothers, their offspring, and grandparents, the level of the grandfather's nurturance had a more direct influence on the grandchild's well-being than did the grandmother's nurturance.

Grandparental influence can be powerful on the negative side as well. Simons investigated the intergenerational transmission of harsh parenting and found that grandmothers and grandfathers affect subsequent generations differently: a grandmother's harsh parenting was found to be linked to her son's harsh parenting of his teenage sons and to her daughter's harsh parenting of her adolescent sons and daughters. A grandfather's harsh parenting was strongly linked to his son's harsh parenting of his adolescent daughters.

There is no doubt that as baby boomers age (by the time the leading edge of this cohort reaches sixty-five, they will constitute one quarter of our country's entire population), grandfatherhood will become better understood as a major contributor to the fatherneed. Ready or not, here they come.

CONCLUSION

A final word: our understanding of the myriad ways fatherneed is expressed in other cultures is very limited. There are major ideologies, cultures, and religions (such as Islam, Hinduism, and Buddhism), which touch millions of lives, that have yet to be heard from in our research efforts to date. Traditional and current fathering traditions have been our focus here, but be forewarned: cultural forces, America being what it is, are in constant flux. New developments in the expression of fatherneed will surely follow.

7

Mothers and Fatherneed

WHEN I FINISHED my lecture in Phoenix on recent changes in the role of the American father, I noticed that the audience was about one-third men, a vast improvement over the ratio of women to men in audiences that used to attend such lectures. "Still," I puzzled aloud, "it never got much better than this, even with plenty of publicity that fathers' issues would be addressed at the conference."

Then, during the question-and-answer session just before lunch (after which I met little Small Hawk), a woman came to the microphone not so much to ask a question as to share an epiphany she'd had. "As I left to come to this conference this morning, I reminded my husband where I was going. My mother lives with us and helps with the kids, so they were covered and we could've both come. So I asked him like this: 'Honey, I'm going to those parenting lectures we'd talked about this morning—you don't want to come, do you?'" A wave of laughter washed over the audience, followed by a short pause; then a louder and darker wave of laughter drove over the first, as the double message in her question dawned on the crowd. The woman continued her story: "My husband laughed and said, 'Well, no, now that you put it *that* way.' 'What way?' I asked. 'You're practically telling me not to come, right?' And it hit me—I *was* asking him not to come!" I asked if she knew why, and she didn't miss a beat: "For all my talk about sharing the raising of our kids—and he's great at it and I love him for it—I still feel deep down this is my world and I'm not sharing all of it." Applause from the women, nervous laughter from the men. Okay, so that's how it is, is it?

I hate these polarizing moments, real as they are, because there's not one iota of concern for a kid's well-being within a country mile of these disputes over territorial power. Still, I deeply appreciated the woman's candor, and I'd much rather have these discussions occurring *between* men and women than hear them bashing away at each other *in absentia* in same-gender groups. Having mothers and fathers discuss the issue together is a way to get the kids' well-being back in the room. This chapter is not about the gender wars or the family as the seat of feminist power. It is about the role of mothers—the women they are and the role they play in shaping the fatherneed in their children, their partner, and themselves. We will explore how women's feelings and attitudes toward fathering are shaped by their experiences with their own fathers ("the father in the mother"), how women shape the access their men have to the children (gatekeeping), and how their past experiences and feelings about marriage, work, feminism, and men in general prepare them to share their children (or not).

Perhaps the most pressing question may be, How does a single mother address the fatherneed in her son or daughter without feeling unfinished or incomplete as a nurturing being herself? Just as generational changes have muddied the waters of what it means to father, so, too, is there confusion over what mothering means. Women are struggling for clarity in understanding what to expect of their mate in terms of sharing and shaping the shared nurturing domain for their children. The window through which parents used to see what to do is fogged by the heat of expectations on one side and the chill of disappointment on the other.

Let me put my cards on the table. Healthy fatherneed paradigms do not happen at the expense of women or their relationships with their children. On the contrary. If you want mother bashing, find another book. A major force for sustaining and gratifying the fatherneed in its healthiest state comes from women. Today 76 percent of all women have a job, and most of them share children with men. For men and women to share the responsibilities and gratifications of the nurturing domain, we need readily available (which probably means subsidized) quality child care and ongoing flexibility in the workplace. This is the only way shared parenting will continue, or even start to work, for most families (except the well-heeled, of course, who pay for their own solutions). Otherwise, fatherneed will languish and be pushed back to the margins of family life for yet another era. The problem is one of balance, as Gloria Steinem so wonderfully and succinctly put it in one of her early *Ms.* magazine articles: "It's clear that most American children suffer from too much mother and too little father."

Of course, sorting out the proper proportions with the help of recent science in a way that will serve kids is still hard going. It seemed so much easier and simpler thirty to forty years ago. Prior to the discovery of the father, the study of child development (or trouble therein) was pretty straightforward (and misleading). Mothers were given credit or blame for it all, unless the child was born with the problem. Now the problem stretches out across the laps of us all. Today's working mothers need a lot of help, and they need fathers to do more. Many fathers, meanwhile, are struggling over whether it's safe, or even desirable, to renegotiate the original contract that said that providing was the royal road to parental gratification and self-righteousness.

Making matters worse, our own opinions about roles have changed dramatically. In 1977, 66 percent of all adults agreed that it was better for everyone in the family if the man achieved outside the home and the woman's achievements were primarily domestic. In less than twenty years, that number had dropped to 38 percent. Of the working mothers with preschoolers in that same 1977 survey, 42 percent felt their kids were likely to suffer as a result of their working. In 1996 that number had dropped to 23 percent. Meanwhile, someone is also moving the goalposts: today, as compared to the 1950s, men and women marry four years later, are older when they become parents, have fewer children (but seven times as many are born outside of marriage), and work a significantly greater number of hours. And as life expectancy lengthens, parenting takes up a smaller chink of the life span than it used to, while evolving into more of a social role than a high calling.

Despite these dizzying changes, two presumptions emerge: (1) as much as societal change has affected mothering, it is reshaping fathering even more and (2) mothers' attitudes shape fathering competence and incompetence much more than the reverse. The androgynous male who was a guaranteed joke in the 1950s has been a valued partner in the 1990s. Nurturing men are less suspect than in many previous eras. Mothers happy in their marriage are shown in study after study (by

Volling and Belsky, by Ferketich and Mercer, to name a few) to be more supportive and facilitative of paternal involvement, to the benefit of their children. These changes promote marital cohesion, but what encourages a mother in the first place to even want to consider facilitating paternal involvement in child care?

For one thing, her own fathering.

In 1994 nearly 150 Midwestern families completed questionnaires regarding mothers as influential agents in the father–child relationship. The strongest predictor of a father's involvement was related to nonmaternal factors: the child's age (the younger the child, the more involved the father). But the mother's own growing up experiences strongly predict her husband's involvement. That is, the greater the level of emotional rejection and distance a woman felt from her own father, the more involved she and her husband report him to be in childrearing. Women who felt emotionally rejected by their father so appreciate their husband's involvement with their children because of its stark contrast to their own childhood experience of fatherneed. This is strikingly similar to the reparative model that Snarey reported being used by men whose fathers had been so negative in their development. These men want to repair that wound in the fathering of their own children (See Chapter 8). Mothers who felt rejected by their father want to heal their father-wound by encouraging the fathering of their own children; they seem to have come to some intuitive understanding that what children need is not that Dad become another sort of mother and simply do more of the same kind of parenting but that he instead instill the differentness of his masculinity into his share of the nurturing.

Repair models can't be completely understood, however, without understanding the vital and active role played by the child. Not simply a passive recipient of mothering or fathering alone, an infant actively mediates the world between parents. Infants can either knit parents together through the delicious and sensuous intimacies of their early social appetites or stress and drive apart more vulnerable parental coalitions through their neediness and periodic exquisitely painful distress. Parents can hang together during the bad moments, or they can hang separately. When it goes even reasonably well, it's the infant who teaches the parents how to parent *together* in a kind of shared transformation. As we saw in Chapter 2, infants are "pre-wired" for attachment to both men and women, and a child's early experiences with both parents become integral to the kind of person that child becomes.

I think that there is *always* a father palpably present in the mother's psyche, in addition to his formidable presence in her genetic complement. From pregnancy onward, this father-in-the-mother affects the way the mother promotes or discourages her partner's relationship with her/their child. Without ever consciously discussing the matter, she can convey positive feeling and expectation about their connection to one another through the tone and pitch of her voice and the softness of her body and face. Conversely, she can convey negative feeling through a chilly edge in her voice and an anxious hardness in her facial expressions and body language, thus discouraging, devaluing, or ridiculing the father's approach to *her* child. How a woman imparts to her partner the meaning and significance to her of the father–child transaction—fatherneed itself—is of huge consequence to their children and to the access they will have to their father.

The mother's enthusiasm for promoting father–child connectedness is also shaped by the kind of marriage she finds herself in. Compared to the mother–child relationship, the relationship between father and child, whether within or outside marriage, is more strongly correlated with the quality of the co-parental connection, according to Belsky's research group. Men often withdraw from their child when not doing well with the mother, whereas mothers may draw even closer to the child when they are not doing well with the father. Is this good for the child? A very large "it depends" is the answer. If the mother moves to amputate the fatherneed, the child will suffer; if she moves to separate her needs from her child's in such unhappiness, the child can manage better. Marital satisfaction itself, however, is clearly both a source and consequence of paternal involvement.

My hunch is that the reason fathering is so sensitive to marital fortunes is that expectations for fatherhood wax and wane with economics, politics, religion, the weather, and so on, leaving men, women, and children casting about for the fatherstick or some ideal by which to measure any particular father's performance. Indeed, it is the very dearth of clear expectations that is so disorienting, even toxic, for the men and women doing their best to find the way to keep fathers and children close.

Yet when mother and father can figure out their own version of how to satisfy fatherneed and stick to it over time, the benefits to their children are significant. This holds true even if there is no marriage. In his important Baltimore study of teenage mothers and their kids, University of Pennsylvania professor Frank Furstenberg found that father presence by itself has relatively little impact on outcomes for adolescent children. However, a strong father–child bond, especially if the father lives with the family, is associated with a variety of positive outcomes for the child. And this happens most often when their is good co-parental relationship. Indeed, even the level of attachment to the mother was found to have little impact on the well-being of the children as they entered adulthood unless associated with a good co-parental relationship.

Furthermore, the study concluded that a poor father–son relationship was worse than no relationship at all because they interfered with the child's capacity to develop other, healthier, connections, and they typically rendered the mother less capable. Matrimony for the sake of matrimony does not protect from the toxicity of an unstable, conflict-laden relationship between parents.

But when mothers respect their partner's fathering, kids thrive. Preschoolers whose mothers were proud of the fathering they received did in fact receive measurably more praise and support from those fathers, according to John Snarey's long-term follow-up research. In interactions with their older children, mother-supported fathers were more responsive, encouraging, and communicative with both sons and daughters.

We can imagine how this works. Mothers who feel supported by marital closeness have more patience and resilience in facing the challenges of rearing children. A woman's lifetime of socialization and, typically, her biological predisposition toward connecting to a child prescribe certain parental behaviors more powerfully in her than a man's socialization and biological predisposition do in him; that is, a man's parental behavior is relatively free of biological and ancient social imperatives. A woman's competence in turn encourages her to be more flexible with her child, enabling her to entrust her partner with child care responsibilities more frequently. This gives her respite and lets the child job-train the father (just as he or she has been job-training the mother). The reverse: an unhappy or unsupported mother has more fatigue and stress, leading to less flexibility and creativity in her mothering; she induces less social interaction between father and child, and the subsequent fathering is more shallow and less engaging for the child and the father, since little positive or hopeful encouragement has been imparted to it.

Arlie Russell Hochschild's research on the feelings of 130 men and women about work versus home gratifications and frustrations is eye-opening. "There's No Place Like Work" was the title of a newspaper article (which has been expanded into a book, *The Time Bind*) that strongly hinted that for many parents, especially women, home is becoming work and work is becoming home. Hochschild found women accommodating to work's time bind, incurring more and more "time debt" with their children and spouses, more often than she found them protesting it. Praise, support, and recognition are more forthcoming at work, given new management styles, while divorce rates and stress rise at home. The ancient male secret, that the escape provided by work offers respite, now belongs to women, too. This promises to be a significant new wrinkle in the co-parenting domain. Its impact on fatherneed is yet to be fathomed, but affect it, it shall.

GATEKEEPING

Hidden in the premise that work and home can reverse is the idea that there is a threshold or boundary line somewhere that one crosses, demarcating one world from the other. Who is the sentry at the gate sitting astride that boundary? Man or woman? Father or mother? Whom do you envision? Is it the same gatekeeper whose vigilance governs and titrates the access men have to their children? Remember the woman at the microphone saying, "For all our talk about sharing the raising of our kids . . . this is my world and I'm not sharing all of it"? *There's* a gatekeeper, and she's apparently proud of it.

A father's involvement with his children, especially his young children, when it matters most, is powerfully contingent on the mother's attitude toward, and expectations of, support from him. The National Survey of Families and Households found that mothers' characteristics outweighed fathers' characteristics with regard to predicting father involvement with their children! Responsible mothering, by definition, means support of the father–child bond. And how often is this the expected behavior? In what contexts does this occur, and in what contexts does it fail? And when there is no available father? We'll tackle this critical issue later in this chapter.

Much current research supports the impression I get regularly in my discussions across the country in boardrooms, churches, media studios, and school gyms, namely, that the majority of men want to be more involved in child care and domestic activities. Meanwhile, Joe

Pleck found that only 42 percent of working mothers wanted more help with child care from their husbands. Pamela Jordan's research at the University of Washington tells repeatedly of the desire in women to be "first among equals" when it comes to managing the nurturing domain. Women cling to control to the point of micromanaging, especially when they are working, to reassure themselves and reaffirm their competence and essential goodness as mothers. They often overtly discourage paternal involvement in child and domestic care because of their time-honored belief that men will screw it up. When they do permit access through the gateway, it is done on their terms, thoroughly managing their husband's behavior with the children.

It's done like this (a real scenario reported to me by a new father):

> "Honey, I heard this guy Pruett on the radio say that the best way for you and Ben to get to know each other is through time alone together, so I'm off to my sister's this morning. Be back at noon. You guys will be fine—he'll love being with you. [Great start!] But he'll need about eight ounces of warmed formula at ten. Put him in that matching jacket and booties outfit if you take him out. [Now it's turning sour.] Don't let him sit in a wet diaper for more than few minutes, because his rash is hanging on. Keep the TV off, watch out for the new dog at the corner, give him his eye medicine. Have fun—do whatever you want!"

This mother undoubtedly meant well, but she's essentially told her husband to do it her way or not bother. He's basically working for her while she's out with her sister, and he has no prayer of doing the caretaking *his* way to get to know his son. Instead, all he can do is hold on till she gets back. It is, of course, hard for most mothers to behave in any other way, until they become more aware of what they're doing. They have been socialized all their life to judge their worth by their nurturing competence. As teenagers they were hired to practice on other people's children, and they were praised for their skills and chastened for their errors. They typically arrive in the delivery room with some parenting skills on board—holding, feeding, burping, dressing, possibly bathing (this is all highly variable)—and weighed down by social expectations that their parenting expertise is sufficiently intact.

But little of her past experience prepares a new mom to raise this particular child, with a particular temperament, at this particular time in her life in this context. If she's lucky, she'll feel sufficiently supported in the early months so that her on-the-job training gets under way quickly and she doesn't fall off the learning curve. As a new mother, she's granted a little slack to not know everything, so advice comes unsolicited from everywhere—and I do mean everywhere. Typically, her confidence grows, she falls in love with her babe, a relationship for a lifetime begins, and she settles down to nurture her child's nature in ways that gratify them both.

The experience for the new father couldn't be more different. Not only has he not been prepared, but he has usually been pretty actively discouraged from developing his nurturing competencies. Guys don't need directions, right? Their baby-sitting experience has been practically nil, unless they come from a large or very enlightened family. Furthermore, an interest in one's nurturing competence still raises suspicions about one's gender identity in many corners of male society. Pregnancy itself finds a man drifting backstage while his partner, or at least her growing body, takes center stage. No one asks him about his thoughts or feelings, or even acknowledges his presence, as I discovered during Marsha's (and my) pregnancy with our daughter Olivia Zoey (born Jan. 26, 1999—thanks for asking; do you want to see pictures?). The expectant father needs to repeatedly introduce himself to every nurse, physician, or midwife that attends to the health and delivery of the baby. What could he possibly have to contribute or even want to know? I found it painfully discouraging to see that so little had changed since the birth of my first daughter twenty-six years earlier. It is all too easy to see how fathers come to see themselves as inadequate at worst and marginal at best, especially when they compare themselves to their partner, now ensconced on the throne of societal expectations, a state of affairs unfair to both.

The rewards for the mother's doing this parenting thing right, however, include new status in her family, community, even her workplace or school. Affirmation comes thick and fast, so much so that she begins to wonder, "What was the matter with me *before* I became a mother?" At any rate, she often feels that she now has power, or meaning, or purpose . . . or whatever. And it is hard to ever give up, let alone share, that with anyone else. The mother–child unit is a powerful, delicious duet between two souls that seems so complete in and of itself so much of the time that a new dad often thinks, "Why on earth muck this up by adding a third wheel?" To him (and many others), it seems that the inclusion of a third person will transform the mother–child entity utterly. The idea that anyone else, but particularly the father, might have a vital role in this whole process, in welcoming and supporting a new life, excites resistance. That is why it is called gatekeeping, this vigilant control of the father's access to his baby, and gatekeeping comes in myriad forms. When things are going nicely at home, gatekeeping is a minor league activity and gate openings are frequent and flexible; when they are not, gate opening can seem optional at best and unwise at worst.

In Jack Kammer's *Good Will Toward Men,* Ellen Dublin Levy speaks openly and articulately of her high regard for her ex-husband's relationship with her daughter, then turns to the subject of her conscious awareness of her undermining of her daughter's relationship with her father:

> I know I see myself undermining her relationship with her father, interfering with it, doing everything that women who undermine father–child relationships . . . are guilty of doing . . . I certainly don't do it on purpose . . . I do it because I am so attached to her . . . I don't let him have enough of her. I keep her too much to me . . . Does [she] need my style of parenting? Oh, no, I don't honestly think that—I think that I need it . . . I should step back and give David and [her] the chance to be father and daughter, separate from me.

Levy's candor is liberating here, for her, her ex, and their daughter. She calls it undermining, but it is simply a more subtle way of gatekeeping, writ large in the words of an affectionate, thoughtful mother of a particular daughter in a particular world at a particular time. She knows that gatekeeping addresses *her* needs, not her daughter's. She knows that it is potentially destructive of her daughter's relationship with her father, and she knows what she should be doing about it to make it better. Studies by researchers Pearson and Thoennes have found that 20 to 40 percent of mothers acknowledge that they have actively interfered with their ex's visitation rights. Later in Ellen Dublin Levy's narrative she reveals that only her ex and her trust in his fathering of their daughter helped her open the gate. But even in the best of circumstances, opening the gate feels counterintuitive to countless women.

Milder forms of gatekeeping occur both within and outside of marriage. John Snarey's four-decade study of fathering found that inside marriage a wife's increased breadwinning responsibility predicted increased childrearing by her husband. At all ages, he found kids spending more time alone with their father when their mother worked outside the home. This is especially true when the wife works only part-time, because couples are more able to use a shift-work system.

But gatekeeping isn't an exclusively feminine province. The vaunted Houston Oilers withheld game pay and threatened to fine one of their starters $125,000 for missing a game simply because he was with his wife during childbirth. And staunch support for gatekeeping also comes from writers like William Sears, M.D., in the La Leche League International's publication *Becoming a Father: How to Nurture and Enjoy Your Family.* Despite his wisdom about child care and his personal experience as the father of six, Sears is curiously devoted to vigilant gatekeeping while the mother is breast-feeding and while she and the child are otherwise engaged. He depicts fathers as queasy and incompetent at changing babies and concludes that moms, therefore, should nurse as long as possible. The fathers he knows are inept with diaper pins. "Diaper pins are part of a subversive plot by mothers against their husbands." Ultimately, he arrives at the judgment that "many mothers are justified in their unwillingness to let fathers care for the baby because these fathers have not demonstrated that they are capable of comforting the baby." This is the old gatekeeping double bind: you were never taught how, because you were a boy, not a girl. You'll never get any good at it, so you shouldn't be allowed near the child until much later, by which point your skills will never catch up.

Look, Dr. Sears: Fathers, like mothers, become nurturing through the daily care of their child, which permits a familiar, competent, and sustained emotional presence in the child's life. Neither mothers nor fathers are natural caregivers. It's incredibly hard work, full of worry and trial and error. Waiting until the mother and child are ready for the father's involvement by your standards means that the horse is long gone from the barn. Remember the research that tells us that the older the child is, the less involved the father? The gate, if there's going to be one, must be opened early and often. Infancy matters, too.

Dr. Sears is not the only man who supports gatekeeping. It seems that many fathers themselves are less enthusiastic about their competence, even once inside the gate, than we might have expected. Diane Willie investigated seventy families with 6-month-olds where fathers were employed outside the home more than mothers. While both parents rated the mother as the better caretaker, the mothers rated the fathers' caretaking competence higher than the fathers rated themselves. Mothers' ratings of their husbands' sensitivity to the baby's cues, his responsiveness, and his ability to meet the needs of the infant surpassed the fathers' self-ratings. The author suggested that this was less a gatekeeping phenomenon than recognition by the fathers of their "lack of experience" and consequent "lack of confidence." I, however, suggest these are merely second generation gatekeeping effects. It is hard even for men to take their potential as competent and devoted caregivers to their kids seriously. (Interestingly, their children do not have this problem, as we'll see in Chapter 10.)

As a sneak preview to Chapter 9, I want to introduce another version of gatekeeping, one that profoundly affects the ability of even our better child care institutions to address the fatherneed in public settings. The experience of This Little Light O' Mine Day Care and Learning Center is illuminating. In the early 1980s, the all-woman staff of this highly regarded children's center decided to initiate a father involvement initiative because of their concern about the male absence in the life of so many of their children. They knew it took mothers and fathers to make things better for their kids. In my consultation to them, it became clear, however, that the joint parent meetings were not getting them where they needed to go. Many of the mothers had been in the parent group a long time, and they couldn't resist using the meetings to express their opinions, concerns, and resentments about being left alone by men so often in the raising of their kids.

Despite the staff's best efforts, they could not keep the men from feeling attacked. Consequently, the men slowly but surely stopped coming. In the interim, I used the opportunity to talk with the staff about the mothers' feelings, and I wondered aloud how many of them thought the moms had a point. For the next two hours we discussed "deadbeat dads," abandoning fathers, and abusive husbands and fathers (some even their own). At the end, we came to the conclusion that, despite their good-hearted and best efforts, the staff members were not yet truly able to help these men feel welcome. They needed to do some more preparatory work before they or their center would ever feel more "father friendly." We decided that while the staff members worked on increasing their sensitivity to these issues by openly exploring their legitimate past concerns, the men would be invited back for their own group for a while, led by a man.

The first meeting of the fathers' group was packed (and their meetings have been ever since). Three months later the men's and women's groups were brought together, and it was decided that the two groups would meet every month for a joint discussion. The center now looks like a place for children of both women *and* men. The magazines in the waiting room reflect men's as well as women's interests. On the walls are posters of children with men and women and art work depicting mother–child and father–child interactions. Some field trips reflect a male interest, others a female interest. Notices to home are addressed to mothers and fathers (and sent separately to nonresidential fathers). All these details have contributed to such extensive change that one father said, "It feels good coming here now as a father to pick up my kid. It used to feel so uncomfortable here for me as a man. It was like I'd walked into the ladies' room by accident!"

What it took to open this gate was not only awareness on the part of the staff that there was a problem but also time, a desire to fix the problem, dialogue about what happened when the gate slammed on their fingers, and renewed efforts to approach the goal, this time in a more effective, sensible way. Once staff members sorted out the problem and were clear about what needed to be done to fix it, they found that staff attendance rates were up, turnover was down, fee collections approached 100 percent, and there was less child absenteeism. The center also had the sharpest, best-equipped playground in the neighborhood—men apparently have their uses.

SINGLE MOTHERS

But what if there are no men? What is the never married or widowed mother to do about fatherneed in her life and in her children's lives? The usual advice centers on making use of the men still in her life to cobble together a "male role model" or "male presence" so that her children can experience the male thing, whatever that may be to her or them. This is not bad advice at all. I've given it myself countless times, telling single mothers to canvas their life for brothers, fathers, male friends, and neighbors, with or without children, who are competent and willing to take their child along on errands, outings, shopping trips, visits to the library, the dump, the recycling center—wherever (and whenever). I tell single mothers to get their kid into activities that are led by good men—coaches, religious leaders, Big Brothers—so that their kid gets a good dose of masculine attitude and behavior.

When I wrote a cover story for the bimonthly periodical *Zero to*

Three, which reaches tens of thousands of early childhood professionals around the country, I titled the issue that dealt with fathers and young children Some Kids Have Dads and Some Don't, Right? *Wrong.* In my article I explained that all children have fathers; whether they know them or not, they have them. All children learn eventually the mystery of their own beginnings. From their own understandings of where babies come from, they know that they could not be here if there was no father. And so they conclude that there's *got* to be one for them, somewhere. This holds true in cases of adoption, desertion, death, or assisted reproductive technology. Kids know the numbers, as is clear by what five-year-old Jake screamed painfully to his grandmother, who told him he didn't have a daddy (he did, via *in vitro* donor sperm): "You lie, Gamma, you lie big! It takes two people to make one!"

The need for a father is so strong in children that they make one up if they don't have one. And they spend a lot of energy looking. A kid will use almost any marginally adequate substitute (sometimes to the mother's alarm). Useful though these substitutes are, they are never really sufficient. Still, it is essential that the child's interest in men be supported by the single mother. By encouraging and providing relationships with men, she helps to detoxify the absence of a father in her child's life. It is likewise destructive for her to convey the message that it is neither necessary nor important to relate to men. Of course, she uses her own judgment about promoting interactions with particular men. Just because her child may be drawn to a particular guy doesn't mean she exercises no caution. Reasonable men respect and appreciate kids for who they are, know their interests and abilities, and support their mother's relationships with them.

Honoring this need in her child can put a lot of stress and strain on the young teenage mother who doesn't know, or doesn't want to know, the father of her child or on the single mother who adopts or conceives by assisted reproductive technology. But the questions from the child will still come, because they must. When it comes to choosing to raise a child without a father, the statistics are sobering: fatherless kids are more prone to depression than kids with a father, are twice as likely to be school dropouts, do less well and are more violent when in school, abuse more drugs, are more criminally active, try (and succeed at) suicide more often, and are at high risk for becoming teenage parents themselves.

Yes, these are statistics, not people, but the numbers tell many truths nonetheless. The pressure on single mothers is intensified by the misogynistic bias against them for raising kids in a deficient environment. Radical feminists shed more heat than light in such debates by charging that it isn't the male *presence* that makes such an environment deficient but only the lack of male *income*. These are not especially helpful, respectful, or encouraging words to little boys, who'd like to matter for something to someone someday. Enough with blaming; there's a surfeit to go around. Penelope Leach tells it like it is: "Why is it socially reprehensible for a man to leave a baby fatherless, but courageous, or admirable, for a woman to have a baby whom she knows will be so?"

Of course, countless single women succeed in raising wonderful sons and daughters. Still, we cannot ignore the fact that raising a boy without an involved father in the home raises the statistical probability of his becoming violent. Boys in school who are violent are *eleven* times more likely to be living without a father. Of course, reasonable parents do not raise their children by statistical probabilities, but this one is risky to ignore. Fatherlessness in any social class seems to catalyze a kind of obsessive hypermasculinity. Beatrice and John Whiting's classic six-culture study of tribal contexts of high and low father involvement found that the most violent cultures had the least paternal involvement. In gang and fraternity violence, males without fathers are the most rabid disparagers of everything female; it's as though they think this is the one true path to a masculine identity. Remember the powerful relationship between empathy and paternal involvement (see Chapter 2)?

Can such probabilities be overcome by any single mother? Of course. They're overcome all the time—but not without help, thought, and a plan. The ones who succeed vouch that their mothering is strengthened, not undermined, by sponsoring and encouraging a paternal presence in the life of their child. First, such a presence relieves mothers of needing to be sun and moon, father and mother, to their children. Mothers can't do it, the kids don't buy it, and it wastes everyone's time trying. Children need you to be who you're best at being, not who you think you should be. Second, having a male presence in the life of her child may help a woman come to terms with her own feelings about men, either in general, or her own life in particular. Given that it's no accident that so many children have no available father in their life, it's important for a mother to sort out why this is so in the case of *her* child so that it doesn't interfere with the relationship she has with her child. Far too often, I've heard a young mother say about her infant, "It's tough feeling love for him sometime, because he came out of me looking just like his father. And that's no good thing." This problem belongs to the mother's life, not the child's, and needs to be kept apart from their emotional connection to each other. Third, a mother's sponsorship of a male presence in her child's life protects the child from needing somehow to be all things to her. The child can think, "I am entitled to relationships with men *and* women, and that's all right with Mom." The corollary to this is the child's sense of relief that Mom has other beings to love besides him or her.

French author Romain Gary, who eventually died by suicide, was raised by his mother before World War II. As depicted in *Promise at Dawn,* the two "owed each other life." In the autobiography he comments on the absence of a father in his life and its impact on his relationship with his mother and vice versa:

> In your mother's love, life makes you a promise at the dawn of life that it will never keep. You have known something that you will never know again. You will go hungry to the end of your days . . . I am not saying that mothers should be prevented from loving their young. I am only saying that they should have something else to love as well. If my mother had a husband or a lover, I would not have spent my days dying of thirst beside so many fountains.

I believe it is the way single mothers *feel* about men in the life of their child, rather than what they *do* about men, that will be more powerful in the long run. Developmentally appropriate explanations to children of how they came to exist and what happened to their biological father, stretched out over the years in increasing detail, helps demystify a lot for them. The positive relationships with men that a woman has in her own life will teach her children more than her words ever will, most of the time, about men and masculinity. Being fatherless does not mean a child is doomed any more than being motherless does. It's risky, yes; doomed, no. It's when the pile of additional risk factors gets high—poverty, illness, abuse, prejudice—that bad stuff enters the life of the fatherless child.

ADVICE TO SINGLE MOTHERS

For those mothers who respect their children's hunger for a male presence in their lives and are thinking about how to sponsor it, here is some advice, cautiously offered. The realm in which children most long for fathering is a private, internal place, a domain of a certain yearning, of a sense of something lost, an incompleteness. It is different from your yearnings, and it's unlikely that your children hold you solely responsible for their father's absence—unless you hold yourself to be so (then they might feel they have to agree). A child's fatherneed is a very deep emotion, and it is not responsive to much rational influence. It hurts, even devastates, to lose a father, and that is what most fatherless kids feel happened to them. Somehow, somewhere they lost a father. Four-and-a-half-year-old Sarah explained to her cousin how it happened to her: "My mom had me in her body, and we weren't looking for my daddy when I was coming out, so we lost him. I look for him every time we go by the hospital, because that's where he got lost."

So a ball game here or there, an occasional camping or bike trip with some men—these will not suffice, as the longing in fatherneed is more emotional than instrumental. Still, do not despair, as your sustained sponsorship over time and your awareness of the importance of this issue in your child's life will benefit both your child and you a great deal. What follows are some suggestions I've shared with other mothers about helping ease a child's fatherneed at different stages of development.

INFANCY

- Take care of yourself first, especially if you are alone. Surround yourself with all the support you can find—emotional, physical, nutritional, spiritual. Don't let loneliness, bitterness, and isolation take root.
- Invite close male relatives and friends to hold, walk, rock, play with, or baby-sit your child. Be sure these men have an important relationship with you, because your kid can tell the difference even at this age. Try to involve these men in your child's life early, before stranger awareness takes hold (around seven to nine months), so your child gets a sense of the body, face, smell, voice, textures, and handling and comforting styles of others.

TODDLERHOOD

- Have close male friends or relatives engage in physical play and rough-and-tumble exploration with your child. These activities are attractive to both boys and girls at this age, and many men feel more comfortable interacting this way than changing diapers. It's a stereotype for a reason.

- Have close male friends or relatives read and comfort your child. The different behavioral styles of other caregivers are stimulating and fascinating to children as they spend more time in the not-the-mother realm.

- Remember that your toddler's search for independence and autonomy, which is normal here, can make you feel that you are losing your baby—because you actually are supposed to. Secure connections can now be made by your child to extended family and friends, and developing language skills in your child make it easier for those men who may be interested in interacting with your child but are not accustomed to physical child care to follow along and communicate.

- Try to find child care arrangements or play groups in which men or older male siblings are involved as staff or regular volunteers. They are increasingly prevalent.

PRESCHOOL YEARS

- Preschoolers love more complex games and have a beginning sense of turn taking and cooperation. And they can be away from you for longer periods of time and feel safe and have fun. Let them go for a few hours with your male buddies if they want to.

- During their toilet training, boys may need or want a demonstration of stand-up peeing, so find a comfortable and competent volunteer in your very immediate circle.

- Reading remains very important to kids at this stage. Press male friends and relatives into this service. Men like to have things to *do* with children, and this is a natural. Be sure to select books that depict men worthy of your and your child's regard, not books that portray those from the bottomless supply of buffoons in the media.

- Since this is the first great age of gender identification, boys are very hungry for masculine role models with whom to practice being a guy. Girls are very interested in exploring the power of their femininity on males, big and small. Either way, make hay while this sun shines. It's a bright one.

PRIMARY AND MIDDLE SCHOOL YEARS

- If there is a golden age of male involvement from a societal standpoint, this is it. Everything from Indian Guides and Princesses to the Pinewood Derby conspire to get men closer to their kids. This is the era in which the civil and civic skills are taught, and—fortunately for kids whose fatherneed is not otherwise being met—the job of fostering decent, productive citizenry in the young seems to be stereotypically granted to males more often than not.
- Religious school starts for the congregation's youngest members, and males are often plentiful around churches.
- Skill mastery in sports, the arts, and educational pursuits bonds kids and teachers in relationships most efficiently, so keep an eye out for male instructors and choose them over female instructors if they have similar competence.

ADOLESCENCE

- By now your children are making most of their own choices about the kind of adults they want to hang out with. They will also be taking a renewed interest in *your* behavior: your dating, ignored by them for years, will now have a powerful effect on their dating.
- An increased appetite for privacy in your children will impose a certain embargo about what you know about their life now. It's important that they have other adults with whom there is an open channel for communication, and a masculine one can help greatly for both sons and daughters.
- Testing of authority and limits is, of course, a natural behavior at this age, and you may need reinforcements from time to time. Affirmation of their safety and clarification of expectations can be very powerful when done in partnership with a male family member who knows and loves your children.
- This is a great time for extended visits with male family members or old family friends as your teens begin to explore their new autonomies in safe and secure venues. Of course, they'll want to bring a friend along. Let them. Boy, will you learn a lot!

CONCLUSION

The way you handle your child's access to the male world matters, but the way you personally feel and act about their right to understand and be a part of it matters more than any particular technique you use or opportunity you provide. The older kids get, the better they are at sniffing out hypocrisies—yours, not theirs—so when you get caught, be honest, not defensive. It'll be a great opportunity to talk together about what they and you feel about fatherneed.

8

How Fathering Changes Men for Good

I was six when my father was called to the pulpit of the Woodward Avenue Baptist Church in Detroit. A foundering church whose physical presence was an inner-city neo-Gothic hulk, it challenged his patience and creativity. One of the few advantages it offered over a regular paycheck and a neo-fancy parsonage was a connection to a network of smaller churches in the Greater Detroit/Windsor (Ontario) region. To "liven up the old places," Dad would sometimes take me or my older brother, Gordon, with him as he supplied the odd pulpit here and there. My favorite trip was the one by train that included a ferry boat connection.

I absolutely loved this time alone with my dad. He was somehow different (as was I) on these trips than he was at home. I did not know then, as I do now, that my father had to skillfully lobby my mother to get her support for these "road shows." They often included an overnight, lots of interaction with strangers (sometimes even staying in their homes), and, if I was lucky, a missed day of school. Gradually, Mom exchanged her vigilance for encouragement, despite withering opposition to these junkets by *her* mother, who felt that "any decent mother simply wouldn't allow it." She eventually told me she gave in because she liked what she saw happening to her husband and his relationship to her sons. For example, after one such adventure, Mom tells me, I draped a scarf around my skinny shoulders (my pastoral robe), grabbed a Bible, and delivered a (mercifully) brief "sermon" of my own composition from the front stair landing (my pulpit). As for what Mom saw happening to Dad: "The more time he spent with you boys, the sweeter he got, and the better he knew how to handle you. When he'd come back from these trips, he also seemed to want to talk more about you, life, the world, us—something about that time with you just opened him up."

This chapter is about understanding the "something about that time." What are the consequences, near and far, in the lives of men who become positively involved fathers? How does generating offspring affect a man's success or failure in love, work, and society?

It might help to understand if I locate my father's experience in the historical context of American maledom. He was born in 1915 in Mangum County, Oklahoma, the youngest of six, to a father who was a rural mail route courier, a cotton farmer, and a deacon and a mother whose family originally emigrated to survive the Irish potato famines. How might this picture compare with my experience or, more importantly, yours? Beyond the biological distinctions that define fatherhood from motherhood lie potent social and cultural traditions and pressures that shape each culture's notion of the ideal father. Each culture endlessly fiddles with variations of the ideal, responding perpetually to conditions that change with time. Sociologist Ralph LaRossa from Georgia State University has shown that the behavior of fathers, as well as the culture in which they are conducting themselves, changes course, generation by generation, depending on the prevailing political and social winds. For example, in our own culture the current interest in and promotion of androgynous traits in men—the mixing of feminine with masculine stereotypes of people's skills and interests—would have been laughable, even thought perverse, just two generations ago. Why the push toward androgyny as a cultural goal? Despite the fact that men and women demonstrate myriad similarities in their interactions with their children, as we saw in previous chapters, their differences are indeed important—and sometimes vital to their children. Children aren't the ones asking their fathers to be more like their mothers or vice versa. The special contribution that men bring to the well-being of their children is so devalued by this enthusiasm for androgyny that I sense this fad has a very short half-life and is already dissipating in our culture.

LaRossa found evidence of culture's complex pull on the expression of fatherhood in a disconnect between our culture's behavioral expectations for fathers and actual paternal conduct in Depression-era America. He found this evidence in an unusual place—the letters written to an advice columnist between 1925 and 1939. In contrast to the "super dad" revered by women in the 1930s—a man who slavishly provided for his children while simultaneously romancing his wife—the men described in these historical documents were found to be actually less involved with their children than were the fathers of the decade before, showing the negative effect the Depression had on father involvement. Job searching consumed time and energy and even those men lucky enough to have jobs were so strained that children were "dropped from the father's calendars." Still, they identified with their kids and felt remorse at their distance, especially when they compared it to the closeness they had felt with their own father (sound familiar?).

Such perspectives encourage us to be cautious in speaking of "revolutions" in fathering or of new kinds of fathering, especially when we consider the familiar myopia of memory-impaired America—fascination with the here and now. As historian Robert Griswold has so skillfully and doggedly reminded us, preindustrial fathering couldn't have been more hands-on. In contrast, the mythical nuclear families of the 1950s had fathers like Ward Cleaver, who apparently worked in la-la land, occasionally consulted a cardboard housewife, and never confronted one serious developmental issue head-on with either of his children. Scavenging the carrion of old *cultural ideals of fatherhood* to flesh out the new ideals will not enlighten us. It is more useful to distinguish between active and passive, involved and disengaged fathering and to try to understand how one becomes the other.

At the age of fifty-five, Buddy Fite was diagnosed with throat cancer. As he tells his interviewer on public radio, Dee Mae Roberts, he'd decided to just let it take him: "If it's time to die, it's time to die." His life had not been dull. He was a legendary guitarist who'd taught himself as a child to pluck a bass line with his thumb and melody with his fingers. At thirteen, he was hired to tour with Willie Nelson, and at a music trade show Les Paul had unplugged his amplifier, saying simply, "Anyone who plays that good just shouldn't be around." Fame did not impress Fite. In fact, his compositions usually went nameless, his albums slipping quietly out of print. He'd spent some of his happiest times motorcycling around with some parachute jumpers from World War II who eventually settled on the name Hells Angels for their little group.

But the reason Fite is still with us five years after his diagnosis has nothing to do with any of the above, he tells the interviewer, but with the fact that he became Michael's father a few months after he had decided to yield to his cancer. As his boy grew, Fite began to feel differently about time, music, and cancer, and he decided to go ahead and let them "yank out" his throat so he could stick around to watch his son "grow where he was going to grow." And, as Dee Mae tells radio listeners, "the man who had never valued his compositions enough to name them is thinking of calling his first lullaby "Michael."

Though divorced from Michael's mother now, Fite sees his boy regularly. He describes to Dee Mae how he set up a little drum set in the corner of his mobile home for his son, then explains: "He gives a pretty good beat and gets in there with his microphone. I play, he sings. He's going to be another one, no question about it." Dee Mae asks if Michael's been a positive influence on him. As a legacy to his son, Fite reveals, he has agreed to publish a guitar instruction book and record a CD to accompany the book. Later in the interview he muses, "Life is here to become aware that you are alive."

THE LIFE-CHANGING EFFECTS OF FATHERHOOD

Something life changing, even life saving happened to Buddy Fite, cancer victim, when he became a father and started to watch his child grow. What does that mean? Where does it start? How does it work?

As turning points go, it's hard to compete with fatherhood for clarity, emotional turbulence, excitement, anticipation, and fear. The closer the turning point is to the emotional side of life and the further from mere biology (i.e., insemination alone), the more critical the balance between things left behind in the past and things found here in the present. Self-absorption, self-involvement, and running in place are essentially over if a man is to be positively involved as a father. Caring behaviors and activities that promote the well-being of others begin to overtake previously more narcissistic pursuits. As John Snarey of Emory University describes it, "The successful realization of generativity gives rise to the ego strength of care—an inclusive concern for what love, necessity, and chance have generated." The effect of this change can be felt in many ways, an important indicator being what many men describe as simply feeling more like an adult. When pressed for further clarification, a new father often says, "I feel more connected to my father and who he is [or was]."

It is, of course, naive to think that this change in a man simply begins with a positive result with a home pregnancy test or, in the case of more resistant men, in the delivery room. Research has shown us frequently that there are many childhood antecedents to being positively involved in the care of one's children. One of the most vigorous predictors of engaged and responsible fathering is the experience the father had growing up in his family of origin. When carefully examined, however, two very divergent paradigms appear to explain the mechanism for such significant influence.

First is the situation where the father mimics the strengths of the fathering he remembers himself receiving. This is called the "modeling" paradigm. Warm, accessible, and authoritative men are particularly accessible models for their sons to emulate. Henry Biller and John Snarey observed that fathers who were encouraging, nurturing, and attentive had sons who were more likely to value masculine nurturing qualities. In the Glueck Longitudinal Study by Snarey, boys elaborated on what they had inherited of their fathers' strengths—strengths documented in the study itself and not simply reported or remembered. Those strengths clustered into being somewhat better educated, having a "better" or more complex job, and having a wife who worked closely with him to make a coherent and interesting home.

An interesting wrinkle in much of the mimicry research is the role that memory, reality, and perception each play in cobbling together a well-remembered paternal role model. Snarey's research gets around the problem of what was real and what was *perceived* as real by the child by recording the data in the actual generation being studied. Although John Snarey had the luxury of time in conducting his research, many other researchers must grapple with the problems produced by the continual refinements subjects make in their judgments and perceptual processes and by the notoriously fickle fluidity of memory. Psychologists, journalists, and historians alike have the same perpetual fears about these problems, because they all know there is a tendency for people to remember things the way they want to remember them, in accordance with their particular current perception of reality. If a man is predisposed to remember his father as a good role model, then so be it, he will, and it will probably work just fine in his day-to-day fathering.

In related research by Anju Jain, Jay Belsky, and Keith Crnic another group of traits was found that preceded positive role modeling in caretaking dads as opposed to disengaged and disciplinarian dads. The former dads tended to be better educated and to have a more valued occupation, were less anxious, had more confidence in the dependability of others, and felt generally less hassled than dads who were harsh disciplinarians or withdrawn.

The other paradigm developed to explain the importance of a father's experience growing up in his own family of origin appears in the motives of men whose childhood experiences were at the opposite end of the spectrum from those who had a caring, involved father. Scholars have called this the "reworking" paradigm, and while it is probably less commonly found among men who are positively fathering their children than the modeling paradigm is, it is nonetheless well known to promote responsible fathering. These sons of passive, nonnurturing, withdrawn, and even abusive, authoritarian fathers can go out of their way to compensate for their own father's weaknesses and failures as a father. In spite of their unhappy childhood experiences and disappointments, such men father their children better than they were fathered. Again, in the Glueck study, Snarey found men who despite their own distant-father experiences provided above-expected levels of care for their own children, particularly in terms of fostering healthy social and emotional development in their children during adolescence. Physical and athletic development in their kids also received above-average support from these compensating men. Finally, men whose fathers had used corporal punishment to instill fear in them as boys tended to be less physically intimidating with their own children.

It has been my repeated clinical experience that such reworking of early negative experiences is easier for men as fathers than for women as mothers precisely because of the larger role that contextual influences, both interpersonal and environmental, play in fatherhood as opposed to motherhood. It's as though societal and cultural supports find their way more easily to the core of fathering than they do in the case of mothering because of the comparatively smaller role that biology plays in fathering. This should truly hearten expectant mothers: there is hope for every father to do better at fathering than did his own father.

Brandon, who could have been a poster child for the "reworking" paradigm, consulted me about a parenting plan for his twin sons after an unwanted divorce. As he reluctantly detailed his history with his own abusive father, he described what he felt fathers should do for their children, having figured this out after going through "the fires of [his] own hell":

Fathers really need to demonstrate their love all the time to their children. It doesn't need to be flashy or expensive. Being around, close—that's most important. It has the effect on your kids of their wanting to feel it in themselves, that closeness and absolute trust. Then, as it grows, they'll just want to pass it along to *their* kids—to be thoughtful and selfless, to nurture them well when they really need it, not just when it's convenient.

Although it was not true in Brandon's case, the first people to notice that fathering has begun to change a man are typically the women in his life. I heard repeatedly from the wives of the men in my longitudinal research on children growing up in homes where the father was the child's first caregiver; they gave descriptions of their husband that were not dissimilar to my mother's description of what happened to my father after he started taking my brother or me on those road trips. Here are some comments from the wives in my study:

"He's getting more mellow, harder to freak out than before Jamie was born."
"He's got a gentle side that I used to only see with our puppies."
"He has settled down a lot and is more responsible about the little things now around the house. The family, even my folks, have noticed."

One of my favorite descriptions of a man changed by fatherhood comes from the mother of one of my patients, a child whom I was treating for posttraumatic symptoms following a school bus accident: "My husband had always had a kind of buzz on for action and teasing—anyone, anytime. After our son was born, he took more responsibility around us and home because he was just less 'ramy' [a reference to testosterone-soaked male sheep?]."

MORE RESPONSIBLE

As we've already heard, first-time fatherhood, in men who feel the desire to engage positively in the well-being of their children, can evoke anxiety about providing security for their wife and child, protecting them from the bad things that can happen to good people, especially little ones. These men also deal with a sudden sense of vulnerability, ineptitude, and uncertainty about what one actually *does* with an infant. The defensive reaction to all these worries can be to "get real" and "get responsible."

A painful Catch-22 can, however, stop a new father in his tracks before he gets started. Those who feel pressure to begin their kid's college fund or who start to worry about private school tuition can easily find themselves with greater work commitments, which can be exactly the worst disincentive to their parental commitment. Greenberger and O'Neill found that fathers of preschoolers feel the highest parental commitment to their children when they feel less strain as a result of a lowered work commitment.

How do men resolve the conflict between wanting to provide more for their family at exactly the same time that they want to be more engaged in caring for a child? Here in the day-to-day decision making of engaged fatherhood, men seem to draw on a whole range of father models. Such a role model isn't derived whole from any specific individual in a father's environment; rather, admired fathering behaviors are picked over and assembled over time into a kind of mosaic of skilled fatherhood behaviors, customized by this particular father at this particular time in his life with this particular child.

An example might be that even though a father has no memory of ever having been taken to the doctor's office by his father, he may now assume responsibility for taking his own child. Indeed, more men are known to now be taking part in the health care decisions and services regarding their kids. The Council of Family Health found in a survey of men and health care issues that a "surprising number of American fathers are taking care of their kids when they're sick . . . 35 percent said they'd missed at least a day of work in the past year to care for their sick kids twelve and under. Sixty-nine percent said they've taken one or more of their children to the doctor's office, and over 80 percent say they're very likely to administer medication to their kids." So where are these men getting the support to do even this much? From their own rising expectations about co-parenting, a supportive and "expectant" spouse, and some mental images of respected pieces of male behavior.

The letter from the venerable Lois Murphy that I shared previously (see end of Chapter 1) has further insights into the development of more responsible fathering from men she knew well. Her research groups at the Menninger Foundation in Topeka, Kansas, were legendary for the thoroughness of their investigations into the lives of the young children and families they studied. Murphy talked to me at length about the dozen or so mothers who had postpartum depression severe enough that if their husbands hadn't taken over the care of the children, I doubt that they or their marriage would have survived. She recalled the resistance among her colleagues to believing that men could manage a baby with sufficient competence to assure its survival in the critical early months. Her own doubts never surfaced, as far as I know, thanks to her experience with her husband: "Gardner was committed to showing the children the world, with endless trips cross-country and to all aspects of New York. He told endless stories—'dragon stories,' which he made up. My daughter remarked, 'He was the only one who could begin a story in New York and continue it till we got to New Hampshire.' He was a *companion* to the children."

MORE COMPASSIONATE

Andrea and Will had been married for six years and had four-year-old twins. Andrea described Will's transformation: "The changes I most appreciated in Will were as he turned from a man into a husband, he seemed less judgmental. In his less attractive moments—before the twins were born—his railings against a disapproved-of neighbor or workmate bordered on the bigoted. Since the twins softened him up, he'll help out a stranger, cook a casserole for a sick friend, give up a Saturday morning to fix up the toy shed at the preschool. He's a better citizen." And such is how Will developed compassion.

Interestingly, recent research in nurse-midwifery has recently highlighted this very change in men as it relates to childbirth and the infant's first hours of life. Although fathers expect to be part of the labor team, they are often surprised at how, once things begin to really happen, they slip from "partnered" to supportive role. The supportive role can be filled by most adult relatives or companions who are there to support the mother through her pain and fear. The partner, however, shares the mother's dreams about and for the baby and her fervent hope that the labor and delivery will go as well as possible.

In the days and weeks after the baby's birth, the new father who accepts true partnership with his mate makes real sacrifices in terms of sleep deprivation and experiences the strain and anxiety inherent in being a parent. Despite their initial confidence in their ability to support their wife through the new experience of parenting, men underestimate the physical demands of the parenting process (who doesn't?). In the end, they come away with greater compassion for their wife and enhanced respect for her as a woman, mother, and partner.

Some suggestions for the expectant father who intends to be a partner in parenting:

- Don't miss a birthing class session, because the skills you learn will keep you at the partner level once that action starts.
- Read all the literature you can get your hands on about birth and delivery. Surprises are just things you didn't think could happen. The more you know, the better prepared you are to stay right with your wife and the less likely you'll be to get overwhelmed and back away.
- Expect to have different questions than your wife will have. She'll worry about pain and anesthesia while you may wonder about fetal monitors and when you'll get your wife back. Just because most of

the attention will be on her and her body, don't assume your questions are less important.

- Talk to other men about the delivery and birth experience. Their wisdom can be very helpful and reassuring.
- Don't let your uncertainty about what is going on moment to moment allow you to get pushed aside by the others in the room. Gently remind nurses and docs that you want to know what is happening and you want to understand. If you understand, your wife will feel partnered. Keep coming back, as she'll need you even closer if things get a little scary.
- Forget the video. You're probably just hiding behind it anyway. Partners are *there,* not filming.

But that is just the beginning. Research into dual-earner families after the birth of the first child reveals that fathers struggle with the demands of child, partner, and job in a way that deepens their appreciation for their spouse's juggling of burdens and opportunities. Recognition of the lack of concurrence between the work and family worlds and their dueling realities leaves fathers feeling closer to their wives' even more complex experience with worlds separated by such competing values.

How long might these effects last? Looking again at the unique observations in John Snarey's forty-year study, we learn that positively involved fathers are more likely to have a successful relationship with their spouse down the road; such men were found to feel more happily married ten or twenty years after the birth of their first child.

African American fathers' involvement with infants has also been shown to profoundly affect their ability to communicate effectively within the family as a whole. Hossain and Roopnarine's research looking at associations between full-time and part-time mothering and father involvement found that although paternal engagement does not correlate with the spouse's work schedule, it is affected by whether or not the father fed or comforted his infant and was responsible for it. Furthermore, engaged parenting was seen by his family to improve his overall "belonging" emotionally to the family and surrounding society as a whole. Of course, what goes around comes around here as well.

An example of the compassion-enabling effect of fathering came through my radio just before Christmas 1998. It is so improbable that I've struggled over whether or not to include it. National Public Radio talk show host Terry Gross was interviewing a man named T. J. Leyden for her December 15, 1998, show *Fresh Air*. A former neo-Nazi white racist skinhead, incongruously now working for the Simon Wiesenthal Center at the Museum of Tolerance, Leyden was sickening to listen to as he spoke of his recruitment of teenagers to violent racist bigotry. As I reached to change stations, Gross asked the only question I might have cared to hear answered: "So, what happened to change your commitment to white racism?"

Leyden haltingly explained that his feelings started to change with the birth of his second son (apparently it doesn't always take the first time around in extreme cases). He began to question where his frenzied bigotry would all end and whether he should be raising his sons to prepare for that end. As his four-year-old (who had never actually encountered any humans other than white racists in his short life) happily spewed forth the epithets his father and mother had so carefully taught him, Leyden found himself shaken that his teachings had already so profoundly shaped his son's expectations of the world. Slowly he began to back away from his bigoted lifestyle. With his mother's persistent efforts over the years to have him renounce his hatred and bigotry, he eventually found his way to the Museum of Tolerance, where he now shares with the staff and occasional visitors his experience, tactics, and knowledge about organized racism. What made him change? "She [mother] helped, but I never would have listened without my boys and becoming a father."

Time will tell what the effect of Leyden's conversation was on his sons' lives. Were there reciprocal changes in them, rendering them more tolerant, more open to the plight of their fellow humans?

MORE COMPETENT

A far too frequently affirmed stereotype in men is their tendency to feel that they are supposed to know how to do a thing, having never previously encountered or practiced it. Raising children is certainly well within that category. The headmaster of a private school once wrote me a letter about this after attending one of my lectures about men in the lives of their children:

> I felt so helped by your statements about reciprocity in parenting. With two daughters, I keep thinking I am always "supposed" to know what to do with the girls, but in fact we learn perpetually

with them and from them. It was a relief to trade in my "supposed-to-know" thoughts and fears for the relieved excitement of reciprocal growth over the years we'll have together. What a nourishing thought.

Nursing research from the University of Arizona looked at predictors of role competence for both experienced and inexperienced fathers. One of the larger surprises in the study was that a quarter of inexperienced fathers reported depression of clinical proportions during the weeks following their child's birth. Although many fathers, especially of breast-fed babies, feel remote from their wife and infant in the first weeks, the depth of the depression in these men was worrisome. The depression affected their ability to work, sleep, and provide support to the mother, and it even interfered with their ability to feel interested in or attached to the new baby. Reactive depression in a father in response to the birth of the child he had only weeks before eagerly anticipated welcoming is far from reassuring; in fact, it can easily complicate any postpartum blues or depression in the mother. A depressed father certainly would have a hard time being the reassuring and supportive partner a tearful, discouraged mother might need, especially one facing a demanding infant for the first time in her life.

This, in fact, was the finding in an important study from the Institute of Biomedical Sciences in Oporto, Portugal, a long-term mental health project involving fifty-four first-time mothers and fathers who rated themselves for depression and anxiety. Postnatal depression in fathers was found to be associated with a personal history of depression and with the occurrence of depression in their spouses during pregnancy and within the first three months after delivery. This is a very important finding to follow up because of the important implications for birth and parent education, particularly if the depression goes untreated or undetected, which it needn't. We have yet to understand, much less study, if the mother's depression impacts upon the father's.

Inexperience alone may not be the only factor in the depression of fathers of young children. Blair and Hardesty's research group proposed that low levels of paternal engagement can lead to depression in men. I find this a fascinating association, suggesting as it does that higher levels of engagement between men and their children may actually play a protective role in mental health in men.

Many men begin to feel an increase in overall competence after the inadequacies of the early months fade in memory. Mary DeLuccie studied predictors of paternal involvement and satisfaction in almost two hundred fathers of firstborn sons and daughters, ages four, eight, twelve, and sixteen years, by evaluating the fathers' childrearing practices, attitudes, involvement, and satisfactions. Measures were made of whether the father was emotionally accepting or rejecting of his kids, whether he was firm or lax in his discipline, and whether he used emotional control or promoted autonomy (particularly in his older children). The study concluded that men who demonstrate warmth and firm control in their childrearing practices feel more effective as parents, are more likely to see their interactions with their kids positively, and feel encouraged to be even more involved.

BETTER BALANCED

The relationship between most men and their work changes profoundly after they become fathers. Further, the more positively active they are as fathers, the more complex the relationship. This is an area of fatherhood that may be undergoing the most rapid change. The number of men reporting a significant conflict between work and family life has increased sevenfold, from 12 percent in 1977 to 84 percent in 1994. While one of the most recent studies on parental employment, reported in a psychological journal in an article titled the "Short-Term and Long-Term Effects of Early Parenting Employment on Children of the National Longitudinal Survey of Youth," concluded that there are "no ill effects from parent's working," most of the media covered it as though it were a study only of working mothers. Family-friendly policies in the workplace are, in fact, implicitly assumed to cover women only, a circumstance hardly ever challenged by men or women. Consequently, where some flexibility regarding mothers is creeping into the workplace, rigidity seems to carry the day for most fathers—hence the increase in the number of men reporting conflict between work and family life.

Dupont's 8,500 employees have been surveyed every five years since 1985 regarding the success of flexible work options in balancing work and family responsibilities: 37 percent of male employees favored such flexibility in 1985, 56 percent did in 1990, and 71 percent did in 1995. As the number of involved fathers rises, so will the pressure on employers for flexible work options, and that pressure must be shared by men and women to successfully resolve the problem. "Working parents should stop assuming that the workplace is incapable of responding to men's family needs. Supervisors are not mind readers; they have to know about those needs to respond," wrote the author of a *New York Times* op-ed piece titled "The Other Working Parent." And, of course, many of those supervisors are men.

In testimony before the House Select Committee on Children, Youth and Families, author Lynn O'Rourke Hayes (*The Best Jobs in America for Parents*) lays out the issue this way: "Interestingly, fathers new and old, are often the gatekeepers to job flexibility. With more management men empathizing with the struggles of their sons and daughters, or, more likely, experiencing their own two-career chaos, the chances of them saying 'yes' to more flexibility and 'no' to more power hours is increasing."

Some forward-thinking companies are already there. The largest government-owned utility in the country is the Los Angeles Department of Water and Power. Of its 12,500 employees, 78 percent are men, with over half of them in skilled jobs in the field; 40 percent of those men participate in programs related to child care, parenting, breastfeeding coaching, single parenting, and stepparents issues. Such family-friendly programming is credited with keeping the employee turnover rate at 2 percent (less than a third of the national average), low absenteeism, and enhanced recruitment.

Elder, Liker, and Cross studied the impact of unemployment on fathering. They discovered that unemployment is far greater in its impact on men's fathering than on women's mothering, reminding us that employment is more salient for fathers than for mothers. Their data indicate that the father's perception of his financial situation, even more than his actual circumstances, influences his fathering behavior overall. Feeling like a failure in the bedrock provider role is very demoralizing for fathers and can cause their relationships with their kids to degrade. McLoyd has shown that this is especially relevant to men of color, who often struggle uphill against compounded odds.

For the large number of men wedged between good employment circumstances and those who don't feel securely or satisfyingly employed, worrying about kids can have an especially corrosive effect. Barnett found than even engaged fathers of "average" employment, in terms of job satisfaction felt increasing job fatigue, increases in random anxiety, headache, low back pain, and sleeplessness when preoccupied by or worried about their children's well-being (sound familiar, mothers?).

Clearly, high levels of paternal engagement are not without cost for fathers, especially when high levels of stress related to work and to family issues combine with lowered self-regard. Interestingly, a man's overall satisfaction with parenthood is not permanently distorted even by these stresses. High involvement may, in fact, have a positive effect on career success down the road and provides strong support for becoming generative in social domains in particular. John Snarey as well as A. J. Hawkins and colleagues argue that despite the significant imbalance and stress in the short run, engaged fathering may actually catalyze men to achieve higher goals and comfort in the workplace later. In his longitudinal study Snarey found that men who had been engaged fathers were more likely to be involved in broader caregiving activities as workplace managers or mentors or as civic and community leaders.

MORE MELLOW

Despite its brief life as a New Age adjective, *mellow* still works for many wives to describe a changing trend in mood in their husbands after they get comfortable as fathers. A certain flexibility seeps into you as daily interaction with children teaches you how little of life you actually *can* control. My cousin David explains it this way: "I wasn't looking for a new perspective on life when I became a father. It just barged in with the baby. My feelings about my work, my religion, health, masculinity— all of it came up for review. It slowed me down, big time. My dreams and daydreams were filled with new ideas about life, its dangers and beauties. It was like getting my battery terminals scrubbed."

Subtle though a mellow mood might be, for many men it may have broader effects. Joseph Pleck reviewed public health implications of men's transitions to fatherhood and found that involved fathers report fewer accidental and premature deaths, less than average contact with the law, less substance abuse, fewer hospital admissions, and a greater sense of well-being overall. How this works—how the engaged raising of one's children, which can seem so exhausting, expensive, depleting, and maddening in the doing of it, could have positive health benefits— doesn't seem intuitive at first glance. Yet, overall, the emotional rewards, combined with the pressure to at least *act* healthier as an adult, accumulate over time to keep a man closer to behavior that promotes health.

MORE DECENT

I've saved decency for last to give it due emphasis. In my own hierarchy it actually goes first, because of its potential to effect lasting change not only in the man-turned-father but in the father's potential to effect lasting change in the world around him. One of the most dramatic findings reflecting the profound change that can occur in men when they nurture actively comes from investigations of the relationship between men's caretaking of infants and subsequent sexual abuse of children.

Hilda and Seymour Parker of the University of Utah compared fifty-six men who were known to have sexually abused their daughters to fifty-four other men who had no known child sexual abuse background. They found a significant correlation between the lack of active involvement in child care and nurturance and eventual child abuse. We know that stepfathers tend to abuse children at considerably higher rates than do biological fathers. The Parkers, however, found no difference in abuse rates when comparing stepfathers who had been involved in the nurturing and physical care of their stepdaughter during the first three years of life and biological fathers similarly involved. The higher rate of stepfathers' sexual abuse appeared related to their higher rate of absence and failure to provide nurturing during the critical period of the stepdaughter's first three years. The Parkers concluded that a man's involvement in the physical care of a child prior to the age of three, whether that child is biologically his or not, significantly reduces the probability that the man will exploit that physical intimacy later on though sexual abuse. It seems that the joint humanization of the father and the child through the father's caring for the helpless infant can immunize the father against crossing that sexual exploitation barrier.

Engaged fathering also helps curb violence through the reduction in rage and in the sense of entitlement that many males express and feel toward women. Our worry over men as perpetrators of violence runs through recorded history. Staggering numbers of men have killed each other across the millennia in wars, gangs, and domestic and ethnic violence. Untold numbers of these men were fathers, and much of their violence was directed at women. Stereotypical views of female and male roles support a male belief in domination.

Because the mother is, and probably always will be, the main caregiver, the infant usually experiences her as the singular, omnipotent source of comfort. This view, of course, is doomed to be disappointing even in the case of the most altruistic of mothers, given the frustrations of everyday life. Sooner or later, children inevitably and normatively resent the fact that Mom can't meet every one of their needs (and immediately!). In particularly vulnerable situations of single parenthood, poverty, and high-risk living of any kind, a child's disappointment can become rage that seethes for years. A man's participation in childrearing and nurturing tends to lessen the unconscious resentment and rage he feels against women, making it easier for him to gratify most of his child's needs and making him less likely to act out his violence.

The classic cross-cultural anthropological study of six cultures by Beatrice and John Whiting found that the most violent tribes were those in which the father was least associated with the family and had minimal to nonexistent involvement in childrearing. Countless studies, meanwhile, affirm our intuition that empathy is inversely related to violent behavior. Professor and author Myriam Miedzian, in her testimony before the Select Committee on Children, Youth and Families, made the following statement:

> Boys raised with nurturant, caring, involved fathers develop a sense of their father's primary male identity on which they can model themselves from the youngest age. They do not need to prove that they are real men by being tough, violent, obsessed with dominance. Their model of masculinity includes nurturance, caring and empathy experienced from their fathers. Since they are secure in their masculinity, they do not have the need to look down on or disparage everything feminine in order to establish a masculine identity.

BOTTOM LINE

If success breeds success, it should be possible to document changes in the way men feel about all the qualities presented in this chapter as life-changing effects of fatherhood—openness, competence, balance, decency, compassion, and responsibility after they become involved in fathering. That is precisely the case in the Haverford Longitudinal Study conducted by Douglass Heath. He found that engaged fatherhood promotes a man's ability to understand himself, to empathically understand others, and to integrate his feelings in an ongoing way. Furthermore, fathers are more likely to want to give back and serve in community leadership positions than are men who have remained childless.

Men, like women, receive their genetic material from the union of male and female. They begin life half male and half female, sort of. Of course, the arranging and pruning of that biological material is what makes each of us unique. Becoming a successful, loved, and loving father might be the highest iteration of reproductive masculinity. But the fullness of fathering lies in the raising, not the having, of children. In the raising of children, men use, just as they do in the loving of women, both halves of their genetic legacy. Being a thoughtful and competent partner and lover, like being a thoughtful and competent father, calls for the joining of a man's feminine and masculine sides into a working whole. That's my take on what we mean when we say a man has gotten it together.

9

Fulfilling Fatherneed

As THIS INK DRIES, a shaken America nervously peeks out from under the pall of yet another school massacre, this time in Littleton, Colorado. We are startled by the sickening violence done to children by children. Of the now half dozen such group murders in 1999 alone, motives range from revenge to no clue. The killers were all teenagers, except for one eleven-year-old, and all male; many, but not all, appear to have been less well fathered than we might have hoped. While it's usually inappropriate to finger a single cause for such horrific events, one cannot help but consider the connection between violence, especially in boys, and absent or inadequate fathering, a worrisome relationship that has been documented for decades. It is equally irresponsible to suggest that adequate fathering will in and of itself always prevent rageful, inhuman violence of this magnitude, but such violence is a far rarer event in the lives of children in whom fatherneed has been fulfilled and satisfied.

This chapter is about the fulfillment of fatherneed at home and in the wider world that influences today's families. While I've offered practical advice throughout this book, this chapter is where the ideas become plans, the visions concrete. Fathers are still the greatest under-mined (double meaning intended) natural resource in the lives of America's children. Furthermore, competent fatherhood is one of the most powerful renewable resources in the life of a family, generation after generation. The potential of every boy and girl born to a family is brought to fruition by involved fathering, or confounded and dissipated by destructive fathering. The absence of a model of involved fathering makes a young boy's acquisition of fathering skills less likely, although, as we've seen, support and encouragement from single mothers can sponsor their growth in their sons.

Now, thanks to societal changes, the excuses for not attending to the fatherneed are fading. Not only are we beginning to resort less to mother-blaming stereotypes, but the more we deconstruct the father-as-bumbler stereotype, the more clearly we see how children interact with fathers to bring out their best over time.

Men can do a lot to help their own cause*—in terms of their attitude and behavior, their relationship with their children, their relationship with their children's mother, their work, their involvement with the community. Shakespeare inspires us with *Macbeth*'s words:

> *I dare do all that becomes a man;*
> *Who dares do more is none.*

All that becomes a man (double-meaning again intended):

IN YOURSELF

- Embrace the irreplaceable value of your fatherhood in your life as a man.
- Think long, hard, and often about what you want to give your children besides your money.
- Acknowledge fatherhood as one of the longest, most creative, and rewarding adventures of your inner life.
- Leave room for failure and forgiveness in yourself (and, of course, others). There is no perfect father—yours wasn't and neither are you.
- Responsibly communicate to abusive or neglecting fathers your concerns about their kids and them.

---

*Although all these ideas can be shared between mothers and fathers, I've chosen to address fathers directly in this chapter, because the workload is largely theirs. Mothers remain critical allies, so their understanding of what you are up to will make your job easier and a lot more fun.

- Look hard at your father in you. He's there. Understand what you are doing with your father's parenting style in the raising of your own child—modeling, overcoming, repairing, emulating?—or a quilt of all these.
- Ask yourself, How do I want the mother of my child to think and feel about me as a father?
- Talk every day with someone outside your family, especially other men, about your fathering. It's called witness.
- Examine your own prejudices regarding men's and women's work.

WITH YOUR CHILDREN

- Your affection is the irreplaceable communication of your child's unique value to you.
- Listen to your child's view of the world, and *share* the last word occasionally.
- Your skills and passions outside work are fascinating to your kids. Share these with them. You are as unique as they are.
- Discipline means to teach, not punish. So forget intimidation and threats, both physical and emotional. They teach your child to fear and avoid, not respect and emulate, you.
- When with your child, be actively attentive and emotionally present. Quality time is a myth. Your children are raised in ordinary time, and being there—being with your kids—gives you the authority you need to do a good job. Fathering takes more than weekends.
- Live the values and habits you'd be thrilled to see in your children. They remember better than you.
- Time alone together is critical at all ages—read when they're little, drive when they're older.
- Know your kids' world, their friends, their doctor. Meet their teachers early and often, and speak up to resist sidelining yourself. Volunteer in the classroom; you'll learn volumes.

WITH YOUR CHILDREN'S MOTHER

- Parenting is an equal partnership emotionally, if not always mathematically, within and outside marriage.

- Engage in discussions with your children's mother about shared authority and power between men and women.
- Ask yourself, how can my relationship with their mother be a positive resource in my kids' life? Start always with what you respect.
- Keep up on your parenting skills together. Share articles or books discussing appropriate expectations for your children at relevant ages.
- When married, carefully maintain your relationship with your kids' mother: date her, snuggle with her, ritualize times to be together. A short talk is better than no talk when you're exhausted.

IN YOUR WORK

- Discourage negative stereotypes of fathers wherever you find them—at the watercooler, in meetings, in policy statements, etc.
- Support family leave for men and women, pitch in to cover, confront the naysayers.
- Bring your children to work. Show them your space. Introduce them to your colleagues. Talk to them about what you do.
- Invite your children to know this side of your world outside home. Ask them what they see and think. Seek their advice occasionally for some eye-opening wisdom.

Now go back and read this list again, and let me know what I've left out. Although gatekeeping by mothers is a significant problem in fulfilling fatherneed, a father's self-hobbling is just as problematic. Becoming a father is less physically frightening than giving birth, but as a threat to a man's status quo, it's without equal. As children, we tend to see our father as someone without much fear on board. But *becoming* a father is very frightening for most of us because of what we think we will lose in the process: freedom, exclusive rights to our partner's love and body, peace and comfort. We expect to be swamped by perpetual anxiety about the child's well-being and to have whatever sense of control and competence we do feel sacrificed to the ego-eroding uncertainties of new parenthood. All this is scary stuff. But it is no excuse for not being prepared and not seeking support and help, for pretending to know everything, or for withdrawing because "I don't do babies." Just do it. "Do it with me," says your baby; he or she doesn't have a choice either.

So here are a few ideas about how to help fathers "do it," beginning with boys, those future fathers. We know that any effort to sustain a boy's rich, nurturing emotional life will probably be a big help to his life as a father, so we need to begin early to help our boys remain emotionally, and not just physically, intact. Because mothering is a more protected system than is fathering, in most societies it is less malleable by social circumstances. But fathering needs help to come to full fruition, and precisely because it *is* more malleable by social circumstances, modeling and teaching can have a bigger impact. And the earlier they occur, the better.

FULFILLING FATHERNEED IN THE EARLY YEARS

The emotional vocabulary we use with boys must invite them, from their earliest years, to be more aware of their inner world: "I could see how angry your coach made you by not playing you. What do you think we should do?" Linking legitimate emotion with an instrumental problem-solving approach is affirming and active. The failure to make this link leaves men so lonely as adults that fathering is often the first time in decades that they feel moved to joy, tears, ecstasy, whatever. We fathers must help our boys remain emotionally alive. We must show them how to sustain friendships and manage competitive feelings; we must let them hear us talk about and see for themselves the warmth and love we have for our friends.

Compassion and empathy are often overlooked in the male world, though they are present and active in boys before school age. In older boys empathy is often lost and courage gets redefined and twisted into dragon slaying, leaving a boy's potential for good fathering headed out to sea on the wrong boat. The violence of sports, on and off the field, and the lessons in sacrificing one's own and the other guy's body are emotionally perverse; they substitute homophobic hypermasculine intimidation for courage. Their violence in TV programs, videos, games, films, and in rock and rap lyrics engages, excites, and overwhelms many boys, especially the ones who already have trouble with impulse controls; without the help of adults and peers pulling on the other side, these boys embrace these expressions of violence in our culture, which foul and degrade their imaginations. Increasingly focused on children and teens, the entertainment media are now so dominated by this carefully managed ubiquitous swamp that boys, particularly, need a lot of help keeping their bearings. Real courage is a matter of character, not muscle mass, and boys need to hear and see this in their interactions with their fathers and other family members.

FULFILLING FATHERNEED IN THE SCHOOL YEARS

Next to home, the school is the institution that shapes our kids most. To fulfill its part, the school needs to ensure that boys feel okay about their learning style and that sons *and* daughters know that teachers value input from fathers as well as from mothers. The latter message must be in the artwork in the halls, the invitations to parents' night, the scheduling options for parent conferences, the choice of field trips, and the composition of the staff. These speak volumes to children and their parents.

The beginning of school is one of the most critical opportunities for father–child engagement and should be thought about carefully. First of all, recognize that boys typically have it harder in kindergarten and first grade in most American schools, especially the overcrowded ones, than do girls. Their predisposition toward activity, which is their way of solving problems and expressing their passions and enthusiasms, is often seen as a problem to a teacher of a large class. The social skills and adaptability of girls and their relative strengths in language and reading readiness make the beginning of school a less shaky time for them than for boys. An involved father is a great help here, affirming his son's competence and ability, supporting his sagging confidence, and stressing the importance of school mastery as a masculine pursuit.

We all need to help our (yes, *our*) schools think actively and regularly about making themselves father-friendly environments. Sadly, awareness of the importance of including fathers doesn't come naturally to every administrator who runs an elementary school. But once administrators understand that schools with involved fathers are better schools, as we've learned over and over again in projects from Head Start to the Comer School Programs, and that it is a good thing for children to know that their school welcomes fathers as enthusiastically as mothers, then progress can at least start.

We can help school administrators begin with the bedrock expectation that fathers will be involved, and we can insist that they ask for fathers' names and addresses at enrollment, that they send fathers announcements about school events, and that they ask them to help out by volunteering in and outside the classroom. We can suggest that administrators ask students' fathers what they might want to contribute to the classroom—perhaps by taking a male interest survey (the kids love these, and they stir up lots of conversation). Schools should make father–child interaction a given; they should make it obvious in the artwork in the halls and classrooms and in the Awards Day recognitions that men matter to children on more than Father's Day.

Next, fathers will have to take on the resistance of the largely female staff to father involvement. It is almost always there, and every teacher has a reason for it—even the men. Failure to welcome father involvement undermines the basic expectation that schools exist to serve the needs of children, not just teachers. Fathers should explore attitudes first and then put this issue on the top of the table, not under it. Think together about why men may not feel welcome in their child's school and whether or not it's a worthy goal to begin with. Over time, you'll identify enough issues so that the teachers' resistance will ease and the fathers will begin to sense that it's safer around the place and will start showing up. While you're at it, try to reduce the amount of gender stereotyping throughout the school. There's probably more of it than you think in the school curriculum and programming, and it harms girls and boys just as much as it does men and women. Male-involvement specialists, employees designated to monitor and promote male inclusion, sometimes fill the bill for keeping men and fathers engaged and welcome while promoting ongoing healthy discussion of the topic. Kids know when men are welcome and when they are not. When they are not, boys and girls both suffer, not to mention the fathers and the school itself, which loses all that talent, know-how, and support. Men vote, too.

A remarkable turnaround occurred at Arlington High School in Indianapolis when its beleaguered, creative principal Jacqueline Greenwood, teamed up with the husband of one of her teachers to found a group called Security Dads. The high school was covered in graffiti and plagued by vandalism, fights in the hallways and cafeteria, and gang politics and mentality. Together, father and principal set up a volunteer thirty-man rotation during the school day simply to have a helpful adult male presence in the hallways, library, cafeteria, and school yard. After some thoughtful training and support (combined with thirty donated T-shirts and hats airbrushed with the Security Dads logo), the volunteer security force was put into service, and life started to improve for everyone in Arlington High School the next week. Six months later the graffiti, gangs, and intimidation are gone and attendance and attitude are up. Dads, never underestimate yourselves.

But helping our schools become more father friendly is window dressing compared to using the power the school has to make competent and involved fathering itself a goal worthy of a man. Beginning in the fourth and fifth grades, discussions of parenting competence, values, and goals have been shown to profoundly affect the way fathering in particular is viewed by boys and girls. Remember our discussion of the particular malleability of fathering? Well, these later grade school years are a good time to hammer away at building parenting competence. This is hardly a new idea. Seventy-five years ago, the National Parent-Teacher Association passed a resolution that parenthood education start before high school. The dawn of pubescence got kids interested in more than sex seventy-five years ago, and it does even more so now; this is precisely the time to teach kids about the responsibilities and skills of parenting.

Education for Parenting, a Philadelphia-based initiative, has set a wonderful standard in this field. It uses thoughtful curricular approaches to involving boys, "fatherless" and otherwise, in exploring their childrearing interests and capacities. When the topic becomes a mandatory consideration for a given individual, his or her shame or embarrassment is less intense. And when the baby or toddler is brought monthly to class so that fellow students can document the little one's growth and progress, the boys are as riveted as the girls. Given half a chance, they are very interested in trying to overcome the message that "nurturing is girl stuff," a message they've heard frequently from their peers.

When this kind of parenting education is followed up in high school with more didactic instruction in child care and the avoidance of child abuse, the principles of good fathering and mothering take root in the imagination, at the very least. Teenage pregnancy rates drop in these programs, once students begin to fathom the daunting responsibility of sustaining another life before you've really started your own. The time is here for a national fatherhood and parenting curriculum. The research is sufficient, the policy ripe. For starters, pioneer fatherhood researcher and activist Jim Levine and expert practitioner Ed Pitt give us a good definition of the responsible father as one who

- Waits to make a baby until he's ready emotionally and financially to support his progeny
- Establishes paternity when he makes that baby
- Shares actively with the child's mother the continuing physical and emotional care of that child from pregnancy on
- Shares in the continuing financial support, with the mother, of their child, from pregnancy on

Parenting education in the schools would help terminate a scene like this: when his third grade teacher asked Sam to draw a picture of his family tree, starting with his mother and father, he got very still. He lowered his eyes, looked down at his desk, and softly said, "My tree's dead. I don't have a father." Not possible, Sam, and your teacher could help you understand that in the proper educational setting.

Boys need many opportunities for physical mastery and discharge, for hands-on learning by doing. They need some single-gender opportunities, just as do girls, to keep gender from being too dominant a factor in their performance. Comfortably masculine boys, given the chance to be who they are in school without shame or guilt, are good learners and citizens. The longer they stay that way, the more they'll have to offer their mates and children in due time.

Our children's first "schools"—their day-care and child care centers—struggle with very similar issues regarding father and male access, and much of the above discussion applies here, too. The earlier fathers find their way into the involved stage, the better it is for them, their child, and their family. The fathers gain more confidence and know their child better; as a consequence, they are less easily discouraged when the going gets tough. But because physical care is still a large proportion of the care given to children of this age, the prejudice runs strong against males as providers of that care, and their caregiving efforts are often viewed as incompetent or irrelevant.

Centers that make fathers welcome find, more often than not, that they are competent, involved, and willing to share their talents and time. The end result is that their kids are less frequently absent from the program and the fees get paid more regularly. Head Start and now Early Head Start have initiatives, supported by federal guidelines, to encourage father and male involvement. Since "father" means different things to different children in these programs, the programs, as James Levine has shown, need to reflect that diversity in their approach. Also, since a nonresidential father is not necessarily uninvolved (as we saw in Chapter 6), creative approaches are required to welcome such a father into these programs. Support in terms of parenting skills is almost always appreciated when provided, but it must be culturally competent.

FULFILLING FATHERNEED AFTER DIVORCE

Another institution reshaping fatherneed is divorce. Although we explored much of that domain in Chapter 5, one area needs revisiting in our present discussion—the issue of timing. Fatherneed is most threatened and the father–child relationship most easily undermined in the first year after divorce. The patterns of involvement are redrawn then, and lack of cooperation and destabilizing conflict at this juncture can erode any foundation for a positive father–child relationship. When the foundation continues to erode, it becomes easier to accept the loss, stop battering against these rocks, and simply accept being less significant or meaningful in each other's life. Therefore, any effort at sustaining, repairing, or fulfilling fatherneed needs to focus on the time period immediately after the divorce as being especially critical. Connecticut's innovative intervention research effort—The Collaborative Divorce Project, which is directed by my wife, psychologist Marsha Kline Pruett—aims to reduce the negative effects of divorce on young children by intervening in this critical time period with families, courts, and lawyers.

FULFILLING FATHERNEED IN THE WORKPLACE

Beyond the home, fulfilling the fatherneed becomes a more complex task as we struggle to weave its demands through the warp and weft of other systems' values, obligations, and subcultures. Many of the values of the workplace—even if the workplace is a local or federal agency or is connected with the legal system or a religious body—compete with, if not erode, the father–child relationship.

As we might expect, the impact of job satisfaction on motherhood is strong indeed. So it is with fatherneed. In working-class families in particular, positive work experience supports self-esteem, which in turn predicts a more flexible, accepting parenting style with preteen kids.

Men who experience autonomy, clarity, innovation, support, peer cohesion, and involvement in their work feel higher self-esteem; this makes them more likely to accept their child's behavioral challenges and to use less punishment, manipulation, or guilt in their discipline.

Surprised that I started out with a positive example of the influence of the workplace on fatherhood? The reverse is certainly more the case in people's minds. It seems that work typically has a more worrisome effect on the fatherneed. Men who are unhappy at their work feel more stress and conflict, which affects their overall sense of well-being. This strain regularly finds its way into their fathering, causing irritability, pessimistic outlook, easy discouragement, and shaky self-regard as a man and consequently as a father (because fatherhood and manhood are so closely woven together in a man's mind).

Some men may feel reasonably sanguine about their work itself but still are in conflict about the role it plays in inhibiting or constraining their fathering. These dads feel stress and strain in fatherneed as well. Such strain affects their work efficiency, attendance, general health, job stability, and overall sense of vulnerability. To be known at work as a man who is a father is not a universally positive achievement (any more than it is for a woman to be known as a mother). A very significant survey in 1997, the Family and Work Institute's National Study of the Changing Workforce, found no significant differences in work–family conflict in dual-earner families between mothers and fathers. But there is serious catch-up to be played in this field by men. The suggestions in the following paragraphs target the workplace's weaknesses in supporting working fathers. Some innovative and parent-friendly companies are models, enjoying growing loyalty from their workforce and plummeting absenteeism; others are draconian in their rigidity and consequently have rapid turnover of employees who feel little satisfaction and loyalty. They are elaborations of the work of my friend Jim Levine, a continuing leader in the father-work-family field.

Existing family-friendly policies should undergo a father interest assessment by management and interested workers because business, like science, doesn't always mean "father" when it uses the word *family*. Once this evaluation is done, a task force can assess workers' family needs, communicate policies, encourage staff development, sensitize management and supervisors, and suggest the expansion of options for work time and place. Today, flextime and flexsite options (such as telecommuting) that pass muster as part of a larger strategic business

plan and not merely as do-gooding are more widely accepted and efficient. These are businesses, after all, not social welfare institutions. Job
sharing and compressed workweek options that also meet appropriate
business criteria can be a godsend to a family balancing critical parenting time. Relocation assistance that addresses father's and mother's
needs, sometimes found in large multisite corporations, is very supportive of continuity in family life. Finance seminars that address college
planning can be hidden support groups for fathers in particular. Cover-
age for absences due to breast-feeding, parent–teacher conferences, a
sick child, or a sick spouse should be planned. Even children-at-work
policies that consider the father's need to take off for snow days, emergencies, vacations, and doctor's appointments would be part of an ideal
company's approach.

Child care opportunities are high-visibility perks these days. When
a day-care center is well run and developmentally appropriate for the
children, it can enhance work satisfaction among the fathers and mothers who make use of it. On-site or near-site *quality* care, or backup care,
referral assistance for good child care off-site, or start-up assistance with
outside child care centers all offer real and substantial support to mothers and fathers. Put fathers on oversight boards because they need and see
different things in their child–work connections. Develop flexible benefit packages that support direct reimbursement of dependent-care costs.

Human resource support of families through parenting programs,
stress-reduction programs, and parent support groups (for both firsttime
and experienced parents) make for a supportive environment. Male focus groups run periodically can keep a business well informed about the
strengths or weaknesses in its father friendliness and avoid paternalism.

PATERNITY LEAVE

Unpaid parental leave is, of course, federally mandated for companies with fifty or more employees, thanks to the 1993 Family and Medical Leave Act. At least get on the table the idea of paid leave for mothers
and fathers.

Taking the time allotted to you at the birth of your child is one of
the best decisions you'll ever make. Remember the attachment and
bonding research that showed this to be the most sensitive time you may
ever have with your child? Make hay while this sun shines. But many of
us worry that the very mention of the phrase *paternity leave* will sour us

in the boss's eyes. So many of us simply cobble together sick days and vacation time (and whatever other time is coming to us) in place of a bona fide paternity leave, since we believe in our heart of hearts that our boss, supervisor, or coworkers will nail us for this some day. Do we want our son and our daughter's husband to have a real choice someday, or should they keep on sneaking around with some kind of informal parental leave? It's still hard to get men to help each other out here on this topic. The Associated Press carried a story on February 5, 1999, of Kevin Kussman, a state trooper from Maryland who finally won a four-year fight against his department for denying him parental leave. He won $375,000 from the jury in the first discrimination case under the 1993 Family and Medical Leave Act—and only two congratulatory phone calls from his male colleagues.

We also know that pay loss plays a big role here. Janet Hyde's research told us that 73 percent of men would take three months or more off if their paternal leave were paid leave. But until paternity leave, paid or not, is more universally applied, we won't know how it really works: Is it economically or fiscally irresponsible in the long run? Is the reluctance of business to grant it to its employees just another form of cultural gatekeeping? Are men themselves reluctant to use it because they are pretty anxious about what babies do to them and their lives?

In the meantime, we do know that paternity does not negatively affect "productivity, profitability, or growth," according to the Commission on Family and Medical Leave. The same research found some interesting trends in reduced turnover and increased advancement with paternity. I advise every expectant father to plan ahead from the beginning of the pregnancy: go public and expect to worry some about your career path. And don't expect to get a lot of sleep once the baby arrives (this is not respite care, it's *that* time of your life, and it will not pass quite this way ever again).

How do we get these father-friendly changes in the workplace started? Begin with an all-employee survey and publish the results. It's the best way to get people to ante up, especially when the questions separately address father and mother needs. It's also a good way to keep from mythologizing or romanticizing fathering or mothering. What mothers and fathers need from their workplace with regard to their lives as parents matters deeply to them, and they share much more than they think. Noting both their similarities and differences allows the workplace to develop parent-supporting benefits that are strategically sound.

FATHERS' AND CHILDREN'S HEALTH

The father's health itself influences his baby long before they even meet. Genetic vulnerabilities may pass to his child through a father's chromosomal share in conception, but beyond these are the father's health-related behaviors and vulnerabilities, which can have substantial impact on the baby's and the mother's well-being.

A history of depression needs to be taken seriously because post-natal depression is a problem for men as well as women. Although little has been written on the subject, experts such as Sandra Ferketich show us that inexperienced fathers may be at somewhat higher risk. Depression in the father at such a time has been shown by psychiatrists Arieas and Kumar in Great Britain to draw a vulnerable mother into a depression herself. With depression in one parent aggravating the condition in the other, early attachment energies that should be devoted to the infant by both parents can be weakened, indicating that early intervention for both parents is a must. Health practitioners and family members need to be vigilant for signs of paternal as well as maternal depression, such as changes in sleep, eating, or drinking patterns, unexplained aches and pains, and deterioration in mood or increased irritability. Right now, I doubt that more than 2 percent of all nurses, midwives, or obstetricians even ask about an expectant father's health in general, much less the history of depression in the father prenatally. Heck, I had to reintroduce myself at every prenatal visit Marsha and I made before Olivia's birth just to get eye contact from the health care provider!

Much is appropriately made of the mother's health habits during pregnancy, but the father's exposure to and use of alcohol, tobacco, illegal substances, certain prescription drugs, and environmental hazards can also harm the fetus, as well as the couple's very ability to conceive. A man's exposure to toxic substances slightly before or around conception and his smoking throughout the pregnancy have been associated with miscarriage, birth defects, and low birth weight. They also raise the child's risk for certain childhood cancers and for learning problems.

Worrisome as these associations are, their statistical likelihood is probably not as strong as the probability that a man's behavior will affect his pregnant partner. The father-to-be can ameliorate or exacerbate the nutritional and emotional challenges of pregnancy. So the advice is obvious: be patient with your partner's discomfort and mood changes, support and practice good nutrition and health habits with her, and participate in her prenatal care. Go to the prenatal exams with her and get your questions answered, too. Do the birth classes (she doesn't know it all either, so why should you?). Plan paternity leave early, think together about how you will make room in your marriage, your living quarters, your wallet, your bed, and your heart for this baby—she or he comes out of you, too.

Beyond the father's workplace are other institutions either whittling away or trying to support the father–child axis. Health care organizations are among the more complex, as they seem determined to do both simultaneously.

In today's health care industry, with its concern for profit taking and downsizing and its maniacal devotion to reducing office visit time, there is plenty of room for improved father friendliness. Just ask any father of a moderately sick child how included he feels in the child's care. Look for health care providers who understand that the father as well as the mother needs to be involved, consulted, and included in the therapeutic plans and decisions. Audit everything from preadmission to discharge follow-up procedures and personal practices at hospitals. Outside of hospital care, ask office managers to review outpatient record keeping, office hours, cover pages with parent contact information, callback practices, and waiting room artwork and reading materials. Ask yourself, Would any self-respecting father choose to come here with his sick child? Those who provide health care to children should never assume that men don't want to be involved. That is a decision that should be the father's alone, not anyone else's, to make. It often looks as if fathers have waived that right, because so many men are uncertain as to how to involve themselves in the child health care system, especially when they are unwelcome there to begin with.

FATHERNEED AND JUSTICE

And then there is the law. Although it touches us all, this institution typically ignores fatherneed until something happens in the child's life that society feels is sufficient to warrant an invitation to the state to enter the nurturing domain in the role of protecting "the best interests of the child." In theory, that's not a bad idea; in practice, the law's intrusion can be terrifying to anyone and everyone near the child. Although we touched on the reach of the law in Chapter 5, we need to further discuss the reach of governmental law into fatherneed of poor, unmarried families. In 1996 the Personal Responsibility and Work Opportunities Reconciliation Act (PRWORA), originally known informally as the workfare reform bill, was passed. It affects fatherneed in such families more than any other piece of federal legislation ever had before.

This is good news or bad news, depending on how your particular state law interfaces with the bill. In a nutshell, the federal government has set the goal of establishing the paternity of 90 percent of all children born outside of marriage. State agencies are motivated by various financial incentives to reach this goal. States, however, must not permit a man's name to be entered on a child's birth certificate until he has voluntarily acknowledged paternity or until there has been a legal determination of same. In the vast majority of circumstances, paternity establishment serves everyone well—child, father, and mother. The man is subsequently the legal father of his child, with all the responsibilities and rights of any father, married or not. He can raise issues of custody and visitation, and he can participate actively in health, schooling, and residency decisions affecting his child. He is expected to supply child support and health care insurance, all the things children have the right to expect from their father.

The law does not permit the father to stop child support if the mother interferes with his visitation rights, any more than any law does. If the father loses his job, he can apply for reduction if he does so in a timely manner. Still, many never-married fathers feel that paternity establishment is the trapdoor for child support enforcement. The reason? Many local and federal policymakers inaccurately view child support enforcement as the vital link to lifting many of these children out of poverty. They feel pressured by the threats to their block grants (their equivalent of child support), and so they pass on the authoritarian punitive attitude down the line to coerce their clients. Mothers, too, feel the squeeze: they stand to lose 25 percent of their benefits if they refuse to cooperate in identifying the father of the child.

Lift out of poverty? The numbers simply do not add up. A third of the nation's noncustodial dads are so poor they qualify for food stamps. Over a third are under thirty-four, and 43 percent didn't finish high school; 45 percent are white and 37 percent are black. Most have no access to job training or employment services. The 30 percent who do have jobs, low paying that they are, already pay child support most of the time, so this system's attempt at reform is going nowhere without a lot of support and help. Clearly, child support agencies will have to facilitate or directly provide social services like family counseling and employment to both parents if anything besides further resentment is going to come out of these enforcement programs.

Woven through these programs must be a recognition that many unwed fathers have experienced the same agonies, loss, and uncertainties as unwed mothers and that they have the same risk factors. Helping them become parents to their kids might be easier if we came at it from this direction, rather than from the courthouse. How on earth could that ever happen? you may well ask. Jeffrey Johnson, president of the National Center for Strategic Nonprofit Planning and Community Leadership, has proposed a creative partnership between community-based organizations and child support enforcement officials that would have them deal with each other in nontraditional ways in an effort to find solutions that fulfill fatherneed for these families in a way that helps them stop reproducing their agonies generation after generation. This partnership needs our strong endorsement. Here are Johnson's main points:

1. Service and enforcement agencies need to work together, ditch their old suspicions, tell each other what they are really up to, and figure out how to team up.
2. Enforcement agencies should subcontract paternity establishment to service organizations, helping to stabilize them financially.
3. Enforcement agencies must demonstrate the capacity to modify child support orders in line with the real world of these often young, undereducated, hard-to-employ fathers.
4. Service agencies must teach responsible social and parenting skills to help these men become involved in their child's life; partner with the child's mother, where appropriate; and accept legal and financial responsibility for their child.
5. Enforcement agencies need to assure service agencies that they will not undermine a couple's partnership goals by categorically demanding full, immediate arrearage on job termination or by immediately garnisheeing wages from a father's brand-new job. Each father must be worked with on a case-by-case basis.
6. Service organizations need to focus on their most fragile families.

7. Employment training networks must be developed and supported by service and enforcement agencies working together.

When not being intimidated by the punishment system, unwed fathers repeatedly affirm that access to education, training opportunities, job placement help, parenting classes, and assistance in dealing with child enforcement officials would make them strongly in favor of paternity establishment.

PATERNAL CHILD ABUSE

Another gaping hole that affects us all is the lack of understanding of paternal child abuse. Kathleen Sternberg has summarized the research in this area as characterized by a "conspicuous absence of information from and about fathers in violent families" and calls fathers the "missing parent" in research on family violence. The problems are significant, to be sure, given the need to protect women and children once violence tears at the family. But most of our information comes from frightened and angry women as the only informants about the father–child relationship. This area is so highly charged that it is hard to reliably establish even the rates of abuse in America or to distinguish between abuse perpetrated by men and abuse perpetrated by women. A respected study by the American Humane Society of reports from eleven states identified fathers as abusing more frequently but committing more minor acts of abuse; mothers, on the other hand, tend to engage in more serious, even life-threatening, acts of abuse. Our research into predicting abuse is still hobbled by small sample size in our studies and by our inability to use what we do know in more appropriate ways. We learn daily that leaving fathers out of our research, or including them only as mute perpetrators, erodes confidence in our findings, to say the least, and leads us down blind alleys when we design prevention or intervention programs that attempt to involve men but later prove to be ineffective. According to Sternberg, some of those in the vanguard in this area of research report that men are willing to describe and discuss the nonviolent and violent aspects of their interactions with their children in the context of an attempt to understand their lives, beliefs, and vulnerabilities.

SUMMARY

We've discussed myriad ways to fulfill fatherneed in all manner of settings and stages of development. Lest we get confused, I summarize here what I feel we've learned from research in this field that is true of fatherneed in any setting or stage. We've learned about

- the long-lasting benefits of the paternal presence in the lives of children
- the unique qualities of father care
- the different needs a child has for a father at different stages, especially in early childhood
- the pervasively negative effect of a father's unemployment or underemployment
- the institutional and systemic barriers that constrict father development
- the influences across generations that shape father behavior and attitude, negatively and positively
- the enduring need for support from the extended family, from the community, and from the partner to co-parent effectively.
- the importance of using especially sensitive periods and critical transitions in the life of the father and his child—the child's birth and first days at school, divorce, illness—to make course corrections in fatherneed

George Eliot's *Silas Marner* traveled a tortuous road to fulfill his fatherneed. Shunned by his birth community, he drifted to strange places, relinquishing his dour isolationism only to market his cloth. He hoarded his accumulating wealth, but Eliot ultimately strips him of his gold, leaving him only with a "golden-haired infant":

> In the old days, there were angels who came and took men by the hand and led them away from the tide of destruction. We see no white-winged angels now. But yet men are led away from threatening destruction: a hand is put into theirs, which leads them gently towards a calm and bright land so that they look no more backward; and that hand may be a little child's.

10

The Kids Get the Last Word

Iᴛ's ᴀ ʀᴇᴠᴏʟᴜᴛɪᴏɴᴀʀʏ ǫᴜᴇsᴛɪᴏɴ, really: What do children think about their fathers, who they actually are and what they do together? We've spent tens of thousands of words so far in this book on what adults think of these matters, leaving the questionable impression that grown-ups' perceptions somehow matter more. They don't. Consequently, I've chosen the honored place of the last act, the last chapter, to present the children's words, because they are more straightforward and far more effective.

The way a father is thought about by his child is determined less by their frequency of contact or even by their cultural or ethnic background and more by the child's age, gender, and experience, by the mother's attitudes and behavior, and by what the child has been permitted to say and to whom it is being said.

My wife and I were on Amtrak between Portland and Seattle last spring, giving our three-month-old her first train ride. To settle Liv (and me) down a bit, I took her on a brief walk, which eventually led us to the café car. There I found a little girl of four or five who, from behind a cascade of curls, was looking with great intensity at me carrying my daughter. A woman seated at the same table, whose relationship to the little girl was not obvious to me, seemed uninterested in the girl's curiosity about me and my daughter.

The alert little girl stopped me in my tracks with her penetrating gaze and said, "That man has a baby. Who are you?" It seemed almost rhetorical the way she asked it, but, never one to pass up a chance to talk with anyone about my children, I replied, "This is my little girl, Olivia, and I'm her father."

The little girl's face went strangely quiet, then slid into a pout. She slumped back into her seat and, barely audibly, said, "I wish I had a father." Her companion said to her with the twang of reprimand, "Now, Sally, you *know* we've talked about this; you don't *have* a father. This man is *his* little girl's father, but you don't have one." The little girl looked back at me with a searing sadness I can still recall, her pain palpable. Her face also betrayed a hint of incredulity, revealing that she knew this was an unacceptable answer.

Sally's intense but forbidden curiosity reminded me of another story regarding children's hunger to know about fathers—all fathers and not simply their own—a hunger that solicits versions of fatherhood that tax the imagination but are becoming increasingly common in this era of assisted reproductive technology. A patient of one of the early leaders in the field of *in vitro* fertilization came to consult me about her concern regarding what to say to her very verbal five-year-old daughter about "who or what" had fathered her. The child had recently begun to press the mother more forcefully for answers to these questions about the whereabouts of her father: "Mommy, what did you do with my daddy?" "Did you get mad at him and make him go away? Didn't you like him? Didn't he like me?" "Does he have other children?" "Where can I find him?" "Could we ever get married?" "Can I write him a letter?" "Has he ever seen me?" "Do you have a picture of him with me?"

The mother's inability to answer such questions in any useful way had become increasingly upsetting to them both. In her attempt to find better answers, she came to speak with me. Not that she hadn't sought advice previously. The gynecologist who had treated her for her infertility, successfully implanting a fertilized ovum in her uterus, had given her a very clear suggestion when she asked him what she should say to her child once the child began to ask about the whereabouts of her father. This was his advice: "Tell her that she does not have one. You loved her so much you made her all by yourself."

The woman remembered feeling strangely anxious at the time, but her gynecologist was a hero in her eyes and she had found it hard to question his advice and its seductive bell-like clarity. Now, after five years of parenthood, its ring was ridiculously hollow. She reflected back on the moment, recalling that this man had four children of his own. "How could he get so far into parenthood and know so little about children?" she asked rhetorically.

These stories are introductions to our spending some time with children's incredibly active imaginations and thoughts about what their father is to them, even in circumstances of fathering that are not mysterious or high-tech. These thoughts are illustrative of the potentially huge discrepancy between the adult's and the child's concept of a father's place in a child's life. Having opened your eyes to such discrepancies with these somewhat extreme examples, I would like to introduce you to children's thoughts, organized by their developmental age, and I encourage you to listen carefully.

I begin with what children say when they first begin talk that relates to their understanding of the role fathers play in bringing them into being.

I was chatting with an acquaintance as we stood in line at the post office in Guilford. Her four-year-old daughter was clinging to her skirt and playing ring-around-the-rosy around her legs. Finally tired of being ignored by the adults, she stopped her play, squarely took the space between her mother and me, and asked, "Are you my daddy?" I had known that this woman had chosen to have a child alone after two failed pregnancies and a subsequent divorce and that this child was the result of a pregnancy with a man with whom she had not planned to have a long-term relationship. The couple had agreed that he would leave her and the child and not contact them again. The mother felt that the child was doing reasonably well despite—and, in her own opinion, possibly because of—the father's absence.

But this out-of-the-blue interrogation of me was a striking example of the child's urgent need to seek her father in any man who was even casually in her mother's life. Fatherneed in the raw. To what was she responding? Was it the friendliness in the tone of the conversation I was having with her mother? What made her think that this would even be an all right question to ask or that I was a reasonable candidate? Our best understanding is that the need for a father is so powerful to such children that it is never far from their consciousness.

Stacy, one of four-year-old twins born to a single mother by donor insemination, asked her mother very matter-of-factly after returning home from a birthday party hosted by a friend's mother and father,

"Mommy, what did you do with my daddy? You *know* I need a daddy or I can't *be* a child."

For the very young child, the single most powerful attribute of the father is the nature of the relationship between them. Research by psychologist Judith Solomon tells us that a young child's understanding of who the parents are is related more to the nature of the relationship between them than to the child's idea of biological connectedness or procreation. She points out that it is not until the age of seven that children understand birth as a part of a process that selectively passes on physical traits from parent to child. Before that, they understand only that it is nurturance, the way a man is with his child, that mediates paternity and the passing on of beliefs and values. Out of the mouths of babes . . .

As for what preschool children feel and have to say about what a father means in their life, I have several experts from a day-care center where I regularly consult. Here is Janine, five years two months, talking about her father on Father's Day: "My dad takes me to parks and zoos with my dog and sister. He means lots of things to me. He likes to sing me stories and is top man in my life. He's like almost better to me than God."

Six-year-old Brook lost her father when she was four and a half in an automobile accident. On what would have been her father's birthday, she told her teacher, "My dad was the big person that made me happier than anybody else. I still love him because of all the things that he did for me I didn't ask for. He was funny and he was cool. His friends liked me and I liked them. He had silly little names for me. I wish everyone would call me those names because it makes me feel close to him. I am lucky I had a great dad, but not that I lived longer than him."

Young children who have lost the day-to-day contact with their father through divorce have poignant comments regarding this kind of father loss in their life. In a recent joint research project, the Culture of Litigation, directed by my wife, Marsha Kline Pruett, we asked children under the age of six to tell us what happened to their relationship with their father as a result of divorce. I could barely write down their answers fast enough. Said Sam, four and a half, "Once they got lawyers, they stopped being friends, just like that! It hurts my heart not to have him tuck me in at night . . . but he sings more and doesn't yell the way he used to." Chris, five years and two months old, chose to talk about what happened to his mom and dad's friendship and how it affected him: "I came from the time when they liked each other and it's gone now . . . they don't kiss anymore and I can't believe either one . . . now they hate each other all the time and my family is dead."

When asked what the divorce had done to his relationship with his father, Ben, age six, replied, "I'm mad at my dad *and* my mom. Divorce is when your mom and dad can't stop pushing each other around and they kill your family." Erin, five years old, said she thinks her dad is "happy now," adding, "He sings more. He likes being a dad now." Erin is describing a kind of low-conflict situation in which the father is elevated in the eyes of his children after the divorce and is perceived as more giving and more emotionally connected and available to them. But Erin worried about the relationship between her parents as though it were a vital component of her ongoing relationship with her father (right on! See Chapter 7): "I don't think mommy and daddy are friends anymore. I'm pretty sure they're not. Do you know?"

The last two quotes to be presented in this section are only marginally connected to this topic, but they are so compelling that I wanted you to hear them. First, from Tomas, the oldest child (six years eight months) in the study on what judges and lawyers need to know about how kids understand divorce: "Lawyers and courts don't always work out. If the judge lets Mom win, it hurts Dad's feelings and I get sad. I'd never want to be a judge. It's like being a fake parent—pretending to do the right thing for kids, but they're not yours and you don't love them. It's so weird."

And, finally, from the study's sage, Alan, aged six and a half: "'Fair' deciding doesn't mean it feels all right. If a person lies, the judge should give more to the person that didn't lie. Be careful and listen. Just because a person makes sense, or is more polite, doesn't mean they're telling the truth, or that they are a good parent. Mom and Dad both tell some lies, but it's because they want us more. Lawyers should *always* tell the truth *all* the time and not try to fool people just to win. The kids know what's happening and they can't forget."

What you hear in these comments is children's hunger for an abiding paternal presence in their life, supported to some extent by their mother, even though they don't talk about it very often (frequently because of concern about their mother's feelings). It's as though the children already know that an absent or noninvolved father is growing a hole in the center of their life.

Once children are in school, they are farther down the road of socialization, having learned in their contacts with other families and other children how their father does or does not stack up to other fathers. They by now have also come to understand his idiosyncracies, strengths, and weaknesses—what makes him uniquely *their* father. In their comments about their fathers you hear what makes fathering distinct to them from mothering and what they particularly appreciate about the paternal presence. In a class discussion on Father's Day, Damion, a third grader, talked about his dad as a "big teaser who likes to make us laugh. Sometimes he makes Mom a little mad, because he teases so much it makes me or my sister laugh till we pee." Graphic.

Dawn, a participant in the same discussion, said that without her dad in her life she would "feel like a kite waiting for wind that never comes." Deward, in the same discussion group, talked about what it's like when his father has to be away for a month at a time as a salesman for his computer company: "I don't see him very much, and I almost forget what he's like. But when he comes home, I get so excited my mother is always telling me to calm down. He's such a hard worker, sometimes I wish I had my dad instead of his money."

Sandra, a child who was visiting the class for the day, also wanted to be heard. She gave this account of her dad:

> My sister—she's fifteen—she doesn't like my dad much right now because he's always telling her no—that she can't go to parties, that she can't have too many boyfriends, that she can't scream at my mother. But I love him so much and feel sorry he has to spend so much time being mean. He doesn't like being mean, he likes being kind and generous. He makes sure that the leftover food we have at Christmas and Thanksgiving and other big eating days goes to people who don't have enough to eat. I like going with him to give the food to the homeless people. When I grow up, I want to act just like my dad, even though I'm a girl. He's so big—actually he's a little fat—but I love to feel his arms around me. He protects me.

Joanna is eleven, her father is sixty, and she is the last of his three children. Her older half siblings are in their thirties. Joanna adores and appreciates her father and has great respect for him, but she worries frequently about his health and well-being:

> I get tired of everybody asking if he's my grandfather, but I suppose that's because he does look more like a granddad. To me he's been my lifeline. My mother loves me, but she works too hard to make me into something she wanted to be herself. My dad just takes me

right where I am—good, bad or in between. He's quirky and cute, strong and smart, but so conservative I don't dare have my friends around him for too long. Older dads are different. They're warm and sweet and wise *and* they're around! My friend's fathers are funny, hyperactive, and gone.

A common theme in schoolchildren's descriptions of their father is the emphasis on the father's skills and how he shares them with them. Fathers are often described as "good at math," "a great fisherman," or "a great sportsman." In one children's discussion group I ran at the conclusion of my Lifetime television program, *Your Child Six to Twelve with Dr. Kyle Pruett,* there was considerable discussion about the father's role in helping children learn the difference between right and wrong. Samantha, twelve, said:

My dad is strict but he's very fair. My mom is softer but she changes her mind a lot and sometimes isn't very fair. My dad teaches me what the difference is between right and wrong and makes me say I'm sorry when I do wrong or bad things. When he gets mad at me and punishes me, I feel his loving me at the same time he's trying to make me grow up into a better person.

Ariel joined in the conversation by saying, "I trust my dad a lot because he's fair. He doesn't try to make me feel guilty. He only wants me to behave so I can get along better in the world." Samantha joined in again and said of her father, "The way he teaches me right and wrong makes me feel secure."

There was considerable emphasis in this discussion group on the father's interest in fun and play. Rocky, a fifth grader, said this about his dad:

He takes my family on neat vacations and we have lots of fun. He's different when he's not working. He's more patient, he takes more time teaching me things, and he seems like my "old shoes dad." He wants me to try new things when we're on vacation, and he helps me stay confident even when those things are hard for me to do for the first time.

In a family therapy session with a three-generation family struggling to cope with the death of the matriarch, the younger children in the family wanted to talk about their father. When I asked if they felt things were going to be all right with their grandmother gone and their need to now depend more on their mother and father, they corrected me that he was their *step*father, not their "real father." Nine-year-old Anna said, "But I don't know what a real father is supposed to be. Daddy taught us how to respect each other and that you can love a lot of people all at the same time and that the way you behave doesn't affect the way you get loved. You get loved just because you belong to each other. That's the realest you can get for a dad, I think."

The absence of a father at this age can be exquisitely painful. A young boy in the educational video *Show Your Love,* prepared by Sam Kaufman of Boston University for Vice President Gore's Nashville Family Reunion III, which examined the role of men in the lives of America's children, said loud and clear that he wished that his dad were still in his life:

> If my dad was still around, I wouldn't do so much dumb stuff. I'm pretty sure I'd be a good student, and that I'd have friends that were better for me. When I turn into a dad, I'm going to be different from my dad. I'll stay home and do some dishes and change their clothes and their diapers and stuff, because I want them to love me the way I love my Mom. Don't get me wrong. I've got a grandfather I love tons. He teaches a lot about what it's like to be a man. But I think I would have listened to my dad even better than I listen to my grandpa.

He then looked down at the ground, on the edge of tears, his heart aching.

Adolescence is a very complicated time in the territory shared by teenager and parent. The struggles for separateness and autonomy are so powerful that it's hard to imagine that teenagers would have any warm or positive thoughts about either parent. Most parents of teenagers feel that their only tasks entail providing security, transportation, maintenance, and cash flow. And there is precious little appreciation even for those essential human services. A neighbor with both a daughter and a son in high school had a T-shirt made for himself with the simple inscription ATM MACHINE on the front and an image of a keypad on the back. He said he wore it only when he was in the company of other parents of adolescents, because it brought him and them such great pleasure. His own children were not amused.

This same man was deeply moved on his forty-fifth birthday, when his son, who struggled with him daily about the use of the car, access to the telephone, curfews, and so on, said to him, in front of assembled witnesses, "Dad, I hope you're not even halfway through your life yet so that we can have as much time together as possible. I love you and need you more than when I was a little boy, regardless of how I treat you and act in public."

A theme in many discussions with teenagers about fathers is the role of the father in helping the child get through difficult or bad times. Here is what Suzanne, who was part of an adolescent discussion group about fathers, had to say:

> I trust and respect the way my dad sets limits with me better than Mom. Mom just yells, but Dad means it. With him, it's over fast, and I know there are no hard feelings. With Mom, I have to walk around on eggshells for days, sometimes weeks. I don't think she means to be that way, but I see it with my friends' parents, too—dads and moms are just different when it comes to telling kids no.

Derek, a sixteen-year-old honor roll student raised the issue of the difference in longevity between men and women:

> I read this piece in the paper about some study that said that men don't live as long as women because they get too freaked out about jobs, loneliness, and isolation. They don't do enough looking after themselves or anybody else. So it seems to me a good idea for fathers to spend more time with their children, because it's healthier for them. We know it's healthier for us.*

Alejandro, in the discussion group with Suzanne and Derek, talked with conviction about how this father stuck with him through "good times and bad." Explained Alejandro, "He seems to know how hard it is to say no to your friends or your own instincts to have fun and get into trouble. I am dead sure that I would be on a different track if it weren't for my dad. Even though I don't talk to him a lot, I feel he's around, especially when I'm starting to think about getting into trouble."

*Derek was, in fact, probably referring to some of the work of John Allman of the California Institute of Technology. Allman has examined the connection between longevity and the sharing of parenting chores between adult male and female primates. Among primates that closely share the care of offspring, male and female life spans are more nearly the same.

Akisha was one of the two kids in this discussion group whose father did not live at home. She was very angry with her dad:

> Just when I'm getting to the age where I ought to know something about men, I don't have a clue what they're about or what they want, so I'm always getting into trouble and doing dumb things in my relationships with guys. My dad's around, don't get me wrong, and he gives me things and he tries to act like he really cares. He gives me nice material things, but he's never lived with me—I know he doesn't like my mother. He doesn't help me with my homework, has never been to one of my sports things—and I'm pretty good. I wonder why he *does* give me things. [*Pauses as though she's trying to figure it out*] Maybe that's all he can do is give me things. Maybe I'm too hard on him, I don't know, but I feel lonely for my dad.

Akisha articulated the pervasive sense of longing for a paternal presence that I hear from many teenagers. Some feel relieved that they only have one person telling them what to do, but the vast majority feel that their life would be richer, safer, saner, and more orderly if they had their father at home. Most of all, they complain about feeling very, very lonely without daily, or at least regular, fathering. Elizabeth, a tenth grader in this same discussion group, said, "I feel kind of lost without my dad. I'm doing okay in school and I have some friends, but I think I could be doing a lot better than okay and I'd have different friends if my dad were around. I hang out with too many losers right now."

Crystal entered the essay contest sponsored by the National Center for Fathering, the brainchild of Ken Canfield, the center's energetic founder and president. Her essay was published in a pamphlet called *What My Father Means to Me* and is presented in full here because of its power:

> I am 14 years old and my father left me when I learned to say "daddy." Even though my father's not around, in my heart he is always there. Every birthday and every Christmas I cross my fingers in hopes that my father will come home. Does my wish come true? No, but I never quit looking and hoping.
>
> What really hurts is walking through the mall and seeing little girls with their fathers walking hand in hand. I can see how much he loves his little girl, but I can't see my father loving me as his little girl. See, in my life, there's not "morning daddy" and me, it's just me and "morning."

I see my father a lot in my dreams but never does he turn around. I call for him, but he's just walking away. I'd like to believe he misses me, but how can he miss a stranger? Every time I blow the candles out on my birthday cake I wish the same wish that I have had for the past thirteen years. I wish that stranger would turn around and look at me. Maybe if he saw all the pain and suffering from living without him in my eyes, he would become a part of my life. For now all I can do is to wish and never give up hope, for hope is all I have, to hold on to.

Even though it's hard to say, my father means the world to me, and if I had the chance to tell him all of this, I would not change anything but I would add a couple of "I love you"s.

Erick, another witness in *Show Your Love*, is an articulate, handsome high school junior whose father deeply disappointed him by leaving the family (from his discussion it appears that his father left his mother for another woman). He describes his competitive feelings toward his dad and his anger and, most of all, his devastating disappointment in the choice his father made at a critical point in Erick's life. He felt deprived of his dad's strengths and gifts just as he was "getting ready to turn into myself." Consequently, he moved his loyalties, as well as his trust, to other men in his life.

When I have my own kids, I'm sure I'm going to be more of a pain in the ass to them than my father has been to me. But you have to be there to care. I have needed guidance and consistency in my life, and he's not been there to do it. I will be loyal and committed to my children and not let them down the way he has me. If my dad hadn't walked out on us, I think I'd be a better student, and work harder . . . I sound kind of pissed off, don't I?

In listening to Erick, we are made aware of the huge amount of energy, especially emotional energy, he is expending in dealing with his feelings for his father. This is a significant diversion of his considerable creative and social energies, and we ache to help him with his resentment and disappointment—and feel a strong urge to have a long talk with the father of this obviously able young man.

When another young woman in the aforementioned discussion group for adolescents describes her father's remarriage and new family, she struggles to be respectful and thoughtful of his new wife and life. But when asked what advice she would give fathers, she digs deeply into her soul for this answer: "You have to love your children. They're your own flesh and blood. So please show your love. It's all you really have to do." A single tear rolls down her cheek to join her trembling lower lip as she struggles for composure, giving away the secret of her aching heart.

As the senior consultant in this chapter, nineteen-year-old Stephanie told the following story:

> I have really changed my feelings about my dad a lot since I went off to college. I'm a sophomore now, and I have a boyfriend who really means everything to me. And if we do get married, I'm going to be very different with him than my mom has been with my dad. They've loved each other for a long time, but my mom had this really irritating habit of telling us not to tell our dad things that she didn't think he needed to know—like how much some clothes cost, or that a "last minute plan" had actually been worked out weeks ahead, or that we weren't to discuss "certain things" with Dad about our feelings or our lives because "men just don't understand" those things. "You're better off to just say yes, no, whatever, and go off and do what you want." She joked about how women stay strong by controlling information.
>
> It seemed simple and almost innocent at the time but now I feel kind of irritated by it, because my boyfriend and I feel like equals and I've become aware that my mom and dad don't at all. It's as though she thought it was more important to keep things running smoothly than to respect my dad as her partner or equal. But she wasn't really doing that. She was manipulating him and cutting me and my sister off from him. I resent that now. I know she came from another time, and she was probably better than her mother. I'm trying to talk to her about it, but she doesn't seem to get how important it is to me to do it differently.

I had a father who also "came from another time" and from whom I learned and needed many things. Luckily, it was a wonderful, loving collaboration that had intriguing twists and turns. My Oklahoma-born father, the youngest of six, was a Baptist minister, and some of my early memories are of sitting on the floor just beyond the living room of our home, where Dad often performed weddings for people who could not afford the church, and hearing my mother play the Hammond organ as Dad sang a tune or two for the newlyweds. I was intrigued by the complex leadership role Dad played in the religious community, hearing him struggle at home (respectfully, for the most part) with the personal and administrative burdens while being revered publicly. There were painful ironies that I would only understand later of his being challenged politically by the ungenerous, bigoted members of this Christian congregation to which he and my mother sacrificed so much over so many years.

I was likewise intrigued that he and my mother, both champion college tennis players, never taught us boys to play good tennis, instead encouraging us to take up swimming as a competitive sport. Occasionally, I resented Dad's not sharing this great skill with me. When I was fourteen and considered way too young by my mother to join the other members of our award-winning Gospel Quartet (namely, my older brother and two faster-living twin sisters) in a barely chaperoned two-week train and bus trip to Mexico, my father encouraged Mom to let me go, thus allowing the whole trip to go forward. (As it turned out, they were both right.)

I was moved then, as I am now, by my father's willingness to drive sixteen hours straight, from Indianapolis to New Haven, to attend my first voice recital at Yale so that I could feel his and Mom's presence and support; then, after coffee in the elegant master's house, they turned around and drove back through the night. Dad's startling and impassioned plea that my brothers and I not let our contact with alcohol get out of control, recalling the Skid Row death of his beloved brother, Chris, still scares me.

Once, as a fourteen-year-old, I got too lippy and disrespectful with my mother for Dad's taste. His looming presence, menacing and physically threatening, made the point more powerfully than any cleverly placed words about how out-of-bounds this kind of treatment was for the woman he loved and respected.

I was puzzled by Dad's devotion to the Masons and his cherished thirty-third degree. I was slightly embarrassed by his acceptance of what seemed to me to be charity in our reduced-fee family membership to the Meridian Hills Country Club (a common and appropriate custom for poorly paid clergy, as I would later learn). There we learned how to play golf, a vital social skill for upwardly mobile Hoosiers, and my brothers and I reigned for years as swimming champions for the club's otherwise lackluster swimming team.

I was proud of Dad's wonderful baritone voice, his oratorical style, and his command of language from the pulpit. I hated religious education in church school, feeling that all I really ever needed to learn about religion, the Bible, and what came to be known as "God," I preferred to learn by listening to my dad and his thoughtful, literate, doubting, deeply human faith. He and my mother weathered serious criticism from members of his church when they sent their older sons to that "Commie, Pinko, liberal fleshpot university in New Haven."

As a teenager I learned to occasionally deceive Dad, exploiting his essential sweetness, but I never felt particularly proud of these small-minded victories. I learned how to say difficult things to people by listening to his warm, humorous, and teasing way of telling people things they did not want to hear. He was a master of the wince-inducing corny joke, making him my hero of this art form up until about the age of eleven; after that, for the next six or seven years, this humor mortified me—until it taught me its dry-witted rural roots in my young adulthood.

As a young adolescent, I was embarrassed by Dad's easy affection and physical contact with me, something I rarely saw between other sons and fathers. I was glad to have it intact when as a young adult I returned to being comfortable with my own body and with intimacy.

He died too soon and too painfully seven years ago, leaving a hole in my life. As the only physician in the family for generations, I had slowly smoldered with anger and frustration that he did not take better care of his body or take his health more seriously. If he had, I keep telling myself in my physician's arrogance, he'd be here now, playing with Olivia on Mony Island. But I was one of those lucky children who felt hunger for and satisfaction of their own fatherneed.

What would this book look like if the kids had written it? I hope by now that you have heard in these children's voices some of the very things that we need to believe if fatherneed is ever to be fulfilled. We have heard of the difference that fathers make to a family and have heard children wisely describe how their life is different when their father is involved with them—or how different it would be if only he were. We have seen the impact of divorce and children's attitudes toward it, especially with regard to how they feel they have lost their dad. We have seen how variations in a child's need for respect, safety, security, companionship, and guidance reflect different developmental stages. Finally, we have heard children's impassioned advice about fulfilling the fatherneed.

All the readers of this book have one thing in common: you were all once a child with a father, whether you loved him, or knew him, or not. You would not be here without a father. And by now you know that your relationship with your father has significantly influenced the way you are fathering your own children (or the way you are encouraging your partner to father your children) and supporting the role of men in the lives of all children.

You also know that being available to your children, being involved and connecting with them in a direct way, day after day, taking responsibility for their care and well-being, matters more to your children than they can ever fully articulate. They feel even more trusting of you if you know what they need from you in the way of guidance, assistance, and letting go. You have heard children say that the consistency with which parents share their life matters as much as (if not more than) what their parents actually do with them or give to them in their life together. You've also heard them say over and over again how important it is for parents to show their love to them, not simply feel it. Children can't feel nurtured unless we show them.

Men are the single greatest untapped resource in the lives of American children. Natural, renewable, and by and large nontoxic, they couldn't be healthier for the country's children. We can't afford to let another one get away.

Notes

INTRODUCTION

1 *Over the course of sixteen years, Joseph Pleck:* Joseph H. Pleck, "Paternal Involvement: Levels, Sources and Consequences," in *The Role of the Father in Child Development,* 3rd ed., ed. Michael E. Lamb (New York: Wiley, 1997), pp. 66–103.

6 *In a scathing critique:* Vicky Phares, "Where's Poppa? The Relative Lack of Attention to the Role of Fathers in Child and Adolescent Psychopathology," *American Psychologist* 47 (5): 656–664 (May 1992).

7 *Things have improved:* Michael E. Lamb, ed., *The Role of the Father in Child Development,* 3rd ed. (New York: Wiley, 1997).

10 *Even more intriguing is a finding:* Jay Belsky, "Parent, Infant and Social–Contextual Antecedents of Father–Son Attachment Security," *Developmental Psychology* 32 (5): 905–913 (1996).

10 *John Snarey's four-decade-long study:* John Snarey, *How Fathers Care for the Next Generation: A Four-Decade Study* (Cambridge, MA: Harvard University Press, 1993).

14 *In a four-year National Institute of Mental Health (NIMH) study:* Rosalind Barnett and Caryl Rivers, cited in Susan McHenry, "Study Finds Men Caught in Parent Trap, Too," *Working Woman,* August 1994, p. 13.

1: FATHERS DO NOT MOTHER

18 *As Erik Erikson explained:* Erik Erikson, *Dimensions of a New Identity* (New York: Norton, 1974).

19 *What I mean by "fathering":* Joseph H. Pleck, "Paternal Involvement: Levels, Sources and Consequences," in *The Role of the Father in Child Development,* 3rd ed., ed. Michael E. Lamb (New York: Wiley, 1997), p. 70.

19 *Historian Robert Griswold has described:* Robert L. Griswold, *Fatherhood in America: A History* (New York: Basic Books, 1993).

19   *Today, fathering behaviors:* Pleck, "Paternal Involvement."

19   *Particular fathering traits and behaviors are shaped:* John Snarey, *How Fathers Care for the Next Generation: A Four-Decade Study* (Cambridge, MA: Harvard University Press, 1993), p. 278.

20   *Research also reveals that a more subtle support:* M. J. Cox, "Progress and Continued Challenges in Understanding the Transition to Parenthood," *Journal of Family Issues* 6: 395–408 (1985).

20   *Overall, writes Pedersen:* Frank A. Pedersen, Joan T. D. Suwalsky, Richard L. Cain, Martha J. Zaslow, and Beth A. Rabinovich, "Paternal Care of Infants During Maternal Separations: Associations with Father–Infant Interaction at One Year," *Psychiatry* 50: 203 (August 1987).

22   *The attachment and closeness that mothers and fathers feel:* Sandra L. Ferketich and Ramona T. Mercer, "Paternal–Infant Attachment of Experienced and Inexperienced Fathers During Pregnancy," *Nursing Research* 44 (1): 31–37 (January 1995).

22   *University of California psychologist Ross Parke:* Ross Parke and Armin A. Brott, *Throwaway Dads: The Myths and Barriers That Keep Men from Being the Fathers They Want to Be* (New York: Houghton Mifflin, 1998).

23   *Michael Lamb has written:* Michael E. Lamb, "The Development of Father–Infant Relationships," in *The Role of the Father in Child Development,* 3rd ed., ed. Michael E. Lamb (New York: Wiley, 1997), p. 120.

23   *The latest contribution to the debate is a large meta-analysis:* H. Lytton and D. M. Romney, "Parents' Differential Socialization of Boys and Girls: A Meta-Analysis," *Psychological Bulletin* 109: 267–296 (1991).

25   *Toward the end of the first year, infants protest:* J. Herzog, "On Father and Hunger," in *Father and Child,* ed. S. Cath et al. (Boston: Little, Brown, 1982).

26   *Toddlers seek out and seem to join:* Herzog, "On Father and Hunger."

28   *Infants between the ages of 7 and 13 months:* Jay Belsky, "Mother–Father–Infant Interaction: A Naturalistic Observational Study," *Developmental Psychology* 15: 601–607 (1979).

28   *French psychologist Florence Labrell:* Florence Labrell, "Paternal Play with Toddlers: Recreation and Creation," *European Journal of Psychology of Education* 11 (1): 43–54 (March 1996).

28   *Rough-and-tumble play makes up an important portion:* K. A. Clark-Stewart, "And Daddy Makes Three: The Father's Impact on Mother and Young Child," *Child Development* 49: 466–478 (1978).

28   *What does vary, however, is the amount of rough-and-tumble play:* C. P. Hwang, "The Changing Role of Swedish Fathers," in *The Father's Role: Cross-Cultural Perspectives,* ed. M. E. Lamb (Hillsdale, NJ: Erlbaum, 1987); J. L. Roopnarine, "Personal Well-Being, Kinship Tie and Mother–Infant and Father–Infant Interactions in Single-Wage and Dual-Wage Families," *Journal of Marriage and the Family* 54: 293–301 (1992).

31   *Boston psychoanalyst Lora Tessman's study:* Lora Tessman, "Early Tones, Later Echoes," in *Fathers and Their Families,* ed. Stanley H. Cath, Alan Gurwitt, and Linda Gunsberg (Hillsdale, NJ: Analytic Press, 1989), pp. 197–223.

33 *Over and over again in the science of father care:* M. A. Easterbrooks and W. A. Goldberg, "Toddler Development in the Family: Impact of Father Involvement and Parenting Characteristics," *Child Development* 53: 740–752 (1984).

2: THE DAD DIFFERENCE IN CHILD DEVELOPMENT

36 *In a chapter titled "Fathers, the Missing Parent in Research on Family Violence":* National Institute of Child and Human Development's Kathleen Sternberg: Kathleen J. Sternberg, "Fathers, the Missing Parents in Research on Family Violence," in *The Role of the Father in Child Development,* 3rd ed., ed. Michael E. Lamb (New York: Wiley, 1997), pp. 284–308.

38 *University of Pennsylvania's Frank Furstenberg and Kathleen Harris fine-tuned:* F. F. Furstenberg, Jr., and K. M. Harris, "When and Why Fathers Matter: Impacts of Father Involvement on the Children of Adolescent Mothers," in *Young Unwed Fathers: Changing Roles and Emerging Policies,* ed. R. I. Lerman and T. J. Ooms (Philadelphia: Temple University Press, 1993).

38 *University of Rhode Island's Henry Biller and University of Michigan's Norma Radin:* Henry B. Biller, *Fathers and Families: Paternal Factors in Child Development* (Westport, CT: Auborn House, 1993); Norma Radin, "The Role of the Father in Cognitive, Academic and Intellectual Development," in *The Role of the Father in Child Development,* 3rd ed., ed. Michael E. Lamb (New York: Wiley, 1981), pp. 379–428.

39 *Studies by Jay Belsky of the influence of women's and men's personality traits:* Jay Belsky, Keith Crnic, and Sharon Woodworth, "Personality and Parenting: Exploring the Mediating Role of Transient Mood and Daily Hassles," *Journal of Personality* 63 (4): 905–929 (December 1995).

39 *Studies of mother–child and father–child contact:* R. L. Munroe and R. H. Munroe, "Father in Children's Environments: A Four-Culture Study," in *Father–Child Relations: Cultural and Biosocial Contexts,* ed. B. S. Hewlett (New York: Aldine de Gruyter, 1992), pp. 213–230.

40 *Here we see a fine example:* S. Wolk, C. H. Zeanah, C. T. Garcia-Coll, and S. Carr, "Factors Affecting Parents' Perceptions of Temperament in Early Infancy," *American Journal of Orthopsychiatry* 62: 193–212 (1982).

40 *One of the most influential studies of paternal impact:* M. A. Easterbrooks and W. A. Goldberg, "Toddler Development in the Family: Impact of Father Involvement and Parenting Characteristics," *Child Development* 53: 740–752 (1984).

42 *Research by Henry Biller and Frank Pedersen:* Biller, *Fathers and Families.*

43 *In the early 1960s psychologist Ellen Bing:* Ellen Bing, "The Effect of Child-Rearing Practices on the Development of Differential Cognitive Abilities," *Child Development* 34: 631–648 (1963).

43 *Another important investigation, by Norma Radin:* Norma Radin, "Primary Caregiving and Role-Sharing Fathers," in *Non-Traditional Families: Parenting and Child Development,* ed. M. E. Lamb (Hillsdale, NJ: Erlbaum, 1982), pp. 173–204.

43 *In an earlier study, she had already investigated:* Norma Radin, "Father–Child

Interaction and the Intellectual Functioning of Four-Year-Old Boys," *Developmental Psychology* 6: 353–361 (1972).

44 *In a landmark study of the relationship:* J. Mosley and E. Thompson, "Fathering Behavior and Child Outcomes: The Role of Race and Poverty," in *Fatherhood: Contemporary Theory, Research, and Social Policy,* ed. W. Marsiglio (Thousand Oaks, CA: Sage, 1995), pp. 148–165.

44 *Michael Lamb studied a group of preschool children:* Michael E. Lamb, "Introduction: The Emergent American Father," in *The Father's Role: Cross-Cultural Perspectives,* ed. Michael E. Lamb (Hillsdale, NJ: Erlbaum), pp. 3–25.

44 *Pediatrician Scott Nugent of Boston's Children's Hospital:* K. Nugent, "Cultural and Psychological Influences on the Father's Role in Infant Development," *Journal of Marriage and the Family* 53: 475–485 (1991).

45 *Biller has repeatedly pointed out:* Henry B. Biller, "The Father and Personality Development: Paternal Deprivation and Sex-Role Development," in *The Role of the Father in Child Development,* ed. Michael E. Lamb (New York: Wiley, 1981), p. 104.

45 *Norma Radin found a positive association:* Norma Radin, "Observed Paternal Behavior and the Intellectual Functioning of Preschool Boys and Girls" (paper presented at Society for Research in Child Development annual meeting, Denver, May 1974).

45 *Interestingly, when a daughter shares:* Lora Tessman, "Early Tones, Later Echoes," in *Fathers and Their Families,* ed. Stanley H. Cath, Alan Gurwitt, and Linda Gunsberg (Hillsdale, NJ: Analytic Press, 1989), pp. 197–223.

45 *Psychologists Grolnick and Slowiaczek studied:* Wendy S. Grolnick and Maria L. Slowiaczek, "Parents' Involvement in Children's Schooling: A Multidimensional Conceptualization and Motivational Model," *Child Development* 65: 237–252 (1994).

45 *Yet another pair of research psychologists:* B. M. Wagner and D. A. Phillips, "Beyond Beliefs: Parent and Child Behaviors and Children's Perceived Academic Competence," *Developmental Psychology* 63: 1380–1391 (1992).

47 *A positive marriage and flexible connections:* Jay Belsky, "Parent, Infant and Social–Contextual Antecedents of Father–Son Attachment Security," *Developmental Psychology* 32 (5): 905–913 (1996).

47 *Frank Pedersen found that at one year of age:* Frank A. Pedersen, Joan T. D. Suwalsky, Richard L. Cain, Martha J. Zaslow, and Beth A. Rabinovich, "Paternal Care of Infants During Maternal Separations: Associations with Father–Infant Interaction at One Year," *Psychiatry* 50: 193–205 (August 1987).

47 *In related work, Cox reviewed:* M. J. Cox, M. T. Owen, V. K. Henderson, and N. A. Margand, "Prediction of Infant–Father and Infant–Mother Attachment," *Developmental Psychology* 28: 474–483 (1992).

48 *An important long-term study of seventy-five children:* R. R. Sears, E. E. Maccoby, and H. Levin, *Patterns of Childrearing* (Evanston, IL: Row Peterson, 1957).

48 *When the children in the study were followed up:* R. Koestner, C. Franz, and J. Weinberger, "The Family Origins of Empathic Concern: A 26-Year Longitudinal Study," *Journal of Personality and Social Psychology* 58: 709–717 (1990).

48 *Developmental psychologist Susan Bernadette-Shapiro studied forty-seven:* Susan Bernadette-Shapiro, Diane Ehrensaft, and Jerrold Lee Shapiro, "Father Participation in Childcare and the Development of Empathy in Sons: An Empirical Study," *Family Therapy* 23 (2): 77–93 (1996).

49 *Norma Radin's study of school behavior:* Normal Radin, "Primary-caregiving Fathers in Intact Families," in *Redefining Families: Implications for Children's Development,* ed. A. E. Gottfried and A. W. Gottfried (New York: Plenum, 1994), pp. 55–97.

49 *Finally, Edith Williams and Norma Radin:* E. Williams, N. Radin, and T. Allegro, "Sex-Role Attitudes of Adolescents Raised Primarily by Their Fathers," *Merrill-Palmer Quarterly* 38: 457–476 (1992).

49 *Constance Hardesty of Morehead State University:* Constance Hardesty, DeeAnn Wenk, and Carolyn Stout Morgan, "Paternal Involvement and the Development of Gender Expectations in Sons and Daughters," *Youth and Society* 25 (3): 283–297 (March 1995).

50 *Psychologist Walter Mischel found young children:* W. Mischel, "Father Absence and Delay of Gratification," *Journal of Abnormal and Social Psychology* 62: 116–124 (1961).

50 *In a related study, psychologist Martin Hoffman:* M. L. Hoffman, "Identification and Conscience Development," *Child Development* 42: 1071–1082 (1971).

51 *Educational psychologist Amato evaluated:* P. R. Amato, *Children in Australian Families: The Growth of Competence* (New York: Prentice-Hall, 1987).

52 *Psychologists Eldred Rutherford and Paul Mussen tested:* E. E. Rutherford and P. H. Mussen, "Generosity in Nursery School Boys," *Child Development* 39: 755–765 (1968).

52 *In one of the more highly regarded:* Mosley and Thompson, "Fathering Behavior and Child Outcomes."

52 *An important British study of at-home births:* Joel Richman, "Men's Experiences of Pregnancy and Childbirth," in *The Father Figure,* ed. L. McKee and M. O'Brien (London: Tavistock, 1982), pp. 89–104.

52 *A related study concluded that the father's presence:* Richman, "Men's Experiences of Pregnancy and Childbirth."

53 *Ross Parke, a preeminent fatherhood researcher:* R. D. Parke, *Fatherhood* (Cambridge, MA: Harvard University Press, 1996).

53 *Maternal and paternal behaviors obviously affect one another:* Jay Belsky, "Early Human Experience: A Family Perspective," *Developmental Psychology* 17: 3–17 (1981); J. R. Dickie, "Interrelationships Within the Mother–Father–Infant Triad," in *Men's Transitions to Parenthood: Longitudinal Studies of Early Family Experience,* ed. P. W. Berman and F. A. Pedersen (Hillsdale, NJ: Erlbaum, 1987), pp. 113–144; R. D. Parke and E. R. Anderson, "Fathers and Their At-Risk Infants: Conceptual and Empirical Analyses," in *Men's Transition to Parenthood: Longitudinal Studies of Early Family Experience,* ed. P. W. Berman and F. A. Pedersen (Hillsdale, NJ: Erlbaum, 1987), pp. 197–216.

54 *Michael Yogman conducted an interesting study into the role:* M. W. Yogman, D. Kindlon, and F. Earls, "Father Involvement and Cognitive/Behavioral Out-

comes of Preterm Infants," *Journal of the American Academy of Child and Adolescent Psychiatry* 34: 58–66 (1995).

55 *New Haven psychoanalyst Rosemary Balsam's:* Rosemary H. Balsam, "The Paternal Possibility: The Father's Contribution to the Adolescent Daughter When the Mother is Disturbed and a Denigrated Figure," in *Fathers and Their Families,* ed. Stanley H. Cath, Alan Gurwitt, and Linda Gunsberg (Hillsdale, NJ: Analytic Press, 1989), pp. 245–263.

56 *Vicky Phares's thoughtful review of findings:* Vicky Phares, *Fathers and Developmental Psychopathology* (New York: Wiley, 1996), p. 181.

3: DAD AS THE PRIMARY CAREGIVER

59 *Although descriptions of the outcome for children:* Kyle D. Pruett, *The Nurturing Father* (New York: Warner Books, 1988); Kyle D. Pruett, "Infants of Primary Nurturing Fathers," *Psychoanalytic Study of the Child* 38: 257–281 (1983); Kyle D. Pruett, "The Nurturing Male: A Longitudinal Study of Primary Nurturing Fathers," in *Fathers and Their Families,* ed. Stanley H. Cath, Alan Gurwitt, and Linda Gunsberg (Hillsdale, NJ: Analytic Press, 1989), pp. 389–405.

60 *A clear profile of at-home fathers:* Robert Frank, "Survey Says: Research on At-Home Dads," in *At-Home Dad Handbook,* ed. Barry Reszel (Apple Valley, MN: Curtis Cooper, 1998), pp. 20–25.

72 *In his study of such men and their families:* Graeme Russell, "The Changing of Fathers: Current Understandings and Future Directions for Research and Practice" (paper presented to the World Association for Infant Psychiatry and Allied Disciplines, Melbourne, April 26–28, 1991).

72 *Norma Radin used four- and eleven-year follow-ups:* Norma Radin, "Primary-caregiving Fathers in Intact Families," in *Redefining Families: Implications for Children's Development,* ed. A. E. Gottfried and A. W. Gottfried (New York: Plenum, 1994), pp. 55–97.

73 *In an Israeli study by psychologist Avi Sagi:* Cited in Radin, "Primary-caregiving Fathers in Intact Families," pp. 55–97.

74 *Bem's research in the early 1980s:* Sandra Lipsitz Bem, "Gender Schema Theory and Self-schema Theory Compared: A Comment on Markus, Crane, Bernstein, and Siladi's Self-schemas and Gender," *Journal of Personality and Social Psychology* 43: 1192–1194 (1982); Sandra Lipsitz Bem, "Gender Schema Theory and Its Implications for Child Development: Raising Gender-Aschematic Children in a Gender-Schematic Society," *Signs* 8: 598–616 (1983).

74 *In 1988 I was sent an unsolicited transcript:* Alcini vs. Navarro, State of Michigan Case No. 339327 (Pontiac, Michigan, November 4, 1987).

4: FATHERNEED THROUGHOUT LIFE

78 *Yet much of the current research indicates that:* G. Roberts, J. H. Block, and J. Block, "Continuity and Change in Parents' Child Rearing Practices," *Child Development* 55: 586–597 (1984).

79 *San Diego psychiatrist Martin Greenberg:* Martin Greenberg, *Birth of a Father* (New York: Continuum, 1985).

79 *Researchers Pamela Daniels and Kathy Weingarten called:* Pamela Daniels and Kathy Weingarten, "The Fatherhood Click: The Timing of Parenthood in Men's Lives," in *Fatherhood Today: Men's Changing Role in the Family,* ed. Phyllis Bronstein and Carolyn Pape Cowan (New York: Wiley, 1988), pp. 36–52.

80 *The intimacy needed by children:* F. M. Cancian, "The Feminization of Love," *Signs: Journal of Women in Culture and Society* 11: 692–709 (1986).

83 *Consequently, I recently wrote a book about it:* Kyle D. Pruett, *Me, Myself and I* (New York: Goddard Press, 1999).

84 *Michael Lamb has cautioned that fathers:* Michael E. Lamb, "The Development of Father–Infant Relationships," in *The Role of the Father in Child Development,* 3rd ed., ed. Michael Lamb (New York: Wiley, 1997), p. 114.

87 *Fathers usually rise to the occasion:* K. MacDonald and R. D. Parke, "Parent–Child Physical Play: The Effects of Sex and Age of Children and Parents," *Sex Roles* 15: 367–378 (1986).

87 *Dads seem to have a slight proclivity:* A. U. Siegal, "Are Sons and Daughters More Differently Treated by Fathers Than by Mothers?" *Developmental Review* 7:183–209 (1987).

87 *They do not adapt fully:* B. McLoughlin, C. Schutz, and D. White, "Parental Speech to Five-Year-Old in a Game-Playing Situation," *Child Development* 51: 580–582 (1980).

88 *New developmental sociological research:* Lyn Mikel Brown and Carol Gilligan, *Meeting at the Crossroads: Women's Psychology and Girls' Development* (Cambridge, MA: Harvard University Press, 1992).

91 *John Snarey found that when men:* John Snarey, *How Fathers Care for the Next Generation: A Four-Decade Study* (Cambridge, MA: Harvard University Press, 1993).

91 *Ross Parke discovered that children:* R. D. Parke, *Fatherhood* (Cambridge, MA: Harvard University Press, 1996).

91 *Conversely, authoritarian and intrusive fathering:* Henry B. Biller, "Fatherhood: Implications for Adult and Child Development," in *Handbook of Developmental Psychology,* ed. B. B. Wolman (Englewood Cliffs, NJ: Prentice-Hall, 1982), pp. 702–725; H. B. Biller and R. S. Solomon, *Child Maltreatment and Paternal Deprivation: A Manifesto for Research, Prevention and Treatment* (Lexington, MA: Lexington, 1986); D. B. Lynn, *The Father: His Role in Child Development* (Belmont, CA: Brooks/Cole, 1974); Norma Radin, "The Role of the Father in Cognitive, Academic and Intellectual Development," in *The Role of the Father in Child Development,* ed. Michael E. Lamb (New York: Wiley, 1981), pp. 379–428.

91 *Some research suggests that school-age children perceive:* W. A. Collins and G. Russell, "Mother–Child and Father–Child Relationships in Middle Childhood and Adolescence: A Developmental Analysis," *Developmental Review* 11: 99–136 (1991).

91 *Fourth and fifth grade children were studied:* M. A. Herman and S. M. Mc-

Hale, "Coping with Parental Negativity: Links with Parental Warmth and Child Adjustment," *Journal of Applied Developmental Psychology* 14:121–130 (1993).

92   *A large study by psychologist Grolnick:* Wendy S. Grolnick and Maria L. Slowiaczek, "Parents' Involvement in Children's Schooling: A Multidimensional Conceptualization and Motivational Model," *Child Development* 65: 237–252 (1994).

92   *A companion study of seventy-five high-achieving third graders:* B. M. Wagner and D. A. Phillips, "Beyond Beliefs: Parent and Child Behaviors and Children's Perceived Academic Competence," *Developmental Psychology* 63: 1380–1391 (1992).

92   *Educational psychologist Epstein found that when parents:* Cited in Grolnick and Slowiaczek, "Parents' Involvement in Children's Schooling."

95   *The bottom line, documented over and over again:* P. Amato, "Father Involvement and the Self-Esteem of Children and Adolescents," *Australian Journal of Sex, Marriage and Family* 7: 6–16 (1986).

95   *As for the effect on men on fathering adolescents:* T. W. Julian, P. C. McHenry and M. W. McKelvey, "Mediators of Relationship Stress Between Middle-Aged Fathers and Their Adolescent Children," *Journal of Genetic Psychology* 152: 381–386 (1991).

97   *Psychologist Speicher-Dubin's landmark study:* B. Speicher-Dubin, "Relationships between Parent Moral Judgement, Child Moral Judgement and Family Interaction: A Correlational Study," Abstract in *Dissertation Abstracts International,* 43, 1600B (1982). (University Microfilms International Order no. 8223231).

5: DIVORCE: CHALLENGE TO FATHERNEED

102   *If, however, you choose numbers from Berkeley's Robert Mnookin:* E. E. Maccoby and R. H. Mnookin, *Dividing the Child: Social and Legal Dilemmas of Custody* (Cambridge, MA: Harvard University Press, 1992).

103   *The important research of psychologist John Gottman:* Cited in Ross Parke and Armin A. Brott, *Throwaway Dads: The Myths and Barriers That Keep Men from Being the Fathers They Want to Be* (New York: Houghton Mifflin, 1998), p. 117.

104   *Some research has strongly supported the notion:* Carmelle Minton and Kay Pasley, "Fathers' Parenting Role Identity and Father Involvement: A Comparison of Nondivorced and Divorced, Nonresident Fathers," *Journal of Family Issues* 17 (1): 26–45 (January 1996).

104   *In a study of seventy-five divorced men:* T. Arendell, *Fathers and Divorce* (Thousand Oaks, CA: Sage, 1995).

104   *These are some of the reasons why:* Maccoby and Mnookin, *Dividing the Child.*

105   *Mark Cummings and Patrick Davies' important research:* E. Mark Cummings and Patrick Davies, *Children and Marital Conflict: The Impact of Family Dispute Resolution* (New York: Guilford Press, 1994).

106   *Jean and Jack Block found children exhibiting:* J. H. Block, J. Block and P. J.

Gjerde, "The Personality of Children Prior to Divorce," *Child Development* 57: 827–840 (1983); J. H. Block, J. Block and A. Morrison, "Parental Agreement-Disagreement on Child-Rearing Orientations and Gender-Related Personality Correlates in Children," *Child Development* 52: 965–974 (1981).

106 *Consequently, it's not surprising that one reputable study:* E. M. Hetherington, M. Cox and R. Cox, "Long-Term Effects of Divorce and Remarriage on the Adjustment of Children," *Journal of the American Academy of Child Psychiatry* 24: 518–530 (1985).

106 *In fact, parental fighting has emerged as a better forecaster:* P. R. Amato and B. Keith, "Parental Divorce and the Well-Being of Children: A Meta-Analysis," *Psychological Bulletin* 110: 26–46 (1991).

107 *Academic and cognitive deficits have been described:* J. Guidabaldi, H. K. Cleminshaw, J. D. Perry, B. K. Nastasi and J. Lightel, "The Role of Selected Family Environment Factors in Children's Post-Divorce Adjustment," *Family Relations* 35: 141–151 (1986).

107 *Even six years down the road, according to Shirley Hanson's research:* S. H. Hanson, *Dimensions of Fatherhood* (Beverly Hills, CA: Sage, 1985).

107 *Hanson's important work shows us that boys with fathers:* Hanson, *Dimensions of Fatherhood.*

107 *According to the work of Richard Warshak:* R. A. Warshak and J. W. Santrock, "The Impact of Divorce in Father-Custody and Mother-Custody Homes: The Child's Perspective," in *New Directions for Child Development: Vol. 19. Children and Divorce,* ed. L. A. Kurdek (San Francisco: Jossey-Bass, 1983), pp. 19–46.

107 *According to pioneering researcher and author Judith Wallerstein:* Judith S. Wallerstein and Sandra Blakeslee, *Second Chances: Men, Women and Children a Decade After Divorce* (New York: Ticknor and Fields, 1990).

108 *Psychologist Nicholas Zill looked carefully:* Nicholas Zill, Donna Ruane Morrison, and Mary Jo Coiro, "Long-Term Effects of Parental Divorce on Parent–Child Relationships, Adjustment and Achievement in Young Adulthood, *Journal of Family Psychology* 7 (1): 91–103 (1993).

109 *Companion research from Denmark:* U. Palosaari, H. Aro, and P. Laippala, "Parental Divorce and Depression in Young Adulthood: Adolescents' Closeness to Parents and Self-Esteem as a Mediating Factor," *Acta Psychiatry Scand* 93 (1): 20–26 (January 1996).

109 *In another study, by Nord and Zill:* C. W. Nord and N. Zill, *Non-Custodial Parents' Participation in their Children's Lives: Evidence from the Survey of Income and Program Participation* (available from the Department of Health and Human Services, 370 L'Enfant Promenade, S.W., Washington, D.C. 20447).

109 *The study of 1,100 families that Eleanor Maccoby and Robert Mnookin:* Maccoby and Mnookin, *Dividing the Child* (Cambridge, MA: Harvard University Press, 1992).

111 *But the facts expose these myths for what they are:* Daniel R. Meyer and Steven Garasky, "Custodial Fathers: Myths, Realities and Child Support Policy," *Journal of Marriage and the Family* 55: 73–89 (February 1993).

115 *Increased involvement becomes much less likely:* C. R. Ahrons and R. B. Miller, "The Effect of the Post-Divorce Relationship on Paternal Involvement: A Longitudinal Analysis," *American Journal of Orthopsychiatry* 63: 441–450 (1993).

118 *In the research of Mavis Hetherington:* E. M. Hetherington, M. Cox, and R. Cox, "Effects of Divorce on Parents and Children," in *Nontraditional Families: Parenting and Child Development*, ed. M. E. Lamb (Hillsdale, NJ: Erlbaum, 1982).

<h2 style="text-align:center">6: Expressions of Fatherneed</h2>

121 *Several groups of investigators have studied how role flexibility:* W. D. Allen and M. Connor, "An African-American Perspective on Generative Fathering," in *Generative Fathering: Beyond Deficit Perspectives*, ed. A. J. Hawkins and D. C. Dollahite (Newbury Park, CA: Sage, 1998).

121 *Norma Radin and her colleagues, in studying Michigan's Ojibwa families:* Edith Williams, Norma Radin, and Kip Coggins, "Paternal Involvement in Childrearing and the School Performance of Ojibwa Children: An Exploratory Study," *Merrill-Palmer Quarterly* 42 (4): 578–595 (1996).

122 *African American fathers have gradually emerged:* Mohammad Ahmeduzzaman and Jaipaul L. Roopnarine, "Sociodemographic Factors, Functioning Style, Social Support, and Fathers' Involvement with Preschoolers in African-American Families," *Journal of Marriage and the Family* 54: 699–707 (August 1992).

122 *John Lewis McAdoo expanded these findings:* John Lewis McAdoo, "Changing Perspectives on the Role of the Black Father," in *Fatherhood Today: Men's Changing Role in the Family*, ed. Phyllis Bronstein and Carolyn Pape Cowan (New York: Wiley, 1988), pp. 79–92.

122 *With other colleagues, Roopnarine affirmed:* Ziarat Hossain and Jaipaul L. Roopnarine, "African-American Fathers' Involvement with Infants: Relationship to Their Functioning Style, Support Education and Income," *Infant Behavior and Development* 17: 175–184 (1994).

123 *McAdoo's research suggests:* J. McAdoo and H. McAdoo, "The Impact of Paternal Interaction Patterns on the Self-Esteem of Black and White Preschool Children" (paper presented at the annual meeting of the National Council on Family Relations, Dallas, November 1986).

123 *Marc Zimmerman and colleagues have shown in their study:* Marc A. Zimmerman, Deborah A. Salem, and Kenneth I. Maton, "Family Structure and Psychosocial Correlates Among Urban African-American Adolescent Males," *Child Development* 66: 1598–1613 (1995).

124 *When researchers ask children:* Jennifer N. Perloff and John C. Buckner, "Fathers of Children on Welfare: Their Impact on Child Well-Being," *American Journal of Orthopsychiatry* 66 (4): 557–571 (1996).

124 *As Norma Radin and her colleagues found:* S. K. Danziger and N. Radin, "Absent Does Not Equal Uninvolved: Predictors of Fathering in Teen Mother Families," *Journal of Marriage and the Family* 52: 636–642 (1990).

125 *Some recent investigations by ethnic sociologist Mirande:* Alfredo Mirandé,

"Chicano Fathers: Traditional Perceptions and Current Realities," in *Fatherhood Today: Men's Changing Role in The Family*, ed. Phyllis Bronstein and Carolyn Pape Cowan (New York: Wiley, 1988), pp. 93–106.

125 *Roopnarine and Ahmeduzzaman looked at father involvement:* Jaipaul L. Roopnarine and Mohammad Ahmeduzzaman, "Puerto Rican Fathers' Involvement with Their Preschool-Age Children," *Hispanic Journal of Behavioral Sciences* 15 (1): 96–107 (February 1993).

126 *Perloff, another ethnic behavioral researcher:* Jennifer N. Perloff and John C. Buckner, "Fathers of Children on Welfare: Their Impact on Child Well-Being," *American Journal of Orthopsychiatry* 66 (4): 557–571 (1996).

127 *In a rare study of relationships between young Chinese adults:* S. Lau, W. J. F. Lew, K. T. Hau, P. C. Cheung and T. J. Berndt, "Relations Among Perceived Parental Control, Warmth, Indulgence and Family Harmony in Chinese in Mainland China," *Developmental Psychology* 26: 674–677 (1990).

128 *Breakfast time is child time for Japanese fathers:* Masako Ishii-Kuntz, "Paternal Involvement and Perception Toward Fathers' Roles: A Comparison Between Japan and the United States," *Journal of Family Issues* 15 (1): 30–48 (March 1994).

128 *Andre Derdeyn and colleagues:* A. Derdeyn, C. Hale, and J. Alvarez, "The Educational Antecedents of Teen Fatherhood," *British Journal of Educational Psychology* 62: 139–147 (1992).

129 *Allen and Doherty's interviews:* W. D. Allen and W. J. Doherty, "The Responsibilities of Fatherhood as Perceived by African-American Teenage Fathers," *Families in Society: The Journal of Contemporary Human Services* 77: 152–155 (1996).

130 *Some researchers believe that the decline:* R. I. Lerman and T. J. Ooms, "Introduction: Evolution of Unwed Fatherhood as a Policy Issue," in *Young Unwed Fathers: Changing Roles and Emerging Policies*, ed. R. Lerman and T. Ooms (Philadelphia: Temple University Press, 1993), pp. 1–23.

131 *This last statement by Kyesha presaged:* Susan A. Brunelli, Gail A. Wasserman, Virginia A. Raugh, Luz E. Alvarado. "Mothers' Reports of Paternal Support: Association with Child-Rearing Attitudes," *Merrill-Palmer Quarterly* 41 (2): 152–171 (1995).

131 *One-third of all American children:* J. A. Seltzer, "Relationships Between Fathers and Children Who Live Apart: The Father's Role After Separation," *Journal of Marriage and the Family* 53: 79–101 (1991).

132 *Mavis Hetherington has shown:* E. M. Hetherington, "An Overview of the Virginia Longitudinal Study of Divorce and Remarriage with a Focus on Early Adolescence," *Journal of Family Psychology* 7: 39–56 (1993).

132 *When remarriage occurs:* E. M. Hetherington, "Coping with Family Transitions: Winners, Losers and Survivors," *Child Development* 60:1–15 (1989).

133 *An important study comparing stepfamilies:* John W. Santrock, Karen A. Sitterle, and Richard A. Warshak, "Parent–Child Relationships in Stepfather Families," in *Fatherhood Today: Men's Changing Role in the Family*, ed. Phyllis Bronstein and Carolyn Pape Cowan (New York: Wiley, 1988), pp. 144–165.

133 *Although there is a worrisome absence:* Frederick W. Bozett, "Gay Fathers: How and Why They Disclose Their Homosexuality to Their Children," *Family Relations* 29: 173–179 (1980).

134 *Furthermore, their reasons for becoming fathers:* J. J. Bigner and R. B. Jacobsen, "The Value of Children to Gay and Heterosexual Fathers," in *Homosexuality and the Family,* ed. F. W. Bozett (New York: Harrington, 1989), pp. 163–172.

134 *Charlotte Patterson, a psychologist:* Charlotte J. Patterson and Raymond W. Chan, "Gay Fathers," in *The Role of the Father in Child Development,* ed. Michael E. Lamb (New York: Wiley, 1997), pp. 245–260.

134 *Furthermore, in an important study of sexual orientation:* J. M. Bailey, D. Bobrow, M. Wolfe, and S. Mikach, "Sexual Orientation of Adult Sons of Gay Fathers," *Developmental Psychology* 31:124–129 (1995).

134 *Consequently, the particular details:* D. Altman, *The Homosexualization of America, the Americanization of the Homosexual* (New York: St. Martin's Press, 1982).

134 *Children are, in general, accepting of their gay fathers:* Bozett, "Gay Fathers."

135 *A companion study comparing gay fathers:* R. M. Scallen, "An Investigation of Paternal Attitudes and Behaviors in Homosexual and Heterosexual Fathers" (Ph.D. diss., California School of Professional Psychology, Los Angeles). Abstract in *Dissertation Abstracts International* 42 (9): 3809-B (1981).

136 *A study by Bigner and Jacobsen challenges:* J. J. Bigner and R. B. Jacobsen, "The Value of Children to Gay and Heterosexual Fathers," in *Homosexuality and the Family,* ed. F. W. Bozett (New York: Harrington, 1989), pp. 163–172.

136 *Researchers Scarr and Weinberg:* S. Scarr and R. A. Weinberg, "IQ Test Performance of Black Children Adopted by White Parents," *American Psychologist* 31: 726–739 (1976).

138 *Vicki Turbeville from the University of Kansas:* Vicki Turbeville, "What Research Says: Fathers, Their Children, and Disability" (Lawrence, KS: University of Kansas, Beach Center on Families and Disability, 1995).

139 *Michael Yogman's study of father involvement:* M. W. Yogman, D. Kindlon, and F. Earls, "Father Involvement and Cognitive/Behavioral Outcomes of Preterm Infants," *Journal of the American Academy of Child and Adolescent Psychiatry* 34: 58–66 (1995).

139 *Seven million American children:* Fox Butterfield, "As Inmate Population Grows, So Does a Focus on Children," *New York Times,* 7 April, 1999, A18.

140 *Michael Murphy, psychologist for the Massachusetts Department of Corrections:* In *Brown University Child and Adolescent Behavior Letter* 13 (9 Sept., 1999).

141 *They can count on more support:* B. Neville and R. D. Parke, "Waiting for Paternity: Interpersonal and Contextual Implications of the Timing of Fatherhood" (unpublished manuscript, University of Washington, 1993).

141 *A nationally representative sample of mature fathers:* T. M. Cooney, F. A. Pedersen, S. Indelicator, and R. Palkovitz, "Timing of Fatherhood: Is 'On-Time' Optimal?" *Journal of Marriage and the Family* 55: 205–215 (1993).

141 *Further qualitative differences between young and mature fathers:* K. MacDonald and R. D. Parke, "Parent–Child Physical Play: The Effects of Sex and Age of Children and Parents," *Sex Roles* 15: 367–378 (1986).

141 *Jay Belsky's research group:* B. L. Volling and Jay Belsky, "Multiple Determinants of Father Involvement During Infancy in Dual-Earner and Single-Earner Families," *Journal of Marriage and the Family* 53: 461–474 (1991).

141 *Heath investigated the impact:* D. Terri Heath, "The Impact of Delayed Fatherhood on the Father–Child Relationship," *Journal of Genetic Psychology* 155 (4): 511–530 (December 1994).

142 *The tag that grandparents and grandchildren:* Margaret Mead, *Blackberry Winter* (New York: Simon & Schuster, 1972), p. 275.

142 *Stanley Cath, a longtime champion:* Stanley H. Cath, "Readiness for Grandfatherhood and the Shifting Tide," in *Fathers and Their Families,* ed. Stanley H. Cath, Alan Gurwitt, and Linda Gunsberg (Hillsdale, NJ: Analytic Press, 1989), pp. 99–118.

142 *This may be particularly true for grandparents:* B. J. Tinsley and R. D. Parke, "Grandparents as Interactive and Social Support Agents for Families with Young Infants," *International Journal of Aging and Human Development* 25: 261–279 (1987).

143 *In fact, psychologist Feldman:* S. S. Feldman, S. C. Nash, and B. G. Aschenbrenner, "Antecedents of Fathering," *Child Development* 54: 1628–1636 (1983).

143 *In a study by sociologist Kornhaber:* A. Kornhaber, *Between Parents and Grandparents* (New York: Berkley Books, 1987).

144 *Simons investigated the intergenerational transmission:* R. L. Simons, L. B. Whitbeck, R. D. Conger, and W. Chyi-In, "Intergenerational Transmission of Harsh Parenting," *Developmental Psychology* 27:159–171 (1991).

7: MOTHERS AND FATHERNEED

147 *The problem is one of balance:* Gloria Steinem, in *MS,* March 1971, p. 37.

147 *Mothers happy in their marriage:* B. L. Volling and Jay Belsky, "Multiple Determinants of Father Involvement During Infancy in Dual-Earner and Single-Earner Families," *Journal of Marriage and the Family* 53: 461–474 (1991); Sandra L. Ferketich and Ramona T. Mercer, "Predictors of Role Competence for Experienced and Inexperienced Fathers," *Nursing Research* 44 (2): 89–95 (March/April 1995).

148 *These men want to repair that wound:* Mary DeLuccie, "Mothers: Influential Agents in Father–Child Relations," *Genetic, Social and General Psychology Monographs* 122 (3): 285–307 (August 1996).

149 *Compared to the mother–child relationship:* Jay Belsky and B. L. Volling, "Mothering, Fathering and Marital Interaction in the Family Triad During Infancy," in *Men's Transitions to Parenthood: Longitudinal Studies of Early Family Experience,* ed. P. W. Berman and F. A. Pedersen (Hillsdale, NJ: Erlbaum, 1987), pp. 37–63.

150 *But when mothers respect their partner's fathering:* John Snarey, *How Fathers Care for the Next Generation: A Four-Decade Study* (Cambridge, MA: Harvard University Press, 1993).

150 *Arlie Russell Hochschild's research:* Arlie Russell Hochschild, "There's No Place Like Work," *New York Times Magazine,* 20 April 1997, p. 51.

151 *The National Survey of Families and Households:* William Marsiglio, "Paternal Engagement Activities with Minor Children," *Journal of Marriage and the Family* 53: 973–986 (1991).

151 *Meanwhile, Joe Pleck found:* Joseph H. Pleck, "Paternal Involvement: Levels, Sources and Consequences," in *The Role of the Father in Child Development,* 3rd ed., ed. Michael E. Lamb (New York: Wiley, 1997), pp. 66–103.

152 *Pamela Jordan's research:* Pamela L. Jordan, "The Mother's Role in Promoting Fathering Behavior," in *Becoming a Father,* ed. Jerrold Lee Shapiro, Michael J. Diamond, and Martin Greenberg (New York: Springer, 1995), pp. 61–82.

154 *In Jack Kammer's Good Will Toward Men:* Jack Kammer, *Good Will Toward Men: Women Talk Candidly About the Balance of Power Between the Sexes* (New York: St. Martin's Press, 1994), p. 208.

154 *Studies by researchers Pearson and Thoennes:* J. Pearson and N. Thoennes, "Custody After Divorce: Demographic and Attitudinal Patterns," *American Journal of Orthopsychiatry* 60: 233–249 (1990).

154 *John Snarey's four-decade study:* Snarey, *How Fathers Care for the Next Generation.*

155 *And staunch support for gatekeeping:* William Sears, "Becoming a Father: How to Nurture and Enjoy Your Family," book review in *Full-Time Dads: The Journal for Caring Fathers* 11:18–19 (September/October 1994).

155 *Diane Wille investigated seventy families:* Diane E. Wille, "The 1990s: Gender Differences in Parenting Roles," *Sex Roles* 33 (11/12): 803–817 (1995).

8: How Fathering Changes Men for Good

166 *Sociologist Ralph LaRossa:* Ralph LaRossa and Donald C. Reitzes, "Continuity and Change in Middle-Class Fatherhood, 1925–1939: The Culture Conduct Connection," *Journal of Marriage and the Family* 55: 455–468 (May 1993).

166 *LaRossa found evidence:* LaRossa and Reitzes, "Continuity and Change."

167 *As historian Robert Griswold:* Robert L. Griswold, *Fatherhood in America: A History* (New York: Basic Books, 1993).

167 *As he tells his interviewer:* Buddy Fite, "Michael," interview by Dee Mae Roberts, *National Public Radio's Weekend Edition with Scott Simon* (11 April 1998).

169 *As John Snarey of Emory University describes it:* John Snarey, *How Fathers Care for the Next Generation: A Four-Decade Study* (Cambridge, MA: Harvard University Press, 1993).

169 *Henry Biller and John Snarey observed that fathers:* Henry B. Biller, *Fathers and Families: Paternal Factors in Child Development* (Westport, CT: Auborn House, 1993); Snarey, *How Fathers Care for the Next Generation.*

169 *In the Glueck Longitudinal Study by Snarey:* Snarey, *How Fathers Care for the Next Generation.*

169 *Psychologists, journalists, and historians alike:* Susan K. Reisch, Lisa Kuester, Denise Brost, and Jane Gilbert McCarthy, "Fathers' Perceptions of How They Were Parented," *Journal of Community Health Nursing* 13 (1): 13–29 (1996).

170   *In related research by Anju Jain and Jay Belsky:* Anju Jain, Jay Belsky, and Keith Crnic, "Beyond Fathering Behaviors: Types of Dads," *Journal of Family Psychology* 10 (4): 431–442 (1996).

170   *Again, in the Glueck study, Snarey found:* Snarey, *How Fathers Care for the Next Generation.*

172   *Greenberger and O'Neill found that fathers:* Ellen Greenberger, Robin O'Neill, and Stacy K. Nagel, "Linking Workplace and Homeplace: Relations Between the Nature of Adults' Work and Their Parenting Behavior," *Developmental Psychology* 30 (6): 990–1002 (1994); Ellen Greenberger, Wendy A. Goldberg, Sharon Hammill, and Robin O'Neil, "Contributions of a Supportive Work Environment to Parents' Well-Being and Orientation to Work," *American Journal of Community Psychology* 17 (6): 755–783 (1989).

173   *The Council of Family Health found in a survey:* Council on Family Health, "Salute to 'Dad, M.D.': More Than Two-Thirds of American Fathers Take Their Sick Kids to the Doctor's Office" (New York, Council on Family Health, May 22, 1997), pp. 1–2.

174   *In the end, they come away with:* S. Chandler and T. A. Field, "Becoming a Father: First-time Fathers' Experience in Labor and Delivery," *Journal of Nurse Midwifery* 42 (1): 17–24 (January 1997).

175   *Research into dual-earner families:* W. A. Hall, "New Fatherhood: Myths and Realities," *Public Health Nursing* 11 (4): 219–228 (August 1994).

175   *Looking again at the unique observations:* Snarey, *How Fathers Care for the Next Generation.*

175   *Hossain and Roopnarine's research:* Ziarat Hossain and Jaipaul L. Roopnarine, "African-American Fathers' Involvement with Infants: Relationship to Their Functioning Style, Support Education and Income," *Infant Behavior and Development* 17: 175–184 (1994).

175   *National Public Radio talk show host Terry Gross:* T. J. Leyden, interview by Terry Gross, *National Public Radio's Fresh Air* (15 December 1998).

177   *Nursing research from the University of Arizona:* Sandra L. Ferketich and Ramona T. Mercer, "Predictors of Role Competence for Experienced and Inexperienced Fathers," *Nursing Research* 44 (2): 89–95 (March/April 1995).

177   *This, in fact, was the finding in an important study:* Ferketich and Mercer, "Predictors of Role Competence."

177   *Blair and Hardesty's research group proposed:* S. L. Blair and C. Hardesty, "Paternal Involvement and the Well-Being of Fathers and Mothers of Young Children," *Journal of Men's Studies* 3: 49–68 (1994).

178   *Mary DeLuccie studied predictors:* Mary DeLuccie, "Predictors of Paternal Involvement and Satisfaction," *Psychological Reports*, 79: 1351–1359 (1996).

178   *The number of men reporting a significant conflict:* Elizabeth Harvey, "Short-Term and Long-Term Effects of Early Parenting Employment on Children of the National Longitudinal Survey of Youth," *Developmental Psychology* 15 (2): 445–449 (1999).

178   *Dupont's 8,500 employees have been surveyed:* James A. Levine and Todd L. Pittinsky, *Working Fathers: New Strategies for Balancing Work and Family* (New York: Addison-Wesley, 1997).

179   *"Working parents should stop assuming . . .":* James A. Levine, "The Other Working Parent," *New York Times,* 4 March 1999, A17.

179   *In testimony before the House Select Committee:* Lynn O'Rourke Hayes, "The Best Jobs in America for Parents," testimony before the House Select Committee on Children, Youth and Families (11 June 1991).

179   *Elder, Liker, and Cross studied:* G. Elder, J. Liker, and C. Cross, "Parent–Child Behavior in the Great Depression: Life Course and Intergenerational Influences," in *Life Span Development and Behavior,* ed. P. Baltes and O. Brim (Orlando, FL: Academic Press, 1984), pp. 109–158.

179   *McLoyd has shown that this is especially relevant:* V. C. McLoyd, "The Impact of Economic Hardship on Black Families and Children: Psychological Distress, Parenting and Socioeconomic Development," *Child Development* 61: 311–346 (1990).

179   *Barnett found that even engaged fathers:* R. C. Barnett, N. L. Marshall and J. H. Pleck, "Men's Multiple Roles and Their Relationship to Men's Psychological Stress," *Journal of Marriage and the Family* 54: 358–367 (1992).

180   *John Snarey as well as A. J. Hawkins:* A. J. Hawkins, S. L. Christiansen, K. P. Sarent and E. J. Hill, "Rethinking Fathers' Involvement in Child Care: A Developmental Perspective," *Journal of Family Issues* 14: 531–549 (1993); Snarey, *How Fathers Care for the Next Generation.*

180   *Joseph Pleck reviewed public health:* Joseph H. Pleck, "Paternal Involvement: Levels, Sources and Consequences," in *The Role of the Father in Child Development,* 3rd ed., ed. Michael E. Lamb (New York: Wiley, 1997), pp. 66–103.

181   *Hilda and Seymour Parker of the University of Utah:* Hilda Parker and Seymour Parker, "Cultural Rules, Rituals and Behavior Regulation," *American Anthropologist* 86 (3): 584–600 (1984).

182   *The classic cross-cultural anthropological study:* Beatrice B. Whiting and John W. M. Whiting, *Children of Six Cultures: A Psycho-Cultural Analysis* (Cambridge, MA: Harvard University Press, 1975).

182   *Professor and author Myriam Miedzian:* Myriam Miedzian, "Babies and Briefcases: Creating a Family-Friendly Workplace for Fathers," testimony before the House Select Committee on Children, Youth and Families (11 June 1991).

183   *That is precisely the case:* Douglass Heath, "The Impact of Delayed Fatherhood on the Father–Child Relationship," *Journal of Genetic Psychology* 155 (4): 511–30 (1994).

9: Fulfilling Fatherneed

192   *Since "father" means different things to different children:* James A. Levine, "Involving Fathers in Head Start: A Framework for Public Policy and Program Development," *Families in Society: The Journal of Contemporary Human Services* 74: 4–21 (1993).

193   *Fatherneed is most threatened:* C. R. Ahrons and R. B. Miller, "The Effect of the Post-Divorce Relationship on Paternal Involvement: A Longitudinal Analysis," *American Journal of Orthopsychiatry* 63: 441–450 (1993).

193 *In working class families in particular:* Karen Grimm-Thomas and Maureen Perry-Jenkins, "All in a Day's Work: Job Experiences, Self-Esteem, and Fathering in Working-Class Families," *Family Relations* 43: 174–181 (1994).

196 *Janet Hyde's research told us that:* Janet Shibley Hyde, Marilyn J. Essex, and Francine Horton, "Fathers and Parental Leave: Attitudes and Experiences," *Journal of Family Issues* 14 (4): 635 (December 1993).

196 *Commission on Family and Medical Leave:* Report to Select Committee on Children, Youth and Families, U.S. House of Representatives, June 11, 1991.

197 *Although little has been written:* Sandra L. Ferketich and Ramona T. Mercer, "Paternal–Infant Attachment of Experienced and Inexperienced Fathers During Pregnancy," *Nursing Research* 44 (1): 31–37 (January 1995).

197 *Depression in the father at such a time:* M. E. G. Arieas, R. Kumar, H. Barrios, and E. Figueiredo, "Correlates of Postnatal Depression in Mothers and Fathers," *British Journal of Psychiatry* 169: 36–41 (1996).

200 *Clearly, child support agencies:* Jeffery Marvin Johnson and Hillard Pouncy, "Developing Creative Ways to Address the Need of Fathers and Fragile Families: A View from the Field," *Harvard Journal of African-American Public Policy* 4: 5–21 (1998).

201 *Kathleen Sternberg has summarized:* Kathleen J. Sternberg, "Fathers, the Missing Parents in Research on Family Violence," in *The Role of the Father in Child Development,* 3rd ed., ed. Michael E. Lamb (New York: Wiley, 1997), p. 284.

201 *A respected study by the American Humane Society:* C. M. Malkin and M. E. Lamb, "Child Maltreatment: A Test of Sociobiological Theory," *Journal of Comparative Family Studies* 25: 121–134 (1994).

10: The Kids Get the Last Word

203 *The way a father is thought about by his child:* Carol S. Michaels, "So Near and Yet So Far: The Nonresident Father," in *Fathers and Their Families,* ed. Stanley H. Cath, Alan Gurwitt, and Linda Gunsberg (Hillsdale, NJ: Analytic Press, 1989), p. 409.

206 *Research by psychologist Judith Solomon:* G. E. Solomon, S. C. Johnson, D. Zaitchick, and S. Carey, "Like Father Like Son: Young Children's Understanding of How and Why Offspring Resemble Their Parents," *Child Development* 67 (1): 151–171 (February 1996).

206 *In a recent joint research project:* Kyle D. Pruett and Marsha Kline Pruett, "Only God Decides: Young Children's Perceptions of Custody and Divorce," *Journal of the American Academy of Child and Adolescent Psychiatry* 38 (12) (December 1999).

Index